LIL' LUNA'S

So Easy & So Yummy

Published by Flashpoint Books™, Seattle
www.flashpointbooks.com

ISBN (hardcover): 978-1-959411-45-1
ISBN (ebook): 978-1-959411-46-8
Printed in China
Design by Weller Smith Design
Author and front cover photographs by Alisha Gregson

Library of Congress Control Number: 2023907923

First Edition

DEDICATION

I would like to dedicate this book to my children, who are the spice of my life;
my husband, who has supported me in my crazy ideas and adventures; and
most of all to my mom, Liv. Without her and her passion for making good food
and even better memories, this book would have never been possible.

LIL' LUNA'S
So Easy &
So Yummy

The Ultimate Resource for Feeding Your Friends and Family

KRISTYN MERKLEY

CONTENTS

Acknowledgments

I would like to thank all the people who make up the "we" in this book. I could not have done it alone!

To Ali Jennings for compiling and editing into the wee hours of the night! She is the only person who has spent more time on this book than me.

To all the Lil' Luna team (especially my main kitchen assistants—Ali; my sister Tara; and my mom), who have researched and tested all of these recipes as well as many more recipes that did not make the cut. Your efforts to research, test and write the recipes help bring so much value to Lil' Luna. I could not ask for a better group of women to work with!

To Katie Wylie for filming and editing all the incredible recipe videos for this book. You have literally worked on these videos for years and have been so amazing to team up with for this project. You have helped put the "So Easy" part in this book with your awesome videos.

To Alicia Skousen for testing and photographing not only many of the recipes in this book, but also many more over the years. I couldn't have made this cookbook without your phenomenal talents.

To Alisha Gregson, whose lifestyle photography made this cookbook look so fun! All the smiles and laughs in the photos are genuine because of your funny and energetic personality. You are an amazing photographer and, more importantly, a cherished friend. Thank you!

To Weller Smith Design, whose team of editors, designers and creators were incredible to work with and are responsible for making this book happen. Your perfect combination of professionalism and genuine care for me and my team made this experience so much easier and enjoyable.

To LeAnna Smith for keeping me sane and on track throughout the whole process. Your constant efforts in making sure the design of this book was fun and beautiful totally paid off! Thank you for your patience, guidance and support as I figured out what my vision for this book would be.

To the readers and the followers of lilluna.com. You have given me the greatest gift ever—I get to do what I love and make a living doing it! I could not have done any of this without you.

To my blogging friends (you know who you are) for the hours and hours on the phone, the late nights talking about blogging strategies and food and for all your support, suggestions, reassurances and honest feedback. I would not still be in this industry without you.

To the Lunas, the source of my love and passion for food and cooking. I am grateful for you and your teaching me the "ways" of the kitchen—especially my sisters, Tara and Kellyn, who have had to live with me and still love me, despite all my shortcomings.

To my six children, Lily, Gavin, Evie, Wesley, Melody and Eliza (Lu). They have been the best taste testers a girl could ask for. Their opinions and suggestions meant so much to me because I knew if they didn't like it, you wouldn't like it. I find no greater joy than spending time with them in the kitchen, and I hope to continue making the best kitchen memories with them for the rest of my life (and hopefully teach them a thing or two along the way).

To my husband, Lo: Thank you, thank you, thank you! From the late-night editing sessions to the brainstorming meetings we had on our walks around the neighborhood, you've had to hear more about cookbooks and recipes than anyone should ever have to. Thank you for encouraging me to do this and for being my number one fan. I am beyond grateful for all your help and to have had you at my side during this crazy adventure (and through life). Я тебя люблю.

Most of all, I would like to thank and dedicate this book to my mom, Olivia Luna Ritchey. No one has impacted my love of the kitchen and cooking as much as she has. Someday my empanadas will taste as good as yours, Mom. I love you.

Thank you!

What Is Lil' Luna?

Hi, I'm Kristyn Merkley!

My mom's maiden name is Luna, and I'm one of the many "Lil' Lunas" in the family who have inherited a love for food.

Coming from a long line of cooks and bakers, it was inevitable that I would fall in love with the same hobbies.

Lilluna.com was born right after my second child in early 2010. I started sharing all of our favorite Mexican recipes I got from my mom, aunts and grandma as well as some of the traditional American recipes that came from my dad's family.

I never intended for it to be anything more than a way to organize and share my recipes. Quickly, more and more people began clicking over to my little blog of creations. It began to grow and grow until it became what it is today.

Now we have thousands of recipes on the website, and through Google, email and various social media platforms, millions of people visit and make recipes every month from lilluna.com. With a team of almost a dozen people working behind the scenes, we continue to create the easiest and yummiest recipes for all to try.

My readers and followers have given me the greatest gift ever—I get to do what I love and make a living doing it! I could not have done it without each of you!

Why Would "We" Write a Cookbook?

Over the past seventeen years, I have been on an awesome and crazy cooking adventure. I have gone from barely being able to cook a handful of meals for my family (my husband would say "a handful" and "barely" is being generous), to studying, practicing and eventually mastering thousands of recipes. My path was extremely enjoyable for many reasons.

My favorite thing about this journey is that I have learned so many amazing recipes and techniques that I've not only been able to share with my own family (again, my husband and kids are very grateful), but also with millions across the internet and on social media platforms. I cannot tell you how happy that makes me! I've always believed that the kitchen is the heart of the home, and I love hearing about the yummy food and great experiences being enjoyed by so many people when friends and family gather around the table to enjoy delicious, homemade recipes. In learning to cook the best recipes, I've learned all the best methods to create them as well, and I have tried to include as many of those treasured tips, tricks and tools as possible for you.

One of my goals for this book is to help everyone feel like cooking and baking are achievable. The recipes in these pages are easy enough that even the most inexperienced person can get in the kitchen and make something extraordinary. Trust me, if this frantic hot mess can do it, you can do it! And not just for yourself—we have put a lot of effort into creating choose-your-own-adventure-style meal plans so you can host all sorts of parties and get-togethers to share that incredible food.

I also hope this book allows you to spend time with your favorite people *making* the food. My kids have provided much of the inspiration (and a good chunk of the necessity, too) behind me perfecting these recipes. I have loved my time with them in the kitchen. When we are cooking or baking, I naturally forget all about them being knuckleheads, and they forget all about me being their nagging mom. Instead, we bond over the yummy food, or the salt and sugar mix-ups and the hilarious prank taste-testing that ensues. So many good memories! I hope you get to make some good memories with others as well while making these recipes.

One thing you should know as you read through this book is that cooking has never been an individual sport for me. Whether it is my Latina mom showing me her authentic ways of preparing a phenomenal Mexican dish, or my team working together to perfect and simplify a tricky recipe, or my kids making a mess in the kitchen with me as we create memories and some delicious food, cooking is about so much more than just me!

For that reason, from now on, you will notice that I never talk about "me" or "I" in this book. It is always "we." That includes myself, my family, my team and now *you*!

Thank you for letting us join your cooking journey. We hope you experience the same joy, learning and sense of fun along the way that we have received from ours.

Thank you!

How to Get the Most out of This Cookbook

We have put *tons* of work into trying to make this cookbook as valuable as possible for you. There is so much more here than just recipes. Here are some highlights from the book to help you get the most out of it.

SUBSTITUTIONS AND GENERAL TIPS: Cooking does not always go as planned. We are here to help! In this book you will find substitutions for ingredients that you might not have on hand, tips on what to do when things do not come out how you had hoped and tricks that make cooking easier in general—we've got your back.

EXTENSIVE INDEXES: We want to make sure it is as easy as possible to find the perfect recipe you need for any given moment. To do this there are several indexes, located on pages 289–312, that list our recipes by name and image, by category, by occasion and by tag, to help you find exactly what you want.

HOLIDAY MENU BUILDER: This mix-and-match holiday helper makes it easy to create an awesome menu for almost any holiday gathering. Pick your main dish, appetizer, side, bread and/or dessert and get tips on when to make them.

CHAPTER INTRODUCTIONS: Don't skip these! At the beginning of each chapter, we've included useful information specific to the recipes found within that section.

1 **TAGS:** This book was created for the busy individual who loves cooking for themselves and others. To make finding the right recipe quicker and easier, we have included tags to help you navigate quickly to the recipe that will work best for the situation or the occasion that you are planning for. These color-coded tags are found on each recipe, as well as in an index located on page 290.

2 **VIDEOS:** To make sure you have all the information you could possibly need to be able to successfully create each and every recipe in this book, we have provided video instructions for every recipe as a reference. These videos are great for seeing the order of ingredients and the desired consistencies and textures of the doughs and mixes. Just point your phone camera at the QR code on any recipe page to get the link to the video for that specific recipe.

3 **VARIATIONS:** Occasionally, recipes can be easily tweaked to create a completely new taste. We have included these possible variations on select recipes.

4 **BONUS RECIPES:** Some recipes can easily be turned into a bonus recipe, like making muffins out of a bread batter or turning homemade tortillas into quesadillas. Other recipes are just made to be served with a partner, like Grilled Cheese with Tomato Basil Soup or Buttermilk Syrup with Swedish Pancakes. These bonus recipes can be found below the main recipe. Be sure to check them out!

5 **RECIPE TIPS:** Here we list some of the best tips and tricks that we've learned for that recipe through research and trial and error. These include information on what can be made ahead of time, how to store leftovers, how to tweak these recipes to make them your own, slow cooker adaptations and much more.

Scan me!

A message from Kristyn about this book

Using the Recipe Pages

SWEDISH PANCAKES

🕐 PREP TIME: **5 MINUTES**
⧗ COOK TIME: **30 MINUTES**
♡ MAKES: **12 PANCAKES**

✓ PREPPED IN 5
✓ QUICK & EASY ◄ ①

INGREDIENTS

3 large eggs
3 cups milk
3 tablespoons unsalted butter, melted, plus more
  for the pan
1½ cups all-purpose flour, sifted
2 teaspoons sugar
1 teaspoon salt
TOPPINGS: fruit, syrup, Homemade Whipped
  Cream (page 208)

② *Scan me!*

INSTRUCTIONS

1. In a medium bowl, beat eggs until well combined.
2. Add milk, butter, flour, sugar and salt to eggs and mix until smooth.
3. Heat more butter in a 10-inch nonstick skillet over medium heat, or spray skillet with nonstick cooking spray.
4. Pour about ¼ cup batter into the pan and tilt the pan in circles until the batter is spread all over in a thin layer. Cook for 1–2 minutes. When the edges are bubbled and browned, it is ready to flip.
5. Cook the other side until golden, about 1 minute, then transfer to a plate. Repeat to make the remaining pancakes, stacking them with a piece of parchment paper between each one to keep from sticking.
6. Serve immediately with your toppings of choice.

⊙ **VARIATIONS** ③

FILLINGS: There are many different sweet and savory fillings you can use for Swedish pancakes. Simply place fillings in the center of a pancake and roll up like a crepe.

SWEET: Fruit, Nutella, buttermilk syrup, jam, whipped cream or ice cream.

SAVORY: Eggs, ham, cheese, mushrooms, spinach, steak, pulled pork with barbecue sauce or a caprese version with avocado, tomato, mozzarella and balsamic glaze.

★ BONUS RECIPE

Buttermilk Syrup ④

Melt ½ cup butter in a medium pot over medium-low heat. Once melted, add 1 cup sugar, ½ cup buttermilk and 1 teaspoon vanilla extract. Whisk until sugar has dissolved and mixture is combined and starting to boil. Remove from the heat and whisk in ½ teaspoon baking powder, which will make the syrup foamy. Serve on top of pancakes and top with whipped cream, fruit or any other toppings. Change up the flavor by adding ¼ teaspoon almond or coconut extract or a spice, such as ¼ teaspoon ground cinnamon.

👍 **RECIPE TIPS** ⑤

☺ Make Ahead: *If making a large batch, you can keep the Swedish pancakes warm until ready to serve in an oven heated to about 200 degrees F. You can either roll each pancake and place them side by side in a pan, or stack them on the pan, separating each pancake with parchment paper.*

PAIRINGS: Scrambled Eggs (page 37), Bacon (page 37), Cheesecake Fruit Salad (page 210), Homemade Ice Cream (page 265) ⑥

Breakfast   41   ⑦

---

⑥ **ALSO TRY:** For each dessert and drink recipe, and some bread and appetizer recipes, we have suggested other recipes that are similar that may also fit the situation at hand for more options to choose from as you plan your menu.

⑦ **PAIRINGS:** Most of these recipes are amazing all by themselves, but some occasions might call for something more to go with a particular dish. We have listed the best possible recipes to up your cooking, mealtime and hosting game.

Setting Yourself up for Success

Cooking can be so much fun, but if you are constantly missing ingredients or tools to easily make the recipes, it can be very frustrating. Below we give you some tips and tricks to remove as much frustration as possible.

OUR PANTRY

Here are the staple ingredients we always try to have on hand at home. You can make almost all of the recipes in this book if you have these. We have also highlighted a few brand-specific products we absolutely love, marked with asterisks, which give great flavor to the recipes.

COOKING & BAKING ESSENTIALS
- [ ] ALMOND EXTRACT
- [ ] APPLESAUCE
- [ ] BAKING POWDER
- [ ] BAKING SODA
- [ ] BROWNIE MIXES
- [ ] CAKE MIXES
- [ ] CHOCOLATE CHIPS (MILK, SEMI-SWEET, ETC.)
- [ ] COCOA POWDER (UNSWEETENED)
- [ ] COOKING SPRAY
- [ ] CORN SYRUP
- [ ] CORNSTARCH
- [ ] CREAM OF TARTAR
- [ ] EVAPORATED MILK
- [ ] FLOUR (ALL-PURPOSE and BREAD)
- [ ] HONEY
- [ ] OLIVE OIL
- [ ] SESAME OIL
- [ ] SUGAR (BROWN, GRANULATED and POWDERED)
- [ ] SOY SAUCE
- [ ] SWEETENED CONDENSED MILK
- [ ] VANILLA EXTRACT
- [ ] VEGETABLE OIL
- [ ] VINEGAR (APPLE CIDER, RED WINE and WHITE)
- [ ] YEAST (RAPID RISE)

DRY GOODS
- [ ] BREADCRUMBS
- [ ] BREAKFAST CEREAL
- [ ] CHIPS
- [ ] COOKIES
- [ ] CRACKERS
- [ ] DRIED FRUIT
- [ ] GRAINS (CEREAL, CORNMEAL, ETC.)
- [ ] MAPLE SYRUP
- [ ] MARSHMALLOWS
- [ ] NUTS
- [ ] OATS (OLD-FASHIONED and QUICK-COOKING)
- [ ] PANCAKE MIX
- [ ] PANKO BREADCRUMBS
- [ ] PASTA
- [ ] PEANUT BUTTER (CREAMY, NATURAL)
- [ ] POPCORN
- [ ] PRETZELS
- [ ] RICE (INSTANT and LONG GRAIN)
- [ ] TORTILLAS

FRESH FOOD FOR THE FRIDGE
- [ ] BUTTER (SALTED and UNSALTED)
- [ ] BUTTERMILK
- [ ] CHEESE
- [ ] CREAM CHEESE
- [ ] EGGS
- [ ] FRUIT
- [ ] GARLIC
- [ ] GREENS
- [ ] HALF-AND-HALF or HEAVY CREAM

- [ ] LEMON JUICE
- [ ] LIME JUICE
- [ ] MILK (2 PERCENT or WHOLE)
- [ ] SOUR CREAM
- [ ] VEGETABLES
- [ ] YOGURT

CANNED GOODS
- [ ] BEANS (BLACK, PINTO and KIDNEY)
- [ ] BROTH or STOCK
- [ ] CHILES
- [ ] FRUIT
- [ ] OLIVES
- [ ] SALSA
- [ ] SOUPS (CREAM OF CHICKEN, ETC.)
- [ ] TOMATOES (DICED, PASTE, *Ro-Tel and SAUCE)
- [ ] VEGETABLES

SEASONINGS
- [ ] BASIL
- [ ] BROWN GRAVY MIX
- [ ] CHILI POWDER (*Gebhardt)
- [ ] CINNAMON
- [ ] GARLIC SALT WITH PARSLEY FLAKES (*Lawry's)
- [ ] GARLIC POWDER
- [ ] GROUND CLOVES
- [ ] GROUND CUMIN
- [ ] GROUND GINGER
- [ ] GROUND NUTMEG
- [ ] ITALIAN SEASONING
- [ ] KOSHER SALT
- [ ] ONION POWDER
- [ ] OREGANO
- [ ] PAPRIKA

- [ ] PARSLEY
- [ ] PEPPER
- [ ] PUMPKIN PIE SPICE
- [ ] RANCH DRESSING MIX
- [ ] RED PEPPER FLAKES
- [ ] ROSEMARY
- [ ] SALT
- [ ] SESAME SEEDS
- [ ] TACO SEASONING
- [ ] WHITE PEPPER

CONDIMENTS
- [ ] BARBECUE SAUCE
- [ ] DRESSING
- [ ] JELLY and JAM
- [ ] KETCHUP
- [ ] MAYONNAISE (*Hellmann's)
- [ ] MUSTARD
- [ ] PICKLES

FREEZER
- [ ] BACON
- [ ] BEEF ROAST or STEAKS
- [ ] BREAD
- [ ] CHICKEN
- [ ] FRUIT
- [ ] GROUND BEEF
- [ ] GROUND TURKEY
- [ ] HOT DOGS
- [ ] ICE CREAM
- [ ] PIE DOUGH
- [ ] PIZZA DOUGH
- [ ] PUFF PASTRY
- [ ] SAUSAGE

FOOD SUBSTITUTIONS

Nothing is more frustrating than wanting to try out a recipe and discovering you are missing one or two key ingredients. Here are some substitutions that can give you similar results for the recipes in this book.

INGREDIENT	TO REPLACE:	USE:
Allspice	1 teaspoon	½ teaspoon cinnamon, ¼ teaspoon cloves and ¼ teaspoon nutmeg
Apple pie spice	1 teaspoon	½ teaspoon ground cinnamon, ¼ teaspoon ground nutmeg, ⅛ teaspoon ground allspice and 1 dash ground cloves or ground ginger
Baking powder	3 teaspoons	½ teaspoon cream of tartar and ¼ teaspoon baking soda
Baking soda	¼ teaspoon	1 teaspoon baking powder
Balsamic vinegar	1 tablespoon	1 tablespoon cider vinegar or red wine vinegar
Bread flour	1 cup	1 cup minus 1½ teaspoons all-purpose flour, plus 1½ teaspoons vital wheat gluten, whisked or sifted together
Broth (chicken or beef)	1 cup	1 teaspoon or 1 cube chicken or beef bouillon plus 1 cup hot water
Brown sugar, dark	1 cup packed	1 cup granulated sugar plus 2 tablespoons molasses
Brown sugar, light	1 cup packed	1 cup granulated sugar plus 1 tablespoon molasses
Buttermilk	1 cup	1 tablespoon lemon juice or vinegar plus enough milk to make 1 cup; stir and let stand for 5 minutes before using. Or 1 cup plain yogurt.
Cake flour	1 cup	1 cup minus 2 tablespoons all-purpose flour, plus 2 tablespoons cornstarch, sifted together
Chili powder	1 teaspoon	¼ teaspoon paprika, ¼ teaspoon garlic powder, ¼ teaspoon cumin and ¼ teaspoon cayenne or red pepper flakes
Cornstarch (for thickening)	1 tablespoon	2 tablespoons all-purpose flour
Corn syrup	1 ounce	1 cup sugar combined with ¼ cup water
Cream of tartar	¼ teaspoon	½ teaspoon fresh lemon juice
Eggs	1 whole egg	3 tablespoons mayonnaise
Half-and-half	1 cup	For cooking: 1 tablespoon melted butter plus enough whole milk to make 1 cup For baking: ⅔ cup low-fat milk plus ⅓ cup heavy cream
Heavy cream	1 cup	¾ cup half-and-half plus ¼ cup melted butter
Kosher salt	½ teaspoon	¼ teaspoon iodized salt
Mayonnaise	1:1	Greek yogurt or sour cream
Pumpkin pie spice	1 teaspoon	½ teaspoon ground cinnamon, ¼ teaspoon ground ginger, ¼ teaspoon ground allspice and ⅛ teaspoon ground nutmeg
Self-rising flour	1 cup	1 cup all-purpose flour, 1½ teaspoons baking powder and ¼ teaspoon salt
Stock	1 cup	1 cup water plus 1 tablespoon butter
Sour cream	1:1	Plain yogurt
Whole milk	1:1	Heavy cream or half-and-half

SPICE UP YOUR LIFE

Don't have a certain herb or spice on hand? This list of seasoning substitutes will help out (in a pinch!). Just replace the ingredient you're missing with one of the listed suggestions for a similar flavor profile.

HERBS

BASIL: cilantro, dill, Italian seasoning, mint, oregano, parsley

BAY LEAVES: herbes de Provence, oregano, rosemary, sage, thyme

CHIVES: cilantro, garlic powder, onion powder, parsley

CILANTRO: basil, chives, parsley, mint

DILL: basil, mint, parsley

MARJORAM: herbes de Provence, Italian seasoning, oregano, rosemary, sage, thyme

MINT: basil, cilantro, dill, parsley

OREGANO: bay leaves, herbes de Provence, Italian seasoning, mint, tarragon

PARSLEY: basil, chives, cilantro, dill, Italian seasoning, mint, tarragon

ROSEMARY: bay leaves, herbes de Provence, oregano, thyme, sage

SAGE: bay leaves, herbes de Provence, oregano, rosemary, thyme

THYME: bay leaves, herbes de Provence, oregano, rosemary, sage

SPICES

CAYENNE PEPPER: chili powder, dried chiles, hot sauce, paprika, red pepper flakes

CINNAMON: allspice, apple pie spice blend, cloves, coriander, nutmeg, pumpkin pie spice blend

CLOVES: allspice, cinnamon, nutmeg, black pepper

CUMIN: chili powder, coriander, curry powder, garlic powder, onion powder, turmeric

GINGER: allspice, cinnamon, cloves, coriander

NUTMEG: allspice, cinnamon, cloves, ground ginger

PAPRIKA: cayenne pepper, chili powder, curry powder, black pepper

MEASUREMENT CONVERSIONS

TSP	TBSP	OUNCES	CUPS	PINTS	QUARTS	GALLONS	ML	LITERS
3	1	½	1/16	-	-	-	15	0.015
6	2	1	⅛	1/16	-	-	30	0.03
24	8	4	½	¼	⅛	-	125	0.125
48	16	8	1	½	¼	1/16	250	0.25
96	32	16	2	1	½	⅛	500	0.5
-	-	32	4	2	1	¼	950	0.95
-	-	128	16	8	4	1	3800	3.8

OUR FAVORITE COOKING SUPPLIES

There are so many amazing cooking and baking utensils out there, but not all of them are created equal. We have found several that make things so much easier, and we wanted to share our must-have kitchen tools with you. To check out some of the specific brands we use in our kitchen, scan the QR code to be taken to an Amazon list highlighting our favorites.

Scan me!

☐ BAKING SHEETS
☐ BAKEWARE SET
☐ CAKE PANS
☐ CAN OPENER
☐ CANDY THERMOMETER
☐ COLANDER
☐ COOKIE SCOOPS
☐ COOKIE SHEETS
☐ COOKWARE SET
☐ CUTTING BOARD
☐ DOUGH BLENDER
☐ DUSTING WAND
☐ FLOUR SIFTER
☐ HAND MIXER
☐ ICE CREAM SCOOP
☐ KITCHEN SHEARS
☐ KNIFE SET
☐ MEASURING CUPS
☐ MEASURING SPOONS
☐ MEAT THERMOMETER

☐ METAL SPATULA
☐ METAL TONGS
☐ MIXING BOWL SET
☐ NONSTICK SKILLET
☐ NUT CHOPPER
☐ OVEN THERMOMETER
☐ PASTA POT
☐ PASTRY CLOTH
☐ PASTRY CUTTER
☐ PASTRY ROLLER
☐ ROLLING PIN
☐ RUBBER SPOON SPATULA
☐ SCRAPER AND CHOPPER
☐ SILICONE MEASURING CUPS
☐ SLOW COOKER
☐ STAND MIXER
☐ VEGETABLE PEELER
☐ WHISK
☐ WOODEN SPOON SET
☐ ZESTER

How Do I . . . ?

Separate Eggs

Create a Roux

Soften Butter Quickly

Zest Citrus

Make Buttermilk

Cream Butter and Sugar

Measure Flour

Ripen Bananas

Activate Yeast

Mince Garlic

Grease and Flour Bread/Cake Pans

Line a Pan with Parchment Paper

QUICK AND EASY COOKING

We know it can be a struggle to come up with quick, easy and yummy meals for those busy weeknights, but luckily, a little planning goes a long way. Here are some of our favorite tips for meal planning and creating quick and easy meals.

MAKE A MEAL PLAN. Are meal plans completely necessary? No, but they do help! Making a weekly or even monthly menu has saved us on many occasions. First and foremost, knowing what you plan to serve saves so much time and means no more having to wonder what's for dinner. It also makes grocery shopping easier. If you know the menu, you know which ingredients to buy, so when it's time to cook you'll have everything on hand for your meal. Simply pick a few minutes each week to plan your menu and make your grocery list, and you will see firsthand how helpful it is.

USE OUR TAGS INDEX ON PAGE 290. Look for recipes with the Quick & Easy tag and make those meals on especially busy nights.

USE THE QUICK AND EASY DINNER CHART ON PAGE 25, which includes our go-to list of quick dinner ideas for inspiration.

BUY MEAT IN BULK AND PREPARE IT AHEAD OF TIME. Not only is it less expensive to buy meat in bulk, it also encourages you to prepare it ahead of time. Simply cook the meat using your favorite spices or marinade, store in resealable plastic freezer bags in the portion sizes you desire and freeze. Then, on the morning of a busy day, you can simply pull out the already-cooked meat to defrost in the refrigerator and use in a meal.

COOK IN LARGE BATCHES. Make double batches of recipes on days when you have more time, and freeze them to use for dinners on busy nights.

Look for the Make Ahead and Freezer Friendly tags for ideas.

REPURPOSE LEFTOVERS. Use leftover meat to quickly whip up new recipes, such as tacos, tostadas, casseroles and more.

KEEP YOUR PANTRY STOCKED. If your pantry is stocked on a regular basis, you will have the ingredients necessary to whip something up without having to go to the store. Refer to our pantry staples list on page 18.

READ THE WHOLE RECIPE BEFORE COOKING. You do not want to get through making half of a recipe on a busy night only to discover that the directions call for it to chill for an hour.

USE BIGGER PANS FOR COOKING. Instead of using a small pan, try one with a larger surface area, so the food is more spread out. Your food will be able to receive more direct heat and will cook faster.

TAKE SHORTCUTS WHEN NEEDED. Use ready-made dough for pizza or biscuits, use frozen, chopped vegetables instead of fresh produce or use store-bought sauces rather than making your own from scratch.

IF IT AIN'T BROKE, DON'T FIX IT. If you have found a quick recipe that works really well, use it again and again. Tweak it on occasion to add some variety.

QUICK AND EASY DINNERS FOR BUSY WEEKNIGHTS

All these recipes can be prepped and on the table in 30 minutes or less.

CHICKEN & POULTRY	PASTA	BEEF & BEANS	SOUP	SALAD	SIDE DISHES
Cream Cheese and Chicken Taquitos (pg. 186)	White Sauce Pasta (pg. 192)	Classic Burgers (pg. 160)	Chicken Dumpling Soup (pg. 124)	Caesar Salad (pg. 106)	Green Bean Bundles (pg. 135)
Chicken Nuggets (pg. 178)	Italian Sausage Pasta (pg. 196)	Pigs in a Blanket (pg. 166)	Taco Soup (pg. 130)	Strawberry Salad (pg. 108)	Brown Sugar–Glazed Carrots (pg. 136)
Chicken Tacos (pg. 188)	Cheesy Pasta Bake (pg. 197)	Beef Stroganoff (pg. 200)	White Chicken Chili (pg. 127)	Southwest Salad (pg. 109)	Creamed Corn (pg. 138)
General Tso's Chicken (pg. 180)	Baked Ziti (pg. 201)	Tostadas (pg. 190)	Egg Drop Soup (pg. 131)	Asian Ramen Salad (pg. 110)	Parmesan Sweet Potato Cubes (pg. 141)

We've all been there before. Your day has been busier than expected, and you need to whip up some dinner in a flash. This handy chart has been our go-to for making delicious home-cooked meals for the family when time is tight.

You can choose one entree from this list as a stand-alone meal, or you can add one of our quick side dishes to make it a quick and easy multicourse dinner. A couple of our favorite combos are Cream Cheese and Chicken Taquitos with our Southwest Salad or our White Sauce Pasta with Green Bean Bundles. We also love creating easy soup-and-salad combos using this chart.

DONENESS CHART

Safely Cooked, Internal Temperatures

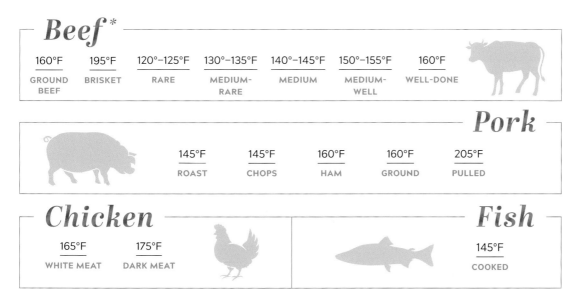

Beef*

160°F	195°F	120°–125°F	130°–135°F	140°–145°F	150°–155°F	160°F
GROUND BEEF	BRISKET	RARE	MEDIUM-RARE	MEDIUM	MEDIUM-WELL	WELL-DONE

Pork

145°F	145°F	160°F	160°F	205°F
ROAST	CHOPS	HAM	GROUND	PULLED

Chicken

165°F	175°F
WHITE MEAT	DARK MEAT

Fish

145°F
COOKED

⊕ *USDA minimum temp for beef to be safely cooked is 145°F.

⊕ **PRO TIP:** Cook to a temperature just below your desired temperature. Carryover cooking can increase the internal temperature by 5–10°F for up to 15 minutes after removing from the heat.

MAKE IT AHEAD

Life can be crazy! A great tip to help you juggle the busy prep time before dinner or hosting and still pull off a great meal is to make the meal ahead of time. The recipes in this chart can almost be completely prepared ahead of time and refrigerated for 24 hours, and many of them can also be frozen for up to two months until you are ready to pop them in the oven right before the meal. A little planning goes a long way in simplifying your life with these recipes.

BREAKFAST

Belgian Waffles (pg. 42)

French Toast Bake (pg. 44)

Coffee Cake (pg. 47)

Potato Breakfast Casserole (pg. 52)

Ham and Cheese Quiche (pg. 54)

BREADS & MUFFINS

Easy Homemade White Bread (pg. 61)

Heavenly Rolls (pg. 68)

Cinnamon Bread (pg. 72)

Banana Bread (pg. 81)

Blueberry Muffins (pg. 77)

APPETIZERS

Spinach Artichoke Dip (pg. 85)

Cream Cheese Bean Dip (pg. 89)

Bacon-Wrapped Smokies (pg. 92)

Fried Egg Rolls (pg. 99)

Slow Cooker Meatballs (pg. 100)

SALADS

Caesar Salad (pg. 106)

Fruit Salad (pg. 105)

Potato Salad (pg. 112)

Pasta Salad (pg. 114)

Chicken Salad (pg. 115)

SOUPS

Slow Cooker Cheesy Potato Soup (pg. 121)

Slow Cooker Beef Stew (pg. 123)

Slow Cooker Spinach Tortellini Soup (pg. 125)

Slow Cooker Chicken Tortilla Soup (pg. 128)

Taco Soup (pg. 130)

SIDES

Green Bean Bundles (pg. 135)

Mashed Potatoes (pg. 145)

Funeral Potatoes (pg. 146)

Homemade Mac and Cheese (pg. 142)

Salsas (pgs. 153, 154 and 155)

MAIN DISHES

Meatloaf (pg. 164)

Pigs in a Blanket (pg. 166)

Sweet Pork (pg. 170)

Green Chile Chicken Enchiladas (pg. 183)

Cream Cheese and Chicken Taquitos (pg. 186)

PASTA & PIZZA

Chicken Tetrazzini (pg. 193)

Beef Goulash (pg. 194)

Cheesy Pasta Bake (pg. 197)

Baked Ziti (pg. 201)

Pizza (pg. 202)

CAKES & CUPCAKES

Jell-O Poke Cake (pg. 208)

Chocolate Sheet Cake (pg. 211)

Vanilla Cupcakes (pg. 215)

Angel Food Ice Cream Cake (pg. 216)

Pumpkin Roll (pg. 218)

BROWNIES, BARS & PIES

Brownies (pg. 220)

Cookie Bars (pg. 223)

Lemon Bars (pg. 226)

Pumpkin Delight (pg. 234)

Scotcheroos (pg. 238)

COOKIES

Chocolate Chip Cookies (pg. 240)

Snickerdoodles (pg. 241)

Sugar Cookies (pg. 242)

Soft Peanut Butter Cookies (pg. 247)

Pumpkin Chocolate Chip Cookies (pg. 251)

CANDY & OTHER DESSERTS

Puppy Chow (pg. 254)

Cookies and Cream Fudge (pg. 256)

Homemade Lollipops (pg. 257)

Candied Almonds (pg.260)

Caramel Dip (pg. 274)

DRINKS

Pink Punch (pg. 279)

Lemonade (pg. 282)

Holiday Punch (pg. 284)

Apple Cider (pg. 286)

Eggnog (pg. 287)

FEEDING A CROWD

We host a lot of get-togethers, especially for the holidays—and we also host a lot of get-togethers just because! We love to invite people into our home to strengthen friendships and to enjoy delicious food. Keep these tips in mind to make feeding a large crowd even easier:

COUNT ON CASSEROLES: Throwing together a casserole or two is a quick and easy way to feed a crowd. They can often be prepared hours before-hand and simply baked in the oven before your guests arrive.

DOUBLE UP: Choose recipes that can be easily doubled so that cooking for a large group does not get overwhelming.

MAKE ASSIGNMENTS: Create your menu ahead of time and when people ask what they can bring, assign a few dishes to those who are coming over.

USE DIFFERENT COOKING METHODS: Be sure to plan your menu so that the various recipes do not all require the same method of cooking (oven, stove, slow cooker, etc.). Using different methods for each recipe will allow for them to cook at the same time without backing up the kitchen.

In case you are looking for a little inspiration for what to make, we wanted to share some of our favorite recipes that provide many servings or can easily be doubled or tripled to accommodate even larger crowds.

FEEDING THE MASSES

BREAKFAST	APPETIZERS	SALADS	DINNERS	SIDES	DESSERTS
Pancakes (pg. 39)	Spinach Artichoke Dip (pg. 85)	Fruit Salad (pg. 105)	Brown Sugar Ham (pg. 172)	Funeral Potatoes (pg. 146)	Dirt Cake (pg. 210)
German Pancakes (pg. 40)	Buffalo Chicken Dip (pg. 86)	Potato Salad (pg. 112)	Roast Turkey (pg. 175)	Homemade Mac and Cheese (pg. 142)	Chocolate Sheet Cake (pg. 211)
French Toast Bake (pg. 44)	Guacamole (pg. 88)	Broccoli Salad (pg. 111)	Enchiladas–Chicken (pg. 183) or Cheese (pg. 184)	Spanish Rice (pg. 148)	White Sheet Cake (pg. 212)
Cinnamon Roll Cake (pg. 46)	Queso Blanco (pg. 90)	Pasta Salad (pg. 114)	Cheesy Pasta Bake (pg. 197)	Street Corn (Esquites) (pg. 150)	Pineapple Upside-Down Cake (pg. 213)
Potato Breakfast Casserole (pg. 52)	Pizza Dip (pg. 91)	Chicken Salad (pg. 115)	Baked Ziti (pg. 201)	Salsas (pgs. 153, 154, 155)	Lemon Lasagna (pg. 228)

HOW LONG WILL IT KEEP?

While everything tastes best fresh, we often find ourselves with yummy food left over that we do not want to waste. Certain foods can still be delicious from a few days to a few months after they are prepared, if they are stored properly. The chart below will tell you how to best store food, and how long you can expect it to keep.

	AT ROOM TEMPERATURE	IN THE FRIDGE	IN THE FREEZER
BREAKFAST			
Breakfast casseroles/bakes	-	< 5 days	< 2 months
Stratas, quiches	-	3-4 days	< 3 months
Pancakes, waffles	-	< 3 days	2-3 months
Smoothies	-	1-2 days	< 3 months
Sweet rolls	2-3 days	5-7 days	4-6 weeks
BREADS & MUFFINS			
Yeast breads	3 days	see recipes	4-6 months
Quick breads, muffins, cornbread	2-3 days	5-7 days	3 months
Biscuits	2 days	5-7 days	2-3 months
APPETIZERS			
Warm dips	-	3-4 days	3 months
Cool dips	-	1-2 days	2-3 months
Meatballs, smokies, wings	-	3-4 days	2-3 months
Fried appetizers	-	2-4 days	-
SALADS			
Dressing (creamy and vinaigrette)	-	1-2 weeks	-
Green salads with no dressing	-	4-5 days	-
Green salads with dressing	-	1-2 days	-
Salads with mayo (pasta, potato, chicken), fruit salad, Jell-O salad	-	3-5 days	-
SOUPS			
Soups, stews, chilis	-	3-4 days	4-6 months
SIDE DISHES			
Cooked vegetables	-	2-3 days	6 months
Baked casseroles	-	2-4 days	Up to 3 months
Rice dishes	-	3-4 days	1-2 months
Salsas	-	5-7 days	3-4 months
MAIN DISHES / MEAT DISHES			
Beef, pork, fish	-	3-4 days	2-3 months
Chicken, turkey	-	3-4 days	3-4 months
Hot dogs, pigs in a blanket	-	2-3 days	1 month
Enchiladas	-	3-5 days	2-4 months

	AT ROOM TEMPERATURE	IN THE FRIDGE	IN THE FREEZER
MAIN DISHES / PASTA & PIZZA			
Pasta	–	3–4 days	3 months
Pizza	–	3–4 days	1–2 months
DESSERTS / CAKES & CUPCAKES			
Unfrosted cakes and cupcakes	2–3 days	3 days	3 months
Frosted cakes and cupcakes	3 days	1 week	3–6 months
DESSERTS / BROWNIES, BARS AND PIES			
Brownies, blondies, cookie bars	3–4 days	5–7 days	3 months
Baked fruit pies	2 days	2–3 days	4 months
Cream and pumpkin pies	–	3–4 days	6 months
Cobblers, crisps	24 hours	2–3 days	3 months
Pie crusts, graham cracker crusts	1–2 days	3 days	3–4 months
DESSERTS / COOKIES			
Drop cookies	3–5 days	–	3–6 months
Sugar cookies	4–5 days	–	3 months
Shortbreads	1–2 weeks	–	2–3 months
No-bake cookies	5–7 days	1–2 weeks	3–4 weeks
DESSERTS / CANDY & OTHER DESSERTS			
Sweet dips (caramel, apple brickle, cream cheese)	–	5–7 days	–
Beignets, funnel cakes, churros	2–4 days	–	2–3 months
Ice cream	–	–	2–4 weeks
DRINKS			
Punch	–	2–3 days	3 months
Lemonade	–	4–5 days	4–6 months
Cider	–	5–7 days	12 months

Holiday Menu Builder

Holidays and special occasions are great reasons to gather with friends and family to enjoy one another's company and to eat delicious food. Our family often hosts these get-togethers, and we love to plan these gatherings around a menu. Making a holiday menu does not have to be stressful! It just takes a little bit of planning and organization to make your event tasty *and* amazing.

When building a menu for a special occasion, be sure to keep these tips in mind:

⊘ Assign dishes to your guests to minimize the work. Most guests are happy to help, so let them.

⊘ Make your menu at least one week before your event.

⊘ Print, bookmark or tag all the recipes you plan to use and make your grocery list.

⊘ Do all the shopping a few days before your event.

⊘ Write out a schedule of when to make your recipes and stick to it! Be sure to take into account prep times, preheating times, cook times and what appliances might already be in use for other recipes when creating your schedule.

To make your special occasions even easier, we have listed our top-choice recipes for all the major holidays below. Simply pick your favorites from each section to build your own delicious menu and then use our scheduling tips below to make execution a breeze. And when someone asks, "What can I bring?" remember, executing your menu will be easier if you assign some of the recipes to your guests!

NEW YEAR'S or SUPER BOWL, serves 8

PICK 2: APPETIZERS	**Spinach Artichoke Dip** (pg. 85), **Buffalo Chicken Dip** (pg. 86) or **Slow Cooker Meatballs** (pg. 100)
PICK 1: MAIN DISH	**Pizza** (delivery or homemade, pg. 202) or **Buffalo Wings** (pg. 96)
PICK 1: DESSERT	**7-Layer Bars** (pg. 225), **Brownies** (pg. 220) or **Blondies** (pg. 221)
PICK 1: DRINK	**Holiday Punch** (pg. 284) or **Eggnog** (pg. 287)
TO-DO LIST	
DAY BEFORE OR MORNING OF	⊘ Make dessert; cover and store.
4 HOURS BEFORE	⊘ Prepare appetizers; cover and store in the refrigerator, or in the slow cooker to keep warm, per recipe directions.
1 (OR 2–3) HOURS BEFORE	⊘ Make the main dish so that it's finishing as guests are arriving.

VALENTINE'S DAY, serves 8

PICK 1: MAIN DISH	**Chicken Tetrazzini** (pg. 193), **Cheesy Pasta Bake** (pg. 197) or **Spaghetti Bake** (pg. 199)
PICK 2: SIDES	**Easy Garlic Knots** (pg. 66), **Roasted Vegetables** (pg. 140) or **Parmesan Sweet Potato Cubes** (pg. 141)
PICK 1: DESSERT	**Chocolate-Covered Strawberries** (pg. 258), **Cream Puff Cake** (pg. 209) or **Fruit Pizza** (pg. 229)
PICK 1: DRINK	**Pink Punch** (pg. 279) or **Cherry Limeade** (pg. 281)

TO-DO LIST

DAY BEFORE OR MORNING OF	⊘ Make the main dish; cover and refrigerate.
4 HOURS BEFORE	⊘ Make dessert and refrigerate. If making Fruit Pizza, wait to add fruit on top until right before serving.
1 HOUR BEFORE	⊘ Make sides and place dinner in the oven to bake.

EASTER, serves 8

PICK 2: APPETIZERS	**Deviled Eggs** (pg. 93), **Charcuterie Board** (pg. 101) or **Cream Cheese Fruit Dip** (pg. 273)
PICK 1: MAIN DISH	**Brown Sugar Ham** (pg. 172) or **Pot Roast** (pg. 165)
PICK 2: SIDES	**Heavenly Rolls** (pg. 68), **Mashed Potatoes** (pg. 145), **Creamed Corn** (pg. 138) or **Brown Sugar–Glazed Carrots** (pg. 136)
PICK 1: DESSERT	**Dirt Cake** (pg. 210), **Pineapple Upside-Down Cake** (pg. 213) or **Lemon Lasagna** (pg. 228)
PICK 1: DRINK	**Lemonade** (pg. 282) or **Pink Punch** (pg. 279)

TO-DO LIST

MORNING OF	⊘ Prepare the main dish and place in a slow cooker, timing it to finish cooking right at dinner time. ⊘ Prepare dessert; cover and refrigerate.
4 HOURS BEFORE	⊘ Prepare appetizers; cover and refrigerate.
1 HOUR BEFORE	⊘ Prepare sides, timing them to finish as guests are arriving.

MOTHER'S DAY OR FATHER'S DAY, serves 8

PICK 1: SALAD	**Strawberry Salad** (pg. 108) or **Caesar Salad** (pg. 106)
PICK 1: MAIN DISH	**Parmesan-Crusted Pork Chops** (pg. 167), **Creamy Swiss Chicken** (pg. 177) or **Marinated Steak** (pg. 161)
PICK 2: SIDES	**Brown Sugar–Glazed Carrots** (pg. 136), **Twice-Baked Potatoes** (pg. 144) or **Roasted Vegetables** (pg. 140)
PICK 1: DESSERT	**Fruit Pizza** (pg. 229), **Cheesecake Fruit Salad** (pg. 210) or **Lemon Bars** (pg. 226)
PICK 1: DRINK	**Pink Punch** (pg. 279) or **Cherry Limeade** (pg. 281)

TO-DO LIST

MORNING OF	⊘ Make dessert; cover and store.
4 HOURS BEFORE	⊘ Prepare salad and dressing and store separately in the refrigerator.
1 HOUR BEFORE	⊘ Make the main dish and sides, timing them to finish as guests arrive.

CINCO DE MAYO, serves 8

PICK 1: APPETIZER	**Flautas** (pg. 187), **Cream Cheese and Chicken Taquitos** (pg. 186) or **Chicken Tacos** (pg. 188)
PICK 1: MAIN DISH	**Green Chile Chicken Enchiladas** (pg. 183), **Cheese Enchiladas** (pg. 184) or **Sweet Pork** (pg. 170)
PICK 1: SIDE	**Spanish Rice** (pg. 148), **Cilantro-Lime Rice** (pg. 149) or **Cream Cheese Bean Dip** (pg. 89)
PICK 1: SALSA	**Homemade Salsa** (pg. 153), **Sweet Salsa Verde** (pg. 154) or **Black Bean and Corn Salsa** (pg. 155)
PICK 1: DESSERT	**Arroz con Leche** (pg. 266), **White Sheet Cake** (pg. 212) or **Churro Popcorn** (pg. 262)
PICK 1: DRINK	**Cherry Limeade** (pg. 281), **Lemonade** (pg. 282) or **Frozen Hot Chocolate** (pg. 285)

TO-DO LIST

DAY BEFORE	⊘ Cook and shred meat for main dish and appetizer. Store in the refrigerator.
MORNING OF	⊘ Prepare main dish and refrigerate. If making the Sweet Pork, place it in the slow cooker and start cooking per directions. ⊘ Make salsa and refrigerate. If making the Black Bean and Corn Salsa, wait to add avocados until right before serving.
4 HOURS BEFORE	⊘ Make dessert; cover and store. If making Arroz con Leche, place in the refrigerator and reheat right before serving.
1 HOUR BEFORE	⊘ Make side and place in a slow cooker to keep warm until dinner. ⊘ Finish main dish, either by baking enchiladas or shredding pork. ⊘ Make the appetizer, timing it to finish as guests arrive.

MEMORIAL DAY/LABOR DAY, serves 8

PICK 1: APPETIZER	**7-Layer Dip** (pg. 87), **Charcuterie Board** (pg. 101) or **Cream Cheese Fruit Dip** (pg. 273)
PICK 1: MAIN DISH	**Classic Burgers** (pg. 160), **Marinated Steak** (pg. 161) or **Pigs in a Blanket** (pg. 166)
PICK 2: SIDES	**Macaroni Salad** (pg. 113), **Fruit Salad** (pg. 105) or **Pasta Salad** (pg. 114)
PICK 1: DESSERT	**Angel Food Ice Cream Cake** (pg. 216), **Cream Puff Cake** (pg. 209) or **Dirt Cake** (pg. 210)
PICK 1: DRINK	**Lemonade** (pg. 282), **Cherry Limeade** (pg. 281) or **Frozen Hot Chocolate** (pg. 285)

TO-DO LIST

DAY BEFORE OR MORNING OF	⊘ Make dessert; cover and store.
4 HOURS BEFORE	⊘ Make appetizer and sides; cover and store in the refrigerator.
1 HOUR BEFORE	⊘ Make the main dish, timing it to finish as guests arrive.

FOURTH OF JULY, serves 8

PICK 1: APPETIZER	**Deviled Eggs** (pg. 93), **Caramel Dip** (pg. 274) or **Apple Brickle Dip** (pg. 275)
PICK 1: MAIN DISH	**Slow Cooker Brisket** (pg. 163) or **Baby Back Ribs** (pg. 168)
PICK 2: SIDES	**Potato Salad** (pg. 112), **Pasta Salad** (pg. 114) or **Broccoli Salad** (pg. 111)
PICK 1: DESSERT	**Jell-O Poke Cake** (pg. 208), **Lemon Lasagna** (pg. 228) or **Homemade Ice Cream** (pg. 265)
PICK 1: DRINK	**Cherry Limeade** (pg. 281) or **Ocean Water** (pg. 280)

TO-DO LIST

MORNING OF	⊘ Start the main dish, timing it to finish as guests arrive. ⊘ Prepare the appetizer; cover and store in the refrigerator.
4 HOURS BEFORE	⊘ Make sides and dessert. Cover and store in the refrigerator.
1 HOUR BEFORE	⊘ Make sure the main dish is ready to serve: slice brisket or brush final coating of sauce onto ribs as guests arrive.

HALLOWEEN, serves 8

PICK 1: APPETIZER	Queso Blanco (pg. 90) or Cream Cheese Bean Dip (pg. 89)
PICK 1: MAIN DISH	Best Chili Soup (pg. 126), White Chicken Chili (pg. 127) or Slow Cooker Green Chile Chicken Enchilada Soup (pg. 129)
PICK 1: BREAD	Cornbread (pg. 71) or Bread Bowls (pg. 64)
PICK 1: SIDE	Homemade Mac and Cheese (pg. 142), Parmesan Sweet Potato Cubes (pg. 141) or Roasted Vegetables (pg. 140)
PICK 1: DESSERT	Popcorn Balls (pg. 263), Pumpkin Delight (pg. 234) or Pumpkin Chocolate Chip Cookies (pg. 251)
PICK 1: DRINK	Apple Cider (pg. 286) or Halloween Punch (pg. 283)

TO-DO LIST

MORNING OF	⊘ Make bread and dessert; cover and store.
2 HOURS BEFORE	⊘ Make main dish and place in the slow cooker on warm.
1 HOUR BEFORE	⊘ Make appetizer and place in a small slow cooker on warm. ⊘ Make side dish, timing it to finish right before guests arrive.

THANKSGIVING, serves 8

PICK 1: APPETIZER	Deviled Eggs (pg. 93), Charcuterie Board (pg. 101) or Cream Cheese Fruit Dip (pg. 273)
PICK 1: MAIN DISH	Roast Turkey (pg. 175) or Brown Sugar Ham (pg. 172)
PICK 1: BREAD	Heavenly Rolls (pg. 68) or Easy Homemade Biscuits (pg. 65)
PICK 2: SIDES	Green Bean Casserole (pg. 137), Mashed Potatoes (pg. 145), Funeral Potatoes (pg. 146) or Homemade Mac and Cheese (pg. 142)
PICK 1: DESSERT	Pumpkin Pie (pg. 235), Pecan Pie Bars (pg. 236), Pumpkin Roll (pg. 218) or Pumpkin Delight (pg. 234)
PICK 1: DRINK	Apple Cider (pg. 286) or Holiday Punch (pg. 284)

TO-DO LIST

MORNING OF	⊘ Make desserts; cover and store in the refrigerator. ⊘ Make appetizer; cover and store in the refrigerator.
4 HOURS BEFORE	⊘ Make the main dish, timing it to finish right before guests arrive. ⊘ Prepare sides up to the point of baking, but do not bake yet. Cover and store in the refrigerator.
1 HOUR BEFORE	⊘ Make bread, timing it to finish as guests arrive. ⊘ Bake sides, timing them to finish as guests arrive.

CHRISTMAS, serves 8

PICK 1: APPETIZER	Slow Cooker Meatballs (pg. 100), Spinach Artichoke Dip (pg. 85) or Charcuterie Board (pg. 101)
PICK 1: MAIN DISH	Garlic Prime Rib (pg. 162), Roast Chicken (pg. 174) or Brown Sugar Ham (pg. 172)
PICK 1: BREAD	Heavenly Rolls (pg. 68) or Easy Garlic Knots (pg. 66)
PICK 2: SIDES	Twice-Baked Potatoes (pg. 144), Funeral Potatoes (pg. 146), Homemade Mac and Cheese (pg. 142) or Green Bean Bundles (pg. 135)
PICK 1: DESSERT	Dirt Cake (pg. 210) or Cream Puff Cake (pg. 209)
PICK 1: DRINK	Holiday Punch (pg. 284), Homemade Hot Cocoa (pg. 285) or Eggnog (pg. 287)

TO-DO LIST

MORNING OF	⊘ Make dessert; cover and store in the refrigerator. ⊘ Prepare sides so they are ready to place in the oven, then cover and store in the refrigerator.
4 HOURS BEFORE	⊘ Start main dish, timing it to finish as guests arrive. ⊘ Make appetizer and store in the refrigerator (for the charcuterie board), or in a slow cooker on the warm setting (for meatballs or dip).
3 HOURS BEFORE	⊘ Make bread, timing it to finish as guests arrive. ⊘ Bake sides, timing them to finish as guests arrive.

BREAKFAST

"I love sleep because it's like a time machine to breakfast!"

They say breakfast is the most important meal of the day. Whether that is true or not, we love breakfast so much that we often have it for dinner (and call it "brinner"!). Although we do not always have time to make a big breakfast on school days, these recipes sure come in handy for weekends, holidays and special occasions. We think you will agree that there's nothing quite like waking up to the smell of delicious food being made in the kitchen.

HELPFUL TIPS + INFORMATION

How Much to Serve?

BACON OR SAUSAGE: 2–3 pieces per person

COFFEE CAKE, SWEET ROLLS OR SWEET BAKES: 1 slice/roll per person

EGGS, ANY STYLE: 2 per person

PANCAKES: 3 per person

QUICHE, STRATAS OR CASSEROLES: 1 slice/piece per person OR mini pieces: 1–2 per person

SMOOTHIES OR JUICE: 1 cup per person

WAFFLES, FRENCH TOAST, BAGELS, MUFFINS, BISCUITS: 2 per person

Make-Ahead Breakfasts

- Breakfast cakes, casseroles, quiches and stratas are all great choices for busy mornings or for hosting a gathering because they can easily be made in advance. Look for "Make Ahead" tips throughout the chapter for instructions on storing and reheating.

- Pancakes, waffles and French toast can all be made ahead and frozen, individually wrapped or separated with parchment paper in a resealable plastic freezer bag, for 1–2 months, so family members can easily grab what they need and reheat in the oven or toaster.

- For super-quick smoothies, create grab-and-go freezer packs: Just prep enough fruits and vegetables to make several smoothies, divide them among individual resealable plastic freezer bags, and freeze. When ready to use, simply blend the contents of one bag with ice and a bit of juice, milk or water.

Smoothie Suggestions

TO MAKE SMOOTHIES HEALTHIER:

- Use low-fat milk and yogurt instead of full-fat, or use unsweetened almond or coconut milk instead of dairy.

- Add more vitamin-rich ingredients. We love adding spinach and kale, chia seeds, fiber, collagen, protein powder, nut butters and/or flaxseed.

- Sweeten your smoothies with honey or stevia instead of white sugar.

FOR THE PERFECT TEXTURE:

- Make your smoothies thinner by adding more liquid, like apple juice, water or milk.

- Make your smoothies thicker with yogurt or fruit. Bananas work especially well.

- To use leftovers: Pour leftover smoothies into a popsicle mold and freeze. Our kids love to eat these as snacks.

SCRAMBLED EGGS

⏱ PREP TIME: **2 MINUTES**

⏳ COOK TIME: **7 MINUTES**

♡ SERVES: **8**

PREPPED IN 5

QUICK & EASY

ON THE TABLE IN 20

FEED A CROWD

GLUTEN-FREE

INGREDIENTS

12 large eggs

¼ cup heavy cream

1 tablespoon unsalted butter

salt and pepper to taste

1 cup shredded cheese (cheddar or Monterey Jack)

Scan me!

INSTRUCTIONS

1. Crack eggs into a large bowl.

2. Add heavy cream and whisk together until smooth.

3. Place butter in a skillet over low heat and let it melt. Add eggs to the skillet and slowly start cooking. Use a rubber spatula to mix eggs around in small circles while they cook.

4. Cook for 2–3 minutes if you want your eggs to be creamier and cook for 5–7 minutes if you want them fluffier.

5. Turn the heat off and season eggs with salt, pepper and cheese. Remove from the skillet once cheese is melted.

★ **BONUS RECIPE**

Bacon (in the oven)

Can't have eggs without bacon! Our favorite way to make it is in the oven. To do that, preheat the oven to 400 degrees F. Line a rimmed baking sheet with aluminum foil (optional, but allows for easy cleanup), and lay out as many bacon slices as you want in a single layer on the sheet. Bake for 18–20 minutes, or until bacon is crisp. Thick-cut bacon may take a few minutes longer.

⚙ VARIATIONS

⊕ **GREEK:** Add chopped spinach, feta cheese and chopped tomatoes

⊕ **DENVER:** Add chopped green onions, peppers and cubed ham

⊕ **SOUTHWEST:** Add some diced green chiles for an amazing flavor

⊕ **MEAT LOVERS':** Add chopped, cooked sausage, ham and/or bacon

PAIRINGS: Bacon (page 37), Breakfast Potatoes (page 38)

BREAKFAST POTATOES

- ⏱ **PREP TIME:** 5 MINUTES
- ⏳ **COOK TIME:** 25 MINUTES
- ♡ **SERVES:** 8

- ✓ PREPPED IN 5
- ✓ QUICK & EASY
- ✓ FEED A CROWD
- ✓ DAIRY-FREE

INGREDIENTS

1½ pounds russet potatoes (about 4 potatoes)
2 tablespoons olive oil
1 teaspoon garlic salt with parsley flakes
½ teaspoon dried parsley
pepper to taste

Scan me!

INSTRUCTIONS

1. Preheat the oven to 400 degrees F. Line a baking sheet with parchment paper and set aside.

2. Peel potatoes and cut into ½-inch cubes.

3. Place potatoes in a large resealable plastic bag and add olive oil, garlic salt, parsley and pepper. Toss until potatoes are coated and pour onto the prepared baking sheet.

4. Bake for 20–22 minutes, then set the oven to broil. Broil for a few minutes to help crisp and brown potatoes.

PAIRINGS: Scrambled Eggs (page 37), Bacon (page 37), Pancakes (page 39), Belgian Waffles (page 42), French Toast (page 43), Fruit Smoothie (page 56)

👍 RECIPE TIPS

☺ **Skillet Directions:** *Combine olive oil and 1 tablespoon butter in a large skillet over medium heat. Add potatoes and cook for 8–10 minutes, tossing occasionally. Season with garlic salt, parsley and pepper while cooking.*

☺ **Serving Idea:** *You can also use these potatoes in breakfast burritos and tacos.*

PANCAKES

PREP TIME: **5 MINUTES**

COOK TIME: **10 MINUTES**

SERVES: **8**

- PREPPED IN 5
- QUICK & EASY
- FREEZER FRIENDLY
- FEED A CROWD

INGREDIENTS

1½ cups all-purpose flour

3½ teaspoons baking powder

1 tablespoon sugar

½ teaspoon salt

1¼ cups milk

1 egg

3 tablespoons unsalted butter, melted

1 teaspoon vanilla extract

TOPPINGS: fruit, Homemade Whipped Cream
(page 208), Buttermilk Syrup (page 41)

Scan me!

INSTRUCTIONS

1. In a large bowl, sift together the flour,
   baking powder, sugar and salt.

2. Make a well in the center of the dry ingredients. Pour in the milk,
   egg, melted butter and vanilla and mix until smooth.

3. Lightly oil a griddle or frying pan and heat to medium-high (about
   375 degrees F).

4. Pour about ¼ cup batter onto the griddle for each pancake. Cook
   until browned (about 3 minutes), then flip and cook 2 minutes more
   until browned on both sides. Serve hot with your favorite toppings.

🔥 RECIPE TIPS

☺ **Make Ahead:** *Pancakes are best made
right before serving. If making a lot, you
can keep them warm by placing them on a
baking sheet in a 200-degree F oven until
you're ready to serve.*

☺ **Want Them Fluffy?** *Let the batter rest for
15 minutes after mixing.*

⚙ VARIATIONS

This recipe is our go-to base for all kinds of
pancakes. Try adding bananas, chocolate
chips, blueberries, oatmeal, strawberries,
raspberries, white chocolate chips, peaches,
brown sugar or cinnamon to the batter before
cooking.

PAIRINGS: Scrambled Eggs (page 37), Bacon (page 37), Breakfast
Potatoes (page 38), Biscuits and Gravy (page 50)

GERMAN PANCAKES

PREP TIME: 5 MINUTES
COOK TIME: 20 MINUTES
SERVES: 8

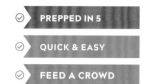

PREPPED IN 5

QUICK & EASY

FEED A CROWD

INGREDIENTS

5 tablespoons unsalted butter

6 large eggs

1 cup all-purpose flour

1 cup milk

½ teaspoon salt

Scan me!

INSTRUCTIONS

1. Preheat the oven to 450 degrees F.

2. Melt butter in a 9-x-13-inch baking dish in the warming oven.

3. In a medium bowl, whisk eggs together. Whisk in flour until clumps are gone.

4. Add milk and salt and whisk until combined (this can also be mixed in the blender to avoid clumps).

5. Pour batter into the pan of melted butter. Bake for 16–20 minutes. The sides will be overflowing and fluffy but will come down a bit once the pan is removed from the oven.

6. Serve immediately with your toppings of choice.

PAIRINGS: Bacon (page 37), Breakfast Potatoes (page 38), Coffee Cake (page 47), Orange Julius (page 57)

👍 RECIPE TIPS

☺ **For Extra Fluffy Puff Pancakes:** *Use the freshest eggs possible and add eggs, one at a time, whisking for 30 seconds after each egg.*

⚙ VARIATIONS

TOPPINGS: There are lots of different toppings you can try! We like to top ours with fruit, powdered sugar and Buttermilk Syrup (page 41).

SWEDISH PANCAKES

🕐 PREP TIME: **5 MINUTES**

⏳ COOK TIME: **30 MINUTES**

♡ MAKES: **12 PANCAKES**

✓ **PREPPED IN 5**

✓ **QUICK & EASY**

INGREDIENTS

3 large eggs

3 cups milk

3 tablespoons unsalted butter, melted, plus more for the pan

1½ cups all-purpose flour, sifted

2 teaspoons sugar

1 teaspoon salt

TOPPINGS: fruit, syrup, Homemade Whipped Cream (page 208)

Scan me!

★ **BONUS RECIPE**

Buttermilk Syrup

Melt ½ cup butter in a medium pot over medium-low heat. Once melted, add 1 cup sugar, ½ cup buttermilk and 1 teaspoon vanilla extract. Whisk until sugar has dissolved and mixture is combined and starting to boil. Remove from the heat and whisk in ½ teaspoon baking powder, which will make the syrup foamy. Serve on top of pancakes and top with whipped cream, fruit or any other toppings. Change up the flavor by adding ¼ teaspoon almond or coconut extract or a spice, such as ¼ teaspoon ground cinnamon.

INSTRUCTIONS

1. In a medium bowl, beat eggs until well combined.

2. Add milk, butter, flour, sugar and salt to eggs and mix until smooth.

3. Heat more butter in a 10-inch nonstick skillet over medium heat, or spray skillet with nonstick cooking spray.

4. Pour about ¼ cup batter into the pan and tilt the pan in circles until the batter is spread all over in a thin layer. Cook for 1–2 minutes. When the edges are bubbled and browned, it is ready to flip.

5. Cook the other side until golden, about 1 minute, then transfer to a plate. Repeat to make the remaining pancakes, stacking them with a piece of parchment paper between each one to keep from sticking.

6. Serve immediately with your toppings of choice.

⚙ **VARIATIONS**

FILLINGS: There are many different sweet and savory fillings you can use for Swedish pancakes. Simply place fillings in the center of a pancake and roll up like a crepe.

SWEET: Fruit, Nutella, Buttermilk Syrup, jam, whipped cream or ice cream.

SAVORY: Eggs, ham, cheese, mushrooms, spinach, steak, pulled pork with barbecue sauce or a caprese version with avocado, tomato, mozzarella and balsamic glaze.

🖒 RECIPE TIPS

☺ **Make Ahead:** *If making a large batch, you can keep the Swedish pancakes warm until ready to serve in an oven heated to about 200 degrees F. You can either roll each pancake and place them side by side in a pan, or stack them on the pan, separating each pancake with parchment paper.*

PAIRINGS: Scrambled Eggs (page 37), Bacon (page 37), Cheesecake Fruit Salad (page 210), Homemade Ice Cream (page 265)

BELGIAN WAFFLES

⏱ **PREP TIME:** 10 MINUTES
⧗ **COOK TIME:** 25–30 MINUTES
♡ **MAKES:** 6–8 WAFFLES

 **FREEZER FRIENDLY**

 MAKE AHEAD

INGREDIENTS

2 cups all-purpose flour
¼ cup sugar
4 teaspoons baking powder
½ teaspoon salt
2 large eggs
2 cups milk
½ cup vegetable oil
1 teaspoon vanilla extract
TOPPINGS: fruit, powdered sugar, Homemade Whipped Cream (page 208), Buttermilk Syrup (page 41)

 *Scan me!*

INSTRUCTIONS

1. In a large bowl, sift flour, sugar, baking powder and salt together.

2. Separate egg whites and yolks into two separate bowls.

3. Beat egg whites until peaks form and set aside.

4. Add milk, oil and vanilla to egg yolks and stir until just combined. Add wet ingredients to dry ingredients and mix well. Fold in egg whites.

5. Grease a waffle iron and preheat to medium-high. Add ½–⅔ cup batter per waffle to the iron and cook for 4–5 minutes, or until waffles are browned and crispy.

6. Serve warm topped with whipped cream, syrup or your favorite fruits.

PAIRINGS: Bacon (page 37), Scrambled Eggs (page 37), Breakfast Potatoes (page 38), Fruit Smoothie (page 56)

👍 **RECIPE TIPS**

☺ **To Freeze:** *Place the waffles on a parchment paper–lined baking sheet. Freeze until frozen (about 2 hours) and then put them in an airtight freezer-safe container. The waffles will stay good for up to 4 months.*

☺ **To Reheat:** *Preheat the oven or toaster oven to 350 degrees F. Bake frozen or refrigerated waffles for 10–15 minutes, or until hot. You can also heat them up in a toaster.*

FRENCH TOAST

PREP TIME: **5 MINUTES**

COOK TIME: **10 MINUTES**

SERVES: **4**

PREPPED IN 5

QUICK & EASY

ON THE TABLE IN 20

MAKE AHEAD

INGREDIENTS

1 cup milk

2 large eggs

2 egg yolks

1 tablespoon sugar

1 teaspoon ground cinnamon

1 pinch salt

1 teaspoon vanilla extract

8 slices brioche bread, toasted or slightly stale

4 tablespoons unsalted butter

TOPPINGS: fruit, powdered sugar, Homemade Whipped Cream (page 208), Buttermilk Syrup (page 41)

Scan me!

INSTRUCTIONS

1. In a medium bowl or cake pan, whisk milk, eggs and egg yolks together. Add sugar, cinnamon, salt and vanilla and whisk until smooth.

2. Soak bread slices in mixture until saturated, 10–15 seconds per side.

3. Heat butter on a griddle or in a frying pan over medium heat. Add bread slices and cook until golden brown, 2–3 minutes per side.

4. Serve hot with your favorite toppings.

PAIRINGS: Bacon (page 37), Scrambled Eggs (page 37), Breakfast Potatoes (page 38), Fruit Smoothie (page 56)

👍 RECIPE TIPS

☺ **Make Ahead:** *Wrap a few slices individually in plastic wrap and freeze them in a resealable plastic freezer bag. Eat within 1–2 months for best quality.*

☺ **To Reheat:** *Place frozen toast on an aluminum foil–lined baking sheet in a single layer. Bake at 375 degrees F for 8–10 minutes. You can also use a toaster.*

☺ **Kick It Up a Notch:** *Try using thick slices of French Bread (page 63), sourdough or even Cinnamon Bread (page 72).*

FRENCH TOAST BAKE

🕐 PREP TIME: 15 MINUTES

⏳ CHILL TIME: 4 HOURS

⏳ COOK TIME: 45 MINUTES

♡ SERVES: 8

FREEZER FRIENDLY

FEED A CROWD

MAKE AHEAD

INGREDIENTS

FRENCH TOAST:

1 loaf sourdough bread (or brioche, challah or French Bread, page 63)

8 large eggs

2 cups milk

½ cup heavy cream

1 tablespoon vanilla extract

¾ cup sugar

TOPPING:

½ cup all-purpose flour

½ cup packed light brown sugar

1 teaspoon ground cinnamon

¼ teaspoon salt

½ cup cold unsalted butter, cut into pieces

Scan me!

INSTRUCTIONS

1. Cut bread into 1-inch cubes and scatter evenly in a greased 9-x-13-inch baking dish.

2. In a medium bowl, mix eggs, milk, heavy cream, vanilla and sugar together, then pour evenly over bread.

3. Cover the dish with plastic wrap and refrigerate for at least 4 hours, or overnight.

4. To make the topping, mix flour, brown sugar, cinnamon and salt in a medium bowl. Cut butter into this mixture until crumbly. Place topping in a small resealable plastic bag and refrigerate overnight as well.

5. When ready to bake, preheat the oven to 350 degrees F.

6. Unwrap the baking dish and sprinkle topping evenly over the bread.

7. Bake, uncovered, for 45–60 minutes, depending on how soft you like it.

👍 RECIPE TIPS

☺ **Make Ahead:** *This bake can be prepared through Step 4 and frozen; store the topping separately and add it once the bake is thawed. It can also be frozen after baking. Wrap the dish with plastic wrap, then aluminum foil and store for up to 2 months in the freezer. When you are ready to eat it, thaw overnight in the fridge. Remove all the wrapping and bake at 350 degrees F. If it has been prebaked, bake for 20 minutes; if not, bake according to the recipe directions above.*

⚙ VARIATIONS

➔ For a more savory casserole, add ham and cheese, chorizo, green chiles, sausage or crumbled bacon.

➔ For a sweet casserole, add thinly sliced apple, orange zest, sliced apricots, sliced pineapple, blueberries or chopped pecans.

PAIRINGS: Scrambled Eggs (page 37), Buttermilk Syrup (page 41), Biscuit Egg Casserole (page 51)

DONUTS

🕐 PREP TIME: 20 MINUTES

⌛ RISE TIME: 3 HOURS

⌛ COOK TIME: 30 MINUTES

♡ MAKES: 30 DONUTS, PLUS DONUT HOLES

✓ **FEED A CROWD**

✓ **MAKE AHEAD**

INGREDIENTS

DOUGH:

2 tablespoons rapid rise yeast

¾ cup warm water (110–115 degrees F)

2 cups milk

½ cup vegetable shortening, room temperature

⅔ cup sugar

2 teaspoons salt

1 teaspoon ground cinnamon

½ teaspoon ground nutmeg

4 large eggs

7–7½ cups all-purpose flour

vegetable oil, for frying

GLAZE:

7 cups powdered sugar, sifted

⅔ cup water

2 teaspoons vanilla extract

Scan me!

👍 RECIPE TIPS

☺ **Make Ahead:** *You can make donut dough ahead up until Step 5, then cover and refrigerate until the next day. When ready to make the donuts, let dough come to room temperature and then rise for an hour.*

☺ **Filled Donuts:** *If you want to fill your donuts, cut whole circles instead of punching out the holes. Make and fry donuts as directed, then use a piping bag to insert your filling of choice (such as pudding, jelly, or Nutella) into the side of each donut when it has cooled.*

☺ **Baked Donuts:** *Once donuts are done rising, you can also bake them instead of frying. Place donuts on a lightly greased baking sheet, brush the tops with melted butter and bake at 375 degrees F for 9–12 minutes. Glaze as directed above while donuts are still warm.*

INSTRUCTIONS

1. Make the dough: Dissolve yeast in lukewarm water. Set aside.

2. Heat milk in the microwave for 2–3 minutes.

3. While milk is heating, place shortening in a large bowl or the bowl of a stand mixer. Pour hot milk over it and whisk until mixed (there will still be a few shortening clumps).

4. Add sugar, salt, cinnamon and nutmeg and mix well with a wooden spoon or the mixer whisk attachment. Add eggs and continue to mix, then stir in yeast mixture.

5. Add 2 cups of flour and mix with a wooden spoon. Continue to add flour 1–2 cups at a time until the batter is no longer runny and is smooth.

6. Place dough on a clean, lightly floured surface and gently knead until the surface of the dough is not too sticky to the touch. The dough should be very soft, but not so sticky that you cannot handle it fairly easily. Place the soft dough into a lightly greased bowl. Cover the bowl and let rise for 1–1½ hours at room temperature. The dough should be about double in size when it is ready.

7. Place dough on a lightly floured surface and roll out to a 1-inch thickness. Use a 3½-inch donut cutter to cut donuts out, cutting as closely as possible together and saving the middles for donut holes. Move donuts and holes to a clean surface, cover and let rise at room temperature for 1–1½ hours.

8. Make the glaze: Mix all ingredients together in a large bowl. Set aside.

9. Once the donuts and holes are done rising, fill a large frying pan with 1½ inches vegetable oil and heat to 365–380 degrees F. Working in batches, fry the donuts and holes until golden brown, 2–3 minutes per side for donuts and about 2 minutes per side for donut holes.

10. Remove each donut from the oil and immediately transfer to the bowl with the glaze. Turn to make sure both sides are coated, then place on a wire rack over parchment paper to let excess glaze drain. Repeat to make the remaining donuts.

PAIRINGS: Homemade Ice Cream (page 265), Homemade Hot Cocoa (page 285)

CINNAMON ROLL CAKE

⏱ PREP TIME: 10 MINUTES

⧗ COOK TIME: 30 MINUTES

♡ SERVES: 12

INGREDIENTS

CAKE:

3 cups all-purpose flour

1 cup sugar

4 teaspoons baking powder

½ teaspoon salt

1½ cups milk

2 large eggs

2 teaspoons vanilla extract

½ cup unsalted butter, melted

CINNAMON TOPPING:

¾ cup unsalted butter, softened

1 cup packed light brown sugar

2 tablespoons all-purpose flour

1 tablespoon ground cinnamon

GLAZE:

2 cups powdered sugar, sifted

5 tablespoons milk

1 teaspoon vanilla extract

Scan me!

INSTRUCTIONS

1. Preheat the oven to 350 degrees F. Grease a 9-x-13-inch baking dish and set aside.

2. Make the cake: In a large bowl, mix flour, sugar, baking powder, salt, milk, eggs and vanilla together.

3. Slowly stir in melted butter and pour batter into the prepared baking dish.

4. Make the cinnamon topping: In another bowl, mix softened butter, brown sugar, flour and cinnamon. Dollop over the top of the cake mixture evenly.

5. Swirl your topping and cake mixture with a knife, only inserting it halfway into the batter and going up and down the length of the pan.

6. Bake for 28–32 minutes.

7. Make the glaze: Mix all glaze ingredients together in a small bowl. Drizzle over the cake while it is still warm.

PAIRINGS: Bacon (page 37), Potato Breakfast Casserole (page 52)

👍 RECIPE TIPS

☺ **Make Ahead:** *We love making this fresh to serve warm, but you can also make it 24 hours in advance and store, unglazed, covered at room temperature. Just reheat it in the oven for a few minutes to get warm before drizzling with the glaze.*

☺ **Frosting:** *This recipe uses a glaze topping, but you can make a cream cheese frosting instead. We love the cream cheese frosting we use on our Easy Cinnamon Rolls (page 48).*

COFFEE CAKE

INGREDIENTS

2 large eggs, lightly beaten

1 cup vegetable oil

1¼ cups milk

1 tablespoon vanilla extract

3 cups all-purpose flour

1 cup sugar

1 tablespoon baking powder

½ teaspoon salt

1¼ cups packed light brown sugar

1 tablespoon ground cinnamon

¼–⅓ cup unsalted butter, melted

Scan me!

INSTRUCTIONS

1. Preheat the oven to 350 degrees F. Lightly grease a 9-x-13-inch baking dish and set aside.

2. In a large mixing bowl, mix eggs, oil, milk and vanilla together.

3. In a medium bowl, blend flour, sugar, baking powder and salt.

4. Add dry ingredients to the wet ingredients and mix well. Pour half the batter into the prepared baking dish.

5. In a medium bowl, combine brown sugar and cinnamon and mix well.

6. Sprinkle half of the cinnamon sugar on top of the batter. Carefully pour the remaining batter over the cinnamon-sugar layer. Sprinkle the remaining cinnamon-sugar mixture on top.

7. Drizzle the melted butter over the top, using more or less as desired.

8. Bake for 35–40 minutes and serve warm.

🖒 RECIPE TIPS

☺ **Make Ahead:** *This cake can be prepared several days in advance and stored in an airtight container in the refrigerator for up to a week. Reheat in the microwave, or in the oven at 350 degrees F for 8–10 minutes.*

PAIRINGS: Bacon (page 37), Biscuit Egg Casserole (page 51), Homemade Hot Cocoa (page 285), Apple Cider (page 286)

EASY CINNAMON ROLLS

⏱ PREP TIME: 20 MINUTES
⧗ REST TIME: 25 MINUTES
⧗ COOK TIME: 20 MINUTES
♡ SERVES: 12

 FREEZER FRIENDLY

 FEED A CROWD

 MAKE AHEAD

INGREDIENTS

DOUGH:

1 cup warm water (110–115 degrees F)

¾ cup buttermilk, room temperature

4 tablespoons unsalted butter, melted

½ cup sugar

3 tablespoons rapid rise yeast

2 large eggs

½ tablespoon salt

5–5½ cups bread flour

FILLING:

⅔ cup granulated sugar

⅔ cup packed light brown sugar

4 tablespoons unsalted butter, melted

3 tablespoons ground cinnamon

FROSTING:

3 cups powdered sugar

4 ounces cream cheese, softened

4 tablespoons unsalted butter, softened

3–4 tablespoons milk (or half-and-half), as needed

1 teaspoon vanilla extract

 Scan me!

INSTRUCTIONS

1. Make the dough: In the bowl of a stand mixer or large bowl, mix water, buttermilk, melted butter, sugar and yeast. Allow to sit for 15 minutes.

2. Add eggs and salt, then mix in flour one cup at a time. Once all flour has been added, mix an additional 5 minutes, then allow to rest for 10 minutes.

3. Meanwhile, prepare your filling. Mix granulated sugar, brown sugar, melted butter and cinnamon together in a medium bowl. Set aside.

4. Preheat the oven to 375 degrees F. Grease a large baking dish or jelly roll pan (or a 9-x-13-inch baking dish if you are fine with your rolls touching).

5. On a lightly floured surface, roll dough into a 12-x-16-inch rectangle. Spread filling over the surface of the dough, leaving a ½-inch border all around. Roll the dough into a log starting at the long edge, making sure the seam is on the bottom.

6. Use a long piece of unflavored dental floss or sewing thread to cut the roll into 12 large rolls or 18 smaller rolls. Gently place the floss under the spot you wish to cut, then bring the ends of the floss up, cross them over the top and pull the ends so it slices right through the dough.

7. Place rolls cut side up in the prepared pan. Bake for 17–20 minutes.

8. While rolls are baking, mix all frosting ingredients together in a large bowl, starting with 3 tablespoons milk and adding more as needed to reach a spreadable consistency.

9. When rolls come out of the oven, immediately spread a layer of frosting on warm rolls. Add another layer of frosting once cooled.

👩‍🍳 RECIPE TIPS

☺ **Flour:** *Bread flour is our preferred choice for this recipe for super soft rolls, but you can substitute all-purpose flour as well. (See notes on page 20 for how to make bread flour.)*

☺ **Make Ahead:** *To freeze rolls unfrosted or frosted, wrap the pan, or individual rolls, with plastic wrap, then with aluminum foil, and freeze for up to 2 months. To reheat, let thaw overnight, then warm the rolls in the oven for a few minutes.*

⚙ VARIATIONS

⊕ Sprinkle raisins or chopped nuts, like walnuts or pecans, over the filling before you roll the dough.

⊕ Use a simple powdered-sugar glaze (like the one on page 46) on top instead of the cream cheese frosting.

⊕ Swap in your favorite frosting—maple and vanilla frosting both taste great.

PAIRINGS: Bacon (page 37), Biscuit Egg Casserole (page 51), Potato Breakfast Casserole (page 52)

BISCUITS AND GRAVY

🕐 **PREP TIME:** 5 MINUTES

⧗ **COOK TIME:** 20 MINUTES

♡ **SERVES:** 6

INGREDIENTS

1 (16.3-ounce) can buttermilk biscuits (or Easy Homemade Biscuits, page 65)

1 (16-ounce) Jimmy Dean sausage roll

½–1 cup all-purpose flour

1–2 cups milk

salt and pepper to taste

Scan me!

INSTRUCTIONS

1. Bake biscuits according to package directions (or recipe).

2. Meanwhile, in a saucepan over medium-high heat, cook sausage while chopping it up into small pieces until browned and cooked through. (Do not drain excess fat from the sausage—it helps bring the flour and milk together.)

3. Once sausage is cooked through, carefully stir in flour ½ cup at a time until sausage has a nice coating.

4. Slowly add milk until you have reached your desired consistency. If you prefer a more runny gravy, add more milk. If you like the gravy to be thicker, add less milk. If you find you have added too much milk, add some flour to thicken it up.

5. Add salt and pepper. Serve gravy immediately over warm biscuits.

PAIRINGS: Bacon (page 37), Breakfast Potatoes (page 38), Fruit Smoothie (page 56)

⚙ VARIATIONS

→ Replace the biscuits with rice, cornbread, toast, or Mashed Potatoes (page 145).

→ Try using ground turkey (plus 2 tablespoons of butter) or ground beef in place of the sausage.

→ Replace the regular milk with buttermilk.

→ Try adding mushrooms, bell peppers or cooked bacon bits to change up the flavor.

BISCUIT EGG CASSEROLE

⏱ **PREP TIME:** 5 MINUTES

⏳ **COOK TIME:** 25 MINUTES

♡ **SERVES:** 12

✓ **PREPPED IN 5**

✓ **QUICK & EASY**

✓ **FEED A CROWD**

✓ **MAKE AHEAD**

INGREDIENTS

1 (16.3-ounce) can Grands! Biscuits (8 count)

1 (8-ounce) package Jimmy Dean precooked sausage crumbles (or 1 cup crumbled cooked sausage)

1 cup shredded mozzarella cheese

1 cup shredded cheddar cheese

8 large eggs, beaten

1 cup milk, room temperature

salt and pepper to taste

 *Scan me!*

INSTRUCTIONS

1. Preheat the oven to 425 degrees F.

2. Line the bottom of a greased 9-x-13-inch baking dish with biscuit dough, firmly pressing to seal and make a bottom crust.

3. Sprinkle sausage and cheeses over crust.

4. In a medium bowl, whisk together eggs, milk, salt and pepper until blended. Pour over sausage and cheeses.

5. Bake for 25–30 minutes, or until set and middle does not jiggle. Let stand for 5 minutes before cutting into squares. Serve warm.

👍 RECIPE TIPS

☺ **Make Ahead:** *Make casserole through Step 4, then cover with aluminum foil and refrigerate overnight. Uncover and bake, adding a few additional minutes to the baking time.*

⚙ VARIATIONS

You can also add onions, green onions, chopped peppers and/or chopped bacon.

PAIRINGS: Pancakes (page 39), French Toast Bake (page 44), Coffee Cake (page 47), Fruit Smoothie (page 56)

POTATO BREAKFAST CASSEROLE

🕐 **PREP TIME:** 5 MINUTES

⏳ **COOK TIME:** 35 MINUTES

♡ **SERVES:** 12

- ✓ **PREPPED IN 5**
- ✓ **QUICK & EASY**
- ✓ **FEED A CROWD**
- ✓ **MAKE AHEAD**

INGREDIENTS

8 large eggs

½ cup milk, room temperature

20 ounces frozen diced hash browns, thawed

9–10 ounces precooked Italian sausage

salt and pepper to taste

1½ cups shredded mild cheddar cheese, divided

Scan me!

INSTRUCTIONS

1. Preheat the oven to 350 degrees F. Grease a 9-x-13-inch baking dish and set aside.

2. In a large bowl, mix eggs, milk, hash browns, sausage, salt, pepper and 1 cup of the cheese until combined. Pour into the prepared baking dish.

3. Bake for 32–35 minutes. Remove from the oven and add remaining ½ cup cheese over the top. Place back in the oven and bake for an additional 3–5 minutes.

🖐 RECIPE TIPS

☺ **Make Ahead:** *Make this breakfast potato casserole through Step 2 up to 24 hours in advance. Just cover and keep in the refrigerator until ready to bake. Uncover and bake; you may need to add a few additional minutes to the baking time.*

☺ **Perfect Prep:** *The milk should be about room temperature before adding the melted butter. Otherwise, the butter will harden up into little flakes or droplets instead of mixing with the other two ingredients.*

⚙ VARIATIONS

⊕ **MEXICAN:** Add chopped bell peppers and use Mexican blend cheese instead of cheddar.

⊕ **MEAT LOVERS':** Add cooked bacon along with the sausage.

⊕ **LOW-FAT:** Omit the meat and add a cup of chopped spinach and other vegetables.

PAIRINGS: French Toast Bake (page 44), Coffee Cake (page 47), Fruit Smoothie (page 56), Orange Julius (page 57)

BREAKFAST STRATA

⏱ **PREP TIME: 10 MINUTES**

⏳ **CHILL TIME: 4 HOURS**

⏳ **COOK TIME: 45 MINUTES**

♡ **SERVES: 8**

✓ **FEED A CROWD**

✓ **MAKE AHEAD**

INGREDIENTS

12 slices white bread, cut into 1-inch squares

2 cups shredded Monterey Jack cheese

2 cups shredded cheddar cheese

2 cups cooked cubed ham

6 large eggs

3 cups milk, room temperature

½ cup unsalted butter, melted

Scan me!

INSTRUCTIONS

1. Grease a 9-x-13-inch baking dish.

2. Layer half of the bread cubes on the bottom of the baking dish, followed by 1 cup of each of the cheeses and 1 cup of the ham. Repeat the layers once more.

3. In a medium bowl, mix eggs, milk and melted butter. Pour over layers.

4. Cover with aluminum foil and refrigerate for at least 4 hours, or ideally overnight.

5. When ready to bake, preheat the oven to 350 degrees F.

6. Bake the strata covered with aluminum foil for 20 minutes, then uncover and continue baking for an additional 25–30 minutes. This will help it cook more evenly without overbaking the top.

PAIRINGS: French Toast (page 43), Cinnamon Roll Cake (page 46), Fruit Smoothie (page 56)

👍 RECIPE TIPS

☺ **Make Ahead:** *This recipe is at its best when made ahead and refrigerated overnight before baking, so making it ahead of time is encouraged.*

☺ **Perfect Prep:** *The milk should be about room temperature before adding the melted butter. Otherwise, the butter will harden up into little flakes or droplets instead of mixing with the other two ingredients.*

HAM AND CHEESE QUICHE

○ **PREP TIME:** 15 MINUTES
⧖ **COOK TIME:** 1 HOUR 5 MINUTES
♡ **SERVES:** 8

○ **FREEZER FRIENDLY**

○ **FEED A CROWD**

○ **MAKE AHEAD**

INGREDIENTS

1 pie crust, unbaked (Perfect Pie Crust, page 232)

1 cup chopped ham

½ cup shredded cheddar cheese

½ cup shredded mozzarella cheese

¼ cup grated Parmesan cheese

1 cup milk (or half-and-half)

4 large eggs, lightly beaten

½ teaspoon garlic salt

¼ teaspoon pepper

Scan me!

INSTRUCTIONS

1. Preheat the oven to 350 degrees F.

2. Place pie crust into a shallow-sided 9-inch glass or ceramic pie plate and crimp the edges. (We like to double fold the edges, then crimp them.) Prebake for 10–12 minutes.

3. Allow crust to cool slightly, then add ham and cheeses to the bottom.

4. In a medium bowl, mix milk, eggs, garlic salt and pepper together. Pour egg mixture into the crust over the ham and cheeses. (NOTE: Do not overfill the crust. The egg will rise a bit, and you do not want it running over the sides.)

5. Bake for 45–50 minutes, or until an inserted knife comes out clean.

6. Allow to set for 5–10 minutes before serving.

⌖ RECIPE TIPS

☺ **Make Ahead:** *Bake the quiche and keep it refrigerated or frozen until you need it. Wrapped airtight, it will last 2–3 days in the refrigerator and 3–4 months in the freezer. Reheat it in the oven for 15–20 minutes at 350 degrees F.*

☺ **Crustless Quiche:** *Simply grease the pie plate with cooking spray and pour the egg mixture straight into the pan.*

☺ **Use It Up:** *You can use store-bought diced ham, but this quiche is also a great way to use up leftover holiday ham (see Brown Sugar Ham, page 172).*

⚙ VARIATIONS

You can add any other mix-ins, such as bacon bits, sliced sausage or chopped veggies, along with the ham and cheeses in Step 3 to change up the flavor.

PAIRINGS: French Toast Bake (page 44), Coffee Cake (page 47), Orange Julius (page 57)

ENERGY BALLS

PREP TIME: **10 MINUTES**

CHILL TIME: **30 MINUTES**

MAKES: **24 ENERGY BALLS**

FREEZER FRIENDLY

MAKE AHEAD

DAIRY-FREE

GLUTEN-FREE

INGREDIENTS

1 cup quick-cooking rolled oats

1 cup shredded coconut

½ cup milled flaxseed

½ cup mini chocolate chips (optional)

¼ cup protein powder (optional)

½ cup creamy natural peanut butter

⅓ cup honey

1 teaspoon vanilla extract

Scan me!

INSTRUCTIONS

1. In a large bowl, combine oats, coconut, flaxseed, chocolate chips and protein powder and mix together.

2. Add peanut butter, honey and vanilla and mix well (I often use my hands to mix to make sure everything is combined). Refrigerate for 30 minutes.

3. Once chilled, use a small cookie scoop to scoop out mixture, and use your hands to help roll it into small, bite-sized balls.

4. Store in an airtight container in the refrigerator. Separate the layers with parchment or wax paper.

PAIRINGS: Pancakes (page 39), Fruit Smoothie (page 56), Orange Julius (page 57)

☺ RECIPE TIPS

☺ **Make Ahead:** *These will keep at room temperature for 1–2 days, in the refrigerator for 1–2 weeks or in the freezer for up to 3 months. Allow frozen bites to thaw before eating.*

⚙ VARIATIONS

Substitute your favorite kind of chips (white chocolate, butterscotch, milk chocolate, etc.) for the mini chocolate chips, if desired.

FRUIT SMOOTHIE

⏱ **PREP TIME: 5 MINUTES**
♡ **SERVES: 2**

✓ **PREPPED IN 5**
✓ **QUICK & EASY**
✓ **FREEZER FRIENDLY**
✓ **MAKE AHEAD**
✓ **GLUTEN-FREE**

INGREDIENTS

1 kiwi, peeled and sliced

1 banana, peeled and sliced

1 cup hulled strawberries

½ cup blueberries

1 cup plain or vanilla Greek yogurt

1 cup ice cubes, plus more as needed

½ cup pineapple juice

 *Scan me!*

INSTRUCTIONS

1. Combine kiwi, banana, strawberries, blueberries, yogurt, ice and pineapple juice in a blender. Blend until smooth.

2. Add more ice and blend for a thicker smoothie. Serve immediately.

👍 **RECIPE TIPS**

☺ **Make Ahead:** *Cut and prepare fruit as directed, then place in a resealable plastic freezer bag and freeze to use later. When ready to use, add frozen fruit to blender and add a half cup ice and more pineapple juice, if needed.*

⚙ **VARIATIONS**

➔ **WANT MORE NUTRITION?** Sneak in some more favorite fruits (like blackberries, raspberries or pineapple) or even veggies (like spinach or kale) for added flavor, vitamins and nutrition.

➔ **FOR ADDED SWEETNESS:** Add stevia, a little sugar, honey or vanilla extract.

PAIRINGS: Pancakes (page 39), French Toast (page 43), Biscuit Egg Casserole (page 51), Energy Balls (page 55)

ORANGE JULIUS

🕐 PREP TIME: **5 MINUTES**

♡ SERVES: **2**

- ✓ PREPPED IN 5
- ✓ QUICK & EASY
- ✓ FREEZER FRIENDLY
- ✓ GLUTEN-FREE

INGREDIENTS

6 ounces frozen orange juice concentrate

1 cup milk (or almond milk for a dairy-free option)

1 cup water

1–2 teaspoons vanilla extract

¼ cup sugar

1 cup ice cubes

INSTRUCTIONS

Combine all ingredients in a blender and blend until smooth. Serve immediately.

Scan me!

👍 RECIPE TIPS

☺ **Freeze It:** *Our favorite thing to do with leftovers is to pour them into a popsicle mold and freeze for a refreshing treat during the summer.*

☺ **Julius with a Twist:** *Add other ingredients to the Orange Julius, like frozen bananas, strawberries or even pineapple juice, for extra flavor.*

PAIRINGS: Scrambled Eggs (page 37), Bacon (page 37), French Toast (page 43), Coffee Cake (page 47), Breakfast Strata (page 53)

BREADS AND MUFFINS

"Happiness is freshly baked bread."

Our whole family would agree that nothing beats the smell of freshly baked bread. Many people find it intimidating to work with yeast to make a delicious loaf of bread—we once did, too. But the yeast-raised recipes in this book are so simple you will feel like a pro making these loaves.

HELPFUL TIPS + INFORMATION

Preparing Your Pans, Doughs and Batters

ALWAYS GREASE AND FLOUR LOAF PANS. To prepare a loaf pan, first grease it with cooking spray. Then add a scoop of flour and move the pan around so that the flour coats all sides. Add more flour if necessary. Once the pan is evenly coated, pour out any excess flour and discard. This will help keep your bread from sticking to the pan. For a video tutorial, scan the QR code on page 23.

DO NOT OVERMIX THE BATTER. Doing so can result in a dense, dry muffin or loaf. Be sure to mix wet and dry ingredients separately first to avoid overmixing. Then mix the wet and dry ingredients together just enough to incorporate them.

FILL MUFFIN TINS CORRECTLY. A good rule of thumb is to fill your muffin cups two-thirds to three-quarters full.

DO YOU HAVE EMPTY MUFFIN CUPS? No worries. Simply add a few tablespoons of water to each empty muffin cup to help with even baking.

Working With Yeast

⊘ **BUYING AND STORING.** One package of yeast contains 2¼ teaspoons yeast. Both active dry yeast and rapid ride yeast can be stored in the refrigerator or freezer, unopened, for 1–2 years. Once opened, a yeast package will last for about 4 months in the fridge or 6 months in the freezer.

⊘ **IS MY YEAST STILL GOOD?** To make sure yeast is still good, mix 2¼ teaspoons yeast with 1 teaspoon sugar and ½ cup warm water. Let sit for 8–10 minutes. If it bubbles and has a yeast-like smell, then it's still good. If it does not, the yeast is too old and no longer working.

⊘ **KNEAD CAREFULLY.** Use as little flour as possible when kneading. Most doughs need to be a bit sticky, but if it's too sticky to handle, add flour sparingly, a tablespoon at a time. Do not over-work your bread when kneading it. You'll know it's been kneaded enough when it is smooth and holds its shape when formed into a ball, but still feels elastic.

⊘ **BE PATIENT.** Give yeast bread dough enough time to rise properly so that the gluten develops effectively. Be sure to follow both the suggested rise times and any visual cues given (such as "until doubled in size") within the recipes.

⊘ **SPEED UP THE RISE TIME.** We all know that bread rising can take some time. To speed up the process, heat the oven to 200 degrees F and then turn the oven off. Make sure the dough is in an oven-safe bowl, then place it in the warm oven and put a damp tea towel over it. The dough will double in size in only 20–30 minutes. Remember, it is more important to pay attention to how much the bread rises than to be a stickler about the rise time. Under-proofing can make the dough more dense and flat. Over-proofing can make the dough rise too much and then fall.

Making Quick Breads and Muffins

⊘ **CHANGE IT UP.** Most quick bread recipes can be adjusted to make mini loaves or muffins, and vice versa. Look for the Bonus Recipes throughout this chapter, and simply use the different pan sizes given and adjust the bake times accordingly.

⊘ Most quick breads and muffins should be removed from their pans immediately or shortly after coming out of the oven for a drier, crispier surface. If the bread is left in the pan too long, it may become too soft from steaming in the pan. Always follow the specific instructions within the recipe for cooling and serving.

EASY HOMEMADE WHITE BREAD

- ⏱ **PREP TIME:** 15 MINUTES
- ⏳ **RISE TIME:** 2 HOURS 30 MINUTES
- ⏲ **COOK TIME:** 30 MINUTES
- ♡ **MAKES:** 2 LOAVES

 **FREEZER FRIENDLY**

 MAKE AHEAD

 DAIRY-FREE

INGREDIENTS

2¼ cups warm water (110–115 degrees F)

2¼ teaspoons rapid rise yeast (1 packet)

3 tablespoons + ½ teaspoon sugar, divided

5–6 cups bread flour, divided

1 tablespoon salt

2 tablespoons canola oil

TOPPING: butter (optional)

 *Scan me!*

INSTRUCTIONS

1. In a large bowl, dissolve yeast and ½ teaspoon sugar in warm water; let stand until bubbles form on the surface.

2. In a large bowl, whisk together 3 cups flour and remaining 3 tablespoons sugar and the salt.

3. Stir oil into yeast mixture, then pour into flour mixture and mix until smooth. Stir in remaining flour ½ cup at a time to form a soft dough.

4. Turn dough onto a lightly floured surface and knead until smooth and elastic, 8–10 minutes. Place in a large, greased bowl, turning once to grease the top. Cover and let rise in a warm place until doubled in size, 1½–2 hours.

5. Punch dough down and place onto a lightly floured surface. Divide dough in half and shape each piece into a loaf.

6. Place in two greased 5-x-9-inch loaf pans. Cover and let rise in a warm place until doubled, 1–1½ hours.

7. When ready to bake, preheat the oven to 375 degrees F.

8. Bake loaves for 26–34 minutes, or until golden brown and bread has reached an internal temperature of 200 degrees F (bread should sound hollow when tapped).

9. Remove bread from pans and transfer to wire racks to cool. Brush tops with butter while warm.

 ★ **BONUS RECIPE**

Honey Butter

In a small bowl, mix ¾ cup salted butter (at room temperature) with ¼ cup honey until smooth. Store, covered, in the refrigerator.

👍 RECIPE TIPS

☺ **Make Ahead:** *Place baked and cooled loaves in a large resealable plastic bag and store on the counter for 3–4 days. Store in the refrigerator for up to 1 week. This bread also freezes beautifully.*

☺ **Use It Up:** *This homemade bread is perfect for making French Toast (page 43), French Toast Bake (page 44), Breakfast Strata (page 53), Homemade Croutons (page 106) and Monte Cristo Sandwiches (page 169).*

PAIRINGS: Strawberry Jam (page 63), Cinnamon Butter (page 68)

WHOLE WHEAT BREAD

⏱ **PREP TIME:** 20 MINUTES
⧖ **REST AND RISE TIME:** 2 HOURS 30 MINUTES
⧖ **COOK TIME:** 25 MINUTES
♡ **MAKES:** 3 LOAVES

✓ **FREEZER FRIENDLY**

✓ **MAKE AHEAD**

INGREDIENTS

SPONGE:

3 cups warm water (110–115 degrees F)

⅓ cup honey

4½ teaspoons rapid rise yeast (2 packets)

5 cups bread flour

DOUGH:

⅓ cup honey

3 tablespoons unsalted butter, melted,
 plus 2 tablespoons for brushing loaves

1 tablespoon salt

3½ cups whole wheat flour

Scan me!

PAIRINGS: Honey Butter (page 61), Cinnamon Butter (page 68), Homemade Croutons (page 106)

INSTRUCTIONS

1. Make the sponge: In a large bowl or the bowl of a stand mixer, stir warm water, honey and yeast together.

2. Mix in bread flour and stir to combine. Let sponge sit for 30 minutes, until bubbly.

3. Make the dough: Add honey, butter, salt and 2 cups of whole wheat flour to sponge and mix with a wooden spoon or the dough hook mixer attachment. Add remaining whole wheat flour ½ cup at a time until the dough comes together and pulls away from the sides of the bowl. Knead until smooth and pliable. (NOTE: If making in your stand mixer, use the bread hook and knead for 6–8 minutes on low speed.)

4. Place the dough in a greased bowl, cover, and let rise in a warm place until doubled in size, about 1 hour.

5. Divide the dough into three equal pieces and roll each piece into a 9-x-13-inch rectangle on a silicone mat. Roll each dough rectangle up into a log starting at the short end. Place each log seam side down in a greased 5-x-9-inch loaf pan. Cover and let rise in a warm place for 1 hour.

6. Toward the end of the rise time, preheat the oven to 350 degrees F. Bake 25–30 minutes, or until golden brown and hollow sounding when tapped. Brush the loaves with melted butter and let cool completely on a cooling rack.

👍 **RECIPE TIPS**

☺ **Make Ahead:** *Place baked and cooled loaves in a large resealable plastic bag and store on the counter for 3–4 days, or in the refrigerator for up to 1 week. This bread also freezes beautifully.*

☺ **Quicker Rise:** *You need to let this bread rise twice, which can easily take 90–120 minutes. We will often use a warm oven to proof the dough faster. Heat the oven to 200 degrees F, then turn the oven off. Be sure the dough is in an oven-safe bowl. Place a damp tea towel over the bowl and put it in the oven. The dough will double in size in only 20–30 minutes.*

FRENCH BREAD

⏱ **PREP TIME:** 15 MINUTES
⏳ **REST AND RISE TIME:** 40 MINUTES
⏳ **COOK TIME:** 20 MINUTES
♡ **MAKES:** 3 LOAVES

✓ **FREEZER FRIENDLY**
✓ **FEED A CROWD**
✓ **MAKE AHEAD**
✓ **DAIRY-FREE**

INGREDIENTS

¼ cup cornmeal

2 tablespoons rapid rise yeast

½ cup warm water (110-115 degrees F)

2 cups hot water

5 tablespoons vegetable oil

3 tablespoons sugar

1 tablespoon salt

6 cups all-purpose flour, divided

1 egg, beaten

INSTRUCTIONS

1. Line a large baking sheet with parchment paper and sprinkle evenly with cornmeal. (Greased baking sheets work, too, but we prefer the cornmeal method.)

2. In a small bowl, dissolve yeast in warm water.

3. In the bowl of a stand mixer, combine hot water, oil, sugar, salt and 3 cups of the flour. Mix together with the paddle attachment.

4. Add yeast mixture and mix to combine.

5. Add remaining 3 cups of flour 1 cup at a time, mixing after each addition. Once all of the flour is added, let dough rest for 10 minutes.

6. Place dough onto a lightly floured surface and divide into three pieces. Roll each piece into a 9-x-12-inch rectangle. Roll each rectangle up from the long edge like a jelly roll.

7. Place each dough roll on a prepared baking sheet, seam side down.

8. Score the bread across the top 3 or 4 times, and brush each loaf with beaten egg for a crisp and shiny crust. Let dough rise, uncovered, for 30 minutes in a warm place.

9. Toward the end of the rise, preheat the oven to 375 degrees F.

10. Bake on the middle rack for 20 minutes or until golden brown.

Scan me!

👍 **RECIPE TIPS**

☺ **Make Ahead:** *To freeze baked loaves, let the bread cool and wrap in parchment paper, then aluminum foil. It can last for up to 3 months in the freezer. When you are ready to eat, remove from the freezer and thaw at room temperature. To reheat, preheat the oven to 400 degrees F and bake for 4–5 minutes, or until warm.*

☺ **Use It Up:** *This recipe is a great bread for some of our other recipes, including French Toast (page 43), French Toast Bake (page 44), Cheesy Garlic Bread (page 67) and Bruschetta (page 94).*

★ **BONUS RECIPE**

Strawberry Jam

Mash 4 cups hulled strawberries with a fork or potato masher. Pour 2 cups mashed berries into a large microwave-safe bowl. Add 4 cups sugar, mix well and microwave for 3 minutes. Mix well again. Let sit for at least 2 hours, stirring occasionally. The sugar should be fully dissolved, and the mixture should not be grainy. In another bowl, combine 2 tablespoons lemon juice and 1 (3-ounce) package liquid pectin. Stir into the strawberry mixture and stir for 3 minutes. Pour jam into clean, dry glass jars, leaving ½ inch space at the top. Cover with clean lids and let sit at room temperature for 24 hours, then refrigerate for 2–3 weeks or freeze for up to 1 year. Makes 5–6 cups.

PAIRINGS: Honey Butter (page 61), Cinnamon Butter (page 68), Strawberry Jam (right)

BREAD BOWLS

⏱ PREP TIME: 20 MINUTES
⏳ RISE TIME: 1 HOUR 30 MINUTES
⏳ COOK TIME: 15 MINUTES
♡ MAKES: 6 BOWLS

✓ MAKE AHEAD

✓ DAIRY-FREE

INGREDIENTS

1½ cups warm water (110-115 degrees F)

2 tablespoons oil

2 tablespoons sugar

1 teaspoon salt

¾ tablespoon rapid rise yeast

4 cups bread flour, plus more as needed

Scan me!

INSTRUCTIONS

1. In a large bowl or the bowl of a stand mixer, mix warm water, oil, sugar, salt, yeast and 2 cups of flour. Add remaining flour ½ cup at a time until the dough pulls away from the sides of the bowl and is smooth, but still slightly tacky.

2. Knead the dough until smooth and elastic. Place in a greased bowl, cover, and let rise in a warm place until doubled in size, about 1 hour.

3. Gently punch down the dough and divide into six equal pieces. Roll each piece of dough into a ball and place on a greased or parchment paper–lined baking sheet.

4. With a sharp knife, cut an X in the top of each dough ball. Cover lightly with a kitchen towel and let rise in a warm place until doubled in size, 30–45 minutes.

5. During the last 15 minutes of rise time, preheat the oven to 400 degrees F.

6. Bake for 15 minutes, or until golden brown and cooked through. Remove to a cooling rack to cool completely.

7. To serve, cut a circle out of the top of each bread bowl, then scoop out the inside of the bread to make a bowl. Ladle hot soup into the bowl and serve immediately. (NOTE: Bread bowls are best served with creamier and chunkier soups, as opposed to broth-based soups.)

👍 RECIPE TIPS

☺ **Make Ahead:** *Place baked and cooled bowls in large resealable plastic bags for 2–3 days. Storing in the refrigerator will extend the shelf life by a few days. You can also wrap each bowl in plastic wrap and then in aluminum foil to freeze for up to 3 months. Thaw at room temperature before cutting and using. You can warm them up in the oven after thawing as well.*

☺ **Dip Bowls:** *We usually divide the dough into six pieces to make bread bowls, and they are the perfect serving size for our family. But you can also divide the dough into fourths for larger bowls to hold a dip, or if you just want a bigger portion size for your soup bowls.*

☺ **For a Crisp, Shiny Finish:** *Make an egg wash by beating 1 egg with 1 tablespoon milk in a bowl. Use a pastry brush to coat the top of each ball of dough right before you score an X on top. For extra crispness, brush again with egg wash halfway through the bake time.*

PAIRINGS: Slow Cooker Cheesy Potato Soup (page 121), Broccoli Cheese Soup (page 122), Best Chili Soup (page 126)

EASY HOMEMADE BISCUITS

⏱ **PREP TIME:** 15 MINUTES

⧗ **COOK TIME:** 10 MINUTES

♡ **MAKES:** 10–12 BISCUITS

✓ **FREEZER FRIENDLY**

✓ **FEED A CROWD**

✓ **MAKE AHEAD**

INGREDIENTS

2 cups all-purpose flour

4 teaspoons baking powder

2 teaspoons sugar

½ teaspoon salt

½ teaspoon cream of tartar

½ cup unsalted butter, chilled, plus melted butter for brushing

¾ cup buttermilk

Scan me!

INSTRUCTIONS

1. Preheat the oven to 450 degrees F.

2. Sift flour, baking powder, sugar, salt and cream of tartar together into a large bowl.

3. Cut in cold butter until the mixture is the consistency of coarse oatmeal.

4. Make a well in the center of the mixture and pour in buttermilk. Stir with a wooden spoon until dough begins to come together. Press dough together, but use your hands as little as possible, since it will warm up the butter in the dough.

5. On a lightly floured surface, roll out dough to about ¾ inch thick. Use a cookie cutter to cut 2-inch round biscuits, then place on an ungreased baking sheet.

6. Bake for 10 minutes, or until golden brown. Brush with melted butter as soon as biscuits come out of the oven. Serve warm.

👍 RECIPE TIPS

☺ **Make Ahead:** *Cut the biscuits from the dough and transfer to a parchment paper–lined baking sheet. Cover lightly with plastic wrap and put the baking sheet in the freezer until biscuits are frozen solid, then transfer to a large resealable plastic freezer bag and freeze for up to 3 months. Thaw at room temperature, and once thawed, bake in the oven for 10 minutes. Fully baked biscuits can be stored in an airtight container on the counter for 1–2 days, or for 1 week in the refrigerator.*

☺ **Cutting-In Butter:** *Use a cheese grater to grate the cold butter into the dry ingredients, then mix it in with a pastry blender.*

PAIRINGS: Biscuits and Gravy (page 50), Honey Butter (page 61), Slow Cooker Beef Stew (page 123)

EASY GARLIC KNOTS

PREP TIME: 10 MINUTES
COOK TIME: 10 MINUTES
MAKES: 16 KNOTS

✓ QUICK & EASY

✓ ON THE TABLE IN 20

✓ FEED A CROWD

✓ MAKE AHEAD

INGREDIENTS

4 tablespoons unsalted butter, melted

2 tablespoons grated Parmesan cheese

¾ teaspoon garlic powder

½ teaspoon dried parsley

½ teaspoon dried oregano

¼ teaspoon salt

1 (16.3-ounce) can refrigerated buttermilk biscuits

Scan me!

INSTRUCTIONS

1. Preheat the oven to 400 degrees F. Lightly spray a baking sheet with cooking spray and set aside.

2. Combine butter, Parmesan, garlic powder, parsley, oregano and salt in a small bowl. Mix and set aside.

3. Open can of biscuits and cut each of the 8 pieces of dough in half so that you have 16 pieces of dough.

4. Roll each piece of dough into a rope about 6 inches long and ½ inch thick.

5. Tie each rope into a knot. Place them on the prepared baking sheet, making sure to tuck the ends of the rope under the knot.

6. Brush dough knots with half the butter mixture. Bake for 9–12 minutes, or until golden brown.

7. Remove knots from the oven and brush with the remaining butter mixture. Serve warm.

☝ RECIPE TIPS

☺ **Make Ahead:** *To freeze baked knots, first place on a baking sheet, or in a container with layers separated by parchment paper, in the freezer until frozen solid. Then wrap in plastic wrap and place in a resealable plastic freezer bag. Freeze for 2–3 months. Reheat in the oven or microwave.*

☺ **Dippable:** *These are delicious all on their own, but they also pair well with some of our favorite dips, including Spinach Artichoke Dip (page 85) and Pizza Dip (page 91).*

PAIRINGS: Garlic Prime Rib (page 162), Italian Sausage Pasta (page 196), Fettuccine Alfredo (page 198), Kid-Friendly Spaghetti (page 199)

CHEESY GARLIC BREAD

⊘ PREPPED IN 5

⊘ QUICK & EASY

⊘ **ON THE TABLE IN 20**

⊘ FREEZER FRIENDLY

⊘ FEED A CROWD

⊘ MAKE AHEAD

INGREDIENTS

½ cup unsalted butter, softened

⅓–½ cup Italian dressing

2 teaspoons minced garlic

1 loaf Italian bread, halved lengthwise

2 cups shredded Colby Jack cheese (or mozzarella cheese)

2 teaspoons dried parsley

Scan me!

INSTRUCTIONS

1. Preheat the oven to 375 degrees F.

2. In a small bowl, blend butter, dressing and garlic.

3. Place bread cut side up on a baking sheet and spread butter mixture over both halves.

4. Top bread with cheese and parsley.

5. Bake, uncovered, for 12–14 minutes, or until cheese is melted and bubbly.

6. Slice and serve warm.

PAIRINGS: Homemade Meatballs (page 100), Pot Roast (page 165), Easy Lasagna (page 195), Italian Sausage Pasta (page 196), Fettuccine Alfredo (page 198), Baked Ziti (page 201)

👍 **RECIPE TIPS**

☺ **Make Ahead:** *You can make this bread ahead of time and freeze for up to 3 months. Once the recipe has been assembled and baked, let cool and slice. Place in a large resealable plastic freezer bag and freeze. To reheat, place frozen pieces on a baking sheet and bake at 400 degrees F for 4–5 minutes.*

HEAVENLY ROLLS

🕐 **PREP TIME:** 20 MINUTES

⏳ **RISE TIME:** 2 HOURS

⏳ **COOK TIME:** 20 MINUTES

♡ **MAKES:** 24 ROLLS

 ✓ **FREEZER FRIENDLY**

 ✓ **FEED A CROWD**

 ✓ **MAKE AHEAD**

INGREDIENTS

1 tablespoon rapid rise yeast

½ cup sugar plus ½ teaspoon sugar, divided

¼ cup warm water (110–115 degrees F)

1 cup warm milk (110–115 degrees F)

½ cup vegetable oil

1 teaspoon salt

4½–5 cups all-purpose flour, divided

2 large eggs

½ cup unsalted butter, melted

salted butter, melted, for brushing

INSTRUCTIONS

1. In a small bowl, mix yeast and ½ teaspoon sugar with warm water. Let stand until bubbly.

2. In a large bowl, mix warm milk, oil, ½ cup sugar and salt with a wooden spoon.

3. Add 1 cup of flour to the mixture and mix well. Add eggs and mix vigorously until smooth. Add yeast mixture and continue to mix until smooth.

4. Add remaining flour to the yeast mixture 1 cup at a time and continue to mix with a wooden spoon until the dough is combined. The dough should be soft and sticky.

5. Place the dough into a large bowl, cover with a tea towel, and let rise until it has doubled in size, about 1 hour.

6. Once the dough has doubled in size, punch down and divide it in half. On a floured surface, roll each piece out into a 12-inch circle. The dough circles should be about ⅜ inch thick.

7. Brush both dough circles with melted unsalted butter. Cut each circle with a pizza cutter into 12 pieces (like a pizza). Roll each piece from the rounded edge to the point to make a crescent roll.

8. Place rolls on a greased baking sheet with the pointed tips down (we use an 11-x-16-inch metal pan and do 3 rows across and 8 rows down).

9. Cover rolls with a tea towel and let rise until they have doubled in size, about 1 hour.

10. When ready to bake, preheat the oven to 375 degrees F.

11. Bake for 16–20 minutes, until lightly browned. (Touch rolls to see if they bounce back—if they do not, bake a little longer.) Brush with melted salted butter while warm. Serve warm.

 *Scan me!*

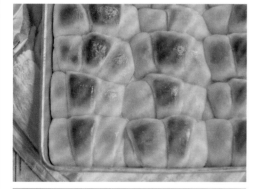

PAIRINGS: Homemade Meatballs (page 100), Green Bean Casserole (page 137), Pot Roast (page 165)

👍 RECIPE TIPS

☺ **Make Ahead:** *Unbaked rolls can be frozen right after they are formed in Step 7. Place unbaked rolls on a baking sheet and freeze immediately. Once frozen, place in resealable plastic freezer bags, seal and place in the freezer. Take them out a couple hours before baking to let them rise to about double the size, which will take longer since the dough is frozen.*

☺ **Using a Stand Mixer:** *You can mix this dough in a stand mixer fitted with the dough hook; just be careful not to overmix the dough because it will make it tougher and not as soft.*

 ★ **BONUS RECIPE**

Cinnamon Butter

In a medium bowl, beat together ½ cup unsalted butter (at room temperature), ¼ cup sifted powdered sugar, 2 tablespoons honey and 1 teaspoon ground cinnamon until smooth. Serve immediately or store in an airtight container in the refrigerator for up to 1 week.

FRY BREAD

⏱ **PREP TIME:** 20 MINUTES
⧗ **REST TIME:** 10 MINUTES
⧖ **COOK TIME:** 5 HOURS 10 MINUTES
♡ **SERVES:** 8

 ✓ **FEED A CROWD**
 ✓ **MAKE AHEAD**
✓ **DAIRY-FREE**

INGREDIENTS

BEAN TOPPING:

2 cups dried pinto beans, rinsed and drained (or
  1 (15-ounce) can pinto beans, rinsed and drained)
water
2–3 slices bacon, chopped and cooked
1 pound ground beef, cooked and drained

BREAD:

2 cups all-purpose flour
1 tablespoon baking powder
1 teaspoon salt
1 cup hot water (130 degrees F)
vegetable oil, for frying

OTHER TOPPINGS: shredded lettuce, sour cream,
  chopped tomatoes, sliced avocados, shredded
  cheese

Scan me!

PAIRINGS: Guacamole (page 88), Cilantro Ranch
Dressing (page 109), Homemade Salsa (page 153)

INSTRUCTIONS

1. Place rinsed dried beans in a slow cooker and cover with water. Cook on low for 4–5 hours, or until beans start to become tender.

2. Add bacon pieces and ground beef to the slow cooker and continue to cook on low for an additional 1–2 hours, or until beans are fully tender. (To make the bean topping using canned beans, combine canned beans, cooked ground beef and cooked bacon and cook in slow cooker on low for 2 hours. Set aside.)

3. Make the bread: Sift flour, baking powder and salt together into a medium bowl. Add hot water and mix with your hands until a dough forms (dough should be a little sticky). Cover and let rest for 10 minutes.

4. While dough is resting, preheat the oven to 200 degrees F. Fill a large saucepan with 1–2 inches of oil and heat over medium-high heat to about 350 degrees F.

5. Break off golf ball–sized pieces of dough and roll into balls about 1½ inches wide.

6. Using a pastry roller and working on a lightly floured surface, roll each dough ball into a thin circle 6–7 inches in diameter.

7. Working in batches, fry each dough piece in hot oil until the dough is golden and puffs up, about 20 seconds, then flip and fry on the other side for 10–20 seconds more. Set on a paper towel–lined plate to drain. Keep the fry bread warm in the oven while frying the remaining pieces.

8. Spread beans over fry bread, top with any other desired toppings and serve warm.

👍 **RECIPE TIPS**

☺ **Perfect Frying:** *Make sure your oil stays at a consistent temperature of about 350 degrees F. If the temp is too low, the bread will be tough. If it is too hot, the outside will burn before the inside cooks through.*

☺ **Soak the Beans:** *To lessen the amount of gas in beans, soak dried beans in a large bowl of water for 8–12 hours. Drain and rinse before use.*

☺ **Serving Suggestions:** *We feel this fry bread is best served with beans, but for a sweeter version, you can also skip the savory toppings and serve it with powdered sugar and/or honey.*

☺ **Make Ahead:** *Mix up the dough and store in a resealable plastic bag for 1–2 days in the refrigerator or portion the dough into 3-inch balls and flash freeze. When ready to fry, remove from the refrigerator or freezer and let the dough come to room temperature. Fry according to recipe instructions.*

FLOUR TORTILLAS

🕐 **PREP TIME:** 20 MINUTES
⏳ **REST TIME:** 10 MINUTES
⏳ **COOK TIME:** 25 MINUTES
♡ **MAKES:** 12 TORTILLAS

✓ **FEED A CROWD**

✓ **MAKE AHEAD**

INGREDIENTS

2 cups plus 2 tablespoons all-purpose flour, plus
   more as needed
1 teaspoon baking powder
1 teaspoon salt
½ cup unsalted butter, melted
¾ cup warm water (110–115 degrees F)

Scan me!

INSTRUCTIONS

1. In a medium bowl, mix flour, baking powder and salt. Add melted butter and water and mix with your hands until combined. Add more flour if needed 1 tablespoon at a time, but the dough should be a little sticky. Let dough rest for 10 minutes.

2. Heat a large skillet over medium heat.

3. While skillet is heating up, divide dough into 12 balls. On a lightly floured surface, use a pastry roller to roll each ball out into a circle about 8 inches wide.

4. Add one tortilla at a time to the hot skillet and cook for about 1 minute on each side, until bubbled and slightly browned on both sides. (NOTE: Carefully wipe flour out of the pan between batches, otherwise it will accumulate in the pan and start to burn.)

★ **BONUS RECIPE**

Quesadilla

Spread butter on one side of a tortilla and place butter side down on a hot skillet. Sprinkle on ½ cup shredded cheese and any other ingredients desired. Butter another tortilla and place it on top of the cheese, butter side up. Cover the pan and let the cheese melt. After 1–2 minutes the cheese should be melted. Flip the quesadilla over and cook 1 minute more, until both sides are browned. Remove from the skillet, cut and serve.

👍 RECIPE TIPS

☺ **Make Ahead:** *Store cooked tortillas in a large resealable plastic bag on the counter for 2–3 days, or in the refrigerator for 1 week. These can also be frozen in a resealable plastic freezer bag for 4–5 months.*

☺ **Serving Tip:** *The easiest way to keep tortillas warm for serving is to use a tortilla warmer. If you do not have one, you can use a pot with a lid that is slightly bigger than the tortillas.*

☺ **Use It Up:** *Tortillas can be used to make Enchiladas (pages 183 and 184), Chimichangas (page 185), Flautas (page 187) and Chicken Tacos (page 188).*

PAIRINGS: Homemade Salsa (page 153), Sweet Salsa Verde (page 154), Creamy Refried Beans (page 190)

CORNBREAD

⏱ **PREP TIME: 5 MINUTES**

⏳ **COOK TIME: 20 MINUTES**

♡ **SERVES: 12**

✓ PREPPED IN 5

✓ QUICK & EASY

✓ FREEZER FRIENDLY

✓ FEED A CROWD

✓ MAKE AHEAD

INGREDIENTS

1 cup yellow cornmeal

1 cup all-purpose flour

⅔ cup sugar

4 teaspoons baking powder

1 teaspoon salt

1 cup milk

2 large eggs, lightly beaten

½ cup unsalted butter, melted

Scan me!

INSTRUCTIONS

1. Preheat the oven to 375 degrees F. Lightly grease an 8-x-10-inch (or 9-x-9-inch) baking dish. Set aside.

2. In a large mixing bowl, combine cornmeal, flour, sugar, baking powder and salt.

3. Make a well in the center of the dry ingredients and pour in milk, eggs and butter. Stir until just combined, then pour batter into the prepared pan.

4. Bake for 20–24 minutes, or until a toothpick inserted in the center comes out clean. Serve warm.

★ **BONUS RECIPE**

Cornbread Muffins

Use the recipe above but divide the batter among the wells of a lined 12-cup muffin tin. Fill each well about two-thirds full and bake at 350 degrees F for 12–14 minutes. Makes 12 muffins.

👍 **RECIPE TIPS**

☺ **Make Ahead:** *To freeze the cornbread, let cool, then wrap the whole block in plastic wrap, or cut into individual portions and wrap. Wrap again with aluminum foil, or place in a large resealable plastic freezer bag, and freeze for 1–2 months. To reheat, thaw at room temperature, remove the plastic wrap, then rewrap in aluminum foil. Bake at 350 degrees F until warm.*

☺ **For a Crispy Crust:** *Try baking the cornbread in a cast iron skillet. Place the empty skillet in the oven for 10 minutes to preheat, then spray with oil, pour in the batter and bake. Check on the bread after 15 minutes by sticking a toothpick in the center. If it comes out clean, the bread is done.*

PAIRINGS: Best Chili Soup (page 126), White Chicken Chili (page 127), Slow Cooker Green Chile Chicken Enchilada Soup (page 129)

CINNAMON BREAD

⏱ **PREP TIME:** 20 MINUTES

⧗ **REST AND RISE TIME:** 2 HOURS

⧗ **COOK TIME:** 40 MINUTES

♡ **MAKES:** 2 LOAVES

✓ **FREEZER FRIENDLY**

✓ **MAKE AHEAD**

INGREDIENTS

DOUGH:

1 cup packed light brown sugar

1 tablespoon salt

1⅓ cups hot water (130 degrees F)

4 tablespoons unsalted butter, softened and cut into pieces

1⅓ cups cold water

1 tablespoon rapid rise yeast

7½–8 cups all-purpose flour

CINNAMON-SUGAR MIXTURE:

1⅓ cups sugar

2 tablespoons ground cinnamon

2 tablespoons all-purpose flour

EGG WASH:

1 egg

1 tablespoon water

Scan me!

INSTRUCTIONS

1. To make the dough: Combine brown sugar, salt, hot water and butter in a large mixing bowl. Stir to mix, break up butter chunks and dissolve brown sugar a bit (there will still be a few butter chunks, which is okay).

2. Add cold water, then sprinkle yeast on top and let sit for 10 minutes. It will not bubble much.

3. Add flour 1 cup at a time and stir together with a wooden spoon until a soft dough forms. Knead the dough for a few minutes to make sure all the flour is well incorporated. (NOTE: This is a very wet dough that will stick to your hands. Dipping your hands in flour before kneading may help, but it will still stick.) Cover with a tea towel and let rise in a warm place for 1½ hours.

4. While bread is rising, grease two 5-x-9-inch loaf pans with cooking spray.

5. To make the cinnamon-sugar mixture, mix sugar, cinnamon and flour together. Set aside.

6. To make the egg wash, whisk egg and water together in a small bowl. Set aside.

7. Once dough has risen, punch it down and place onto a lightly floured surface. Form a ball and divide into 2 equal pieces.

8. Working with one piece at a time on a well-floured surface, roll dough out into a rectangle to about 7x22 inches and about ½ inch thick. Brush with half of the egg wash to help the cinnamon-sugar mixture stick better. Spread ⅔ cup cinnamon-sugar mix evenly over the dough, then lightly spray with water.

9. Roll dough up tightly, lightly pulling as well as tucking in the sides as you roll. Pinch ends closed and drop into the prepared loaf pan seam side down. Repeat with the second piece of dough and the remaining egg wash and cinnamon-sugar mix. Cover and let rise in a warm place for 20 minutes.

10. Meanwhile, preheat the oven to 350 degrees F.

11. Bake for 40–45 minutes. As soon as bread comes out of the oven, brush tops with butter. Let cool completely before slicing.

👍 **RECIPE TIPS**

☺ **Make Ahead:** *Place in a large resealable plastic bag and store at room temperature for 3–4 days or in the refrigerator for 7 days. This bread also freezes well. Wrap each loaf in plastic wrap, then place in a resealable plastic freezer bag and freeze for up to 3 months. Thaw at room temperature before warming to your liking.*

☺ **Use It Up:** *This cinnamon bread is perfect on its own, but it can also be used to make some of our other recipes even better. Try cutting it up and using it to make French Toast (page 43) or our French Toast Bake (page 44).*

PAIRINGS: Honey Butter (page 61), Cinnamon Butter (page 68), Homemade Hot Cocoa (page 285)

SNICKER-DOODLE BREAD

⏱ PREP TIME: 5 MINUTES
⌛ COOK TIME: 40 MINUTES
♡ MAKES: 2 LOAVES

✓ PREPPED IN 5

✓ QUICK & EASY

✓ FREEZER FRIENDLY

✓ MAKE AHEAD

INGREDIENTS

DOUGH:

1 cup unsalted butter, softened

2 cups sugar

2 teaspoons ground cinnamon

½ teaspoon salt

3 large eggs

¾ cup sour cream

1 teaspoon vanilla extract

2½ cups all-purpose flour

2 teaspoons baking powder

1 (10-ounce) package Hershey's Cinnamon Chips

CINNAMON-SUGAR MIXTURE:

3 tablespoons sugar

1½ teaspoons ground cinnamon

Scan me!

INSTRUCTIONS

1. Preheat the oven to 350 degrees F. Lightly grease two 5-x-9-inch loaf pans with cooking spray and set aside.

2. In a large bowl, cream butter, sugar, cinnamon and salt with a hand mixer until fluffy. Add eggs and mix well. Then add sour cream and vanilla and mix well.

3. Mix flour and baking powder in a separate bowl. Add to wet ingredients and mix until combined.

4. Add cinnamon chips and stir into batter.

5. Spoon batter evenly into the prepared loaf pans.

6. To make the cinnamon-sugar mixture, mix sugar and cinnamon in a bowl and sprinkle over the batter in each loaf pan.

7. Tent pans with aluminum foil and bake for 40–45 minutes, or until a toothpick inserted into the middle comes out clean. Let cool before removing from pan and slicing.

🔥 RECIPE TIPS

☺ **Make Ahead:** *Place cooled loaves in a large resealable plastic bag and store at room temperature for 3–4 days or in the refrigerator for 7 days. This bread also freezes well. Wrap each loaf in plastic wrap, then place in a resealable plastic freezer bag and freeze for up to 4 months. Thaw at room temperature before warming to your liking.*

☺ **Cinnamon Chips:** *Although few stores carry cinnamon chips throughout the year, you can always order them online at the Hershey's Store. Having said that, be sure to stock up when you do see them (they last longer in the freezer)! White chocolate chips make a great substitution for this recipe.*

☺ **Keep the Chips from Sinking:** *Toss cinnamon chips in a bowl with 2 tablespoons flour before folding them into the batter to prevent them from sinking to the bottom of the bread.*

★ BONUS RECIPE

Snickerdoodle Muffins

To make Snickerdoodle Muffins, use the recipe above but divide the batter among the wells of two lined 12-cup muffin tins. Fill each well about two-thirds full and bake at 350 degrees F for 18–20 minutes. Makes 18 larger or 24 smaller muffins.

ALSO TRY: French Toast (page 43), Cinnamon Butter (page 68), Snickerdoodles (page 241)

GLAZED LEMON ZUCCHINI BREAD

PREP TIME: 10 MINUTES

COOK TIME: 50 MINUTES

REST TIME: 30 MINUTES

MAKES: 2 LOAVES

FREEZER FRIENDLY

MAKE AHEAD

INGREDIENTS

BREAD:

2 cups cake flour (or all-purpose flour)

2 teaspoons baking powder

½ teaspoon salt

2 large eggs

½ cup canola oil

1⅓ cups sugar

½ cup buttermilk

2 tablespoons lemon juice

zest of 1 lemon

1 cup grated zucchini

GLAZE:

1 cup powdered sugar, sifted

3 tablespoons milk

2 tablespoons lemon juice

Scan me!

ALSO TRY: Snickerdoodle Bread (page 74), Almond Poppy Seed Bread (page 76), Banana Bread (page 81)

INSTRUCTIONS

1. Preheat the oven to 350 degrees F. Grease two 5-x-9-inch loaf pans and set aside.

2. To make the bread, mix flour, baking powder and salt in a medium bowl, and set aside.

3. In a large bowl, beat eggs with a hand mixer. Then add oil and sugar and mix until well blended. Add buttermilk, lemon juice and lemon zest and mix.

4. Wring out zucchini to remove moisture. Fold zucchini into wet ingredients.

5. Add dry ingredients to the wet ingredients and mix until well combined.

6. Pour batter evenly into the prepared loaf pans and bake for 50–60 minutes.

7. To make the glaze, stir all ingredients together in a small bowl. Spoon over the bread while still warm. Let the glaze set for at least 30 minutes before cutting and serving.

🖒 RECIPE TIPS

☺ **Make Ahead:** *Place cooled loaves in a large resealable plastic bag and store at room temperature for 3–4 days or in the refrigerator for 7 days. This bread also freezes well. Wrap each unglazed loaf in plastic wrap, then place in a resealable plastic freezer bag and freeze for up to 4 months. Thaw at room temperature before warming to your liking.*

☺ **Wringing Out Zucchini:** *For this recipe, it is important to remove excess water from the zucchini so the batter is not too runny. To do that, place grated zucchini on the center of a tea towel, fold up the towel, and wring out by twisting over the sink. This is a great way to prepare grated zucchini for most baked goods.*

★ BONUS RECIPE

Glazed Lemon Zucchini Muffins

To make Glazed Lemon Zucchini Muffins, use the recipe above but divide the batter among the wells of a lined 12-cup muffin tin. Fill each well two-thirds full and bake at 350 degrees F for 17–19 minutes. Makes 12 large muffins.

ALMOND POPPY SEED BREAD

⏱ **PREP TIME: 5 MINUTES**

⏳ **COOK TIME: 55 MINUTES**

⏳ **REST TIME: 10 MINUTES**

♡ **MAKES: 2 LOAVES**

✓ **PREPPED IN 5**

✓ **FREEZER FRIENDLY**

✓ **MAKE AHEAD**

INGREDIENTS

BREAD:

3 cups all-purpose flour

2½ cups sugar

1½ tablespoons poppy seeds

1½ teaspoons baking powder

½ teaspoon salt

3 large eggs

1½ cups milk

1⅛ cups vegetable oil

1 cup sour cream

2 teaspoons almond extract

2 teaspoons vanilla extract

GLAZE:

2 cups powdered sugar, sifted

3–4 tablespoons milk

1 tablespoon lemon juice

½ teaspoon almond extract

Scan me!

INSTRUCTIONS

1. Preheat the oven to 350 degrees F. Grease two 5-x-9-inch loaf pans with cooking spray and set aside.

2. To make the bread, mix flour, sugar, poppy seeds, baking powder and salt in a large bowl or the bowl of a stand mixer fitted with the paddle attachment. Add eggs, milk, oil, sour cream and almond and vanilla extracts and mix until smooth. Distribute batter evenly into the prepared loaf pans.

3. Tent loaf pans with aluminum foil and bake for 55–60 minutes, removing the foil for the last 15 minutes. Cool loaves in pans for 10 minutes before removing to a wire rack.

4. While bread is baking, prepare the glaze. Mix powdered sugar, milk, lemon juice and almond extract in a bowl until well combined. Begin with 3 tablespoons milk and add more as needed to make it the consistency you like.

5. Spoon glaze over loaves while they are still warm. Allow to cool completely before serving.

⟳ RECIPE TIPS

☺ **Make Ahead:** *Place cooled loaves in a large resealable plastic bag and store at room temperature for 3–4 days or in the refrigerator for 7 days. To freeze, wrap each loaf in plastic wrap, then place in a resealable plastic freezer bag and freeze for up to 4 months. Thaw at room temperature before warming to your liking.*

★ **BONUS RECIPE**

Almond Poppy Seed Muffins

To make Almond Poppy Seed Muffins, use the recipe above and divide the batter among the wells of two lined 12-cup muffin tins. Fill each well about two-thirds full and bake at 350 degrees F for 17–19 minutes. Makes 24 muffins.

⚙ VARIATIONS

Turn this recipe into a Lemon Poppy Seed Bread (or muffins) by substituting the same amount of lemon extract for the almond extract in the bread and glaze.

ALSO TRY: Snickerdoodle Bread (page 74), Glazed Lemon Zucchini Bread (page 75), Banana Bread (page 81)

BLUEBERRY MUFFINS

🕐 **PREP TIME:** 15 MINUTES

⏳ **COOK TIME:** 20 MINUTES

⏳ **REST TIME:** 30 MINUTES

♡ **MAKES:** 16 MUFFINS

✓ **FREEZER FRIENDLY**

✓ **MAKE AHEAD**

INGREDIENTS

1¼ cups granulated sugar

½ cup unsalted butter, softened

2 eggs

1 teaspoon vanilla extract

2 cups plus 1 tablespoon all-purpose flour, divided

2 teaspoons baking powder

½ teaspoon salt

½ cup milk

2 cups blueberries, rinsed, drained and dried

⅛ cup coarse sprinkling sugar

Scan me!

INSTRUCTIONS

1. Preheat the oven to 375 degrees F. Prepare two 12-cup muffin tins by adding liners. Set aside.

2. In a medium bowl, beat granulated sugar and butter with a hand mixer until well combined. Add eggs one at a time, blending in between additions. Mix in vanilla.

3. In a separate bowl, sift together 2 cups flour, the baking powder and salt. Add to butter/sugar mixture a little bit at a time, alternating with the milk, using a wooden spoon and making sure not to overmix.

4. Using a fork, crush ½ cup of the blueberries and fold into the batter. Toss remaining blueberries in remaining 1 tablespoon flour. Fold these coated blueberries into the batter.

5. Divide batter among the wells of the prepared muffin tins. You will not need to fill all the wells in the second tin; add a few tablespoons of water to each empty well to ensure even baking. Sprinkle coarse sugar over the tops and bake for 20–24 minutes.

6. Remove from muffin tin and allow to cool at least 30 minutes.

PAIRINGS: Scrambled Eggs (page 37), Breakfast Potatoes (page 38), Pumpkin Bread (page 78), Banana Bread (page 81)

🔥 RECIPE TIPS

☺ **Make Ahead:** *Place cooled muffins in a large resealable plastic bag and store at room temperature for 3–4 days or in the refrigerator for 7 days. These muffins also freeze well. Place muffins in a single layer in a resealable plastic freezer bag and freeze for up to 3 months.*

☺ **Sinking Blueberries:** *Tossing the berries in flour before adding them to the mixture should keep them from sinking to the bottom. You can also try adding 1 tablespoon of plain batter to each muffin liner before folding the blueberries into the remaining batter. Finish filling in the muffin tins and bake.*

☺ **Optional Crumb Topping:** *Combine 1⅓ cups flour, ½ cup sugar and 1½ teaspoons ground cinnamon in a bowl. Mix with a fork and sprinkle over the muffins. Bake as directed above.*

★ **BONUS RECIPE**

Blueberry Bread

Pour batter into a parchment paper–lined 5-x-9-inch loaf pan and sprinkle with sugar. Tent with aluminum foil and bake for 70 minutes, or until a toothpick inserted into the middle comes out clean.

PUMPKIN BREAD

⏱ **PREP TIME:** 10 MINUTES
⧗ **COOK TIME:** 1 HOUR 15 MINUTES
♡ **MAKES:** 2 LOAVES

⊘ **FREEZER FRIENDLY**

⊘ **MAKE AHEAD**

⊘ **DAIRY-FREE**

INGREDIENTS

BREAD:

1 (15-ounce) can pumpkin puree
4 eggs
1 cup vegetable oil
⅔ cup water
3 cups sugar
3½ cups all-purpose flour
2 teaspoons baking soda
1½ teaspoons salt
1 teaspoon ground cinnamon
1 teaspoon ground nutmeg
½ teaspoon ground cloves
¼ teaspoon ground ginger

TOPPING:

3 tablespoons sugar
½ tablespoon ground cinnamon

Scan me!

INSTRUCTIONS

1. Preheat the oven to 325 degrees F. Grease and flour two 5-x-9-inch loaf pans and set aside.

2. To make the bread, mix pumpkin puree, eggs, oil, water and sugar in a large bowl until well blended.

3. In a separate bowl, whisk together flour, baking soda, salt, cinnamon, nutmeg, cloves and ginger. Combine dry ingredients with the pumpkin mixture and stir until just blended. Pour evenly into the prepared pans.

4. To make the topping, combine sugar and cinnamon and mix well. Sprinkle topping evenly over the top of both loaves.

5. Tent with aluminum foil and bake for 75–80 minutes, or until an inserted toothpick comes out clean. Serve warm, or let cool before serving.

★ **BONUS RECIPE**

Pumpkin Muffins

To make Pumpkin Muffins, use the recipe above and divide the batter among the wells of two lined 12-cup muffin tins. Fill each well two-thirds full and bake at 350 degrees F for 18–20 minutes. Makes 24 muffins.

⌂ **RECIPE TIPS**

☺ **Make Ahead:** *Place cooled loaves in a large resealable plastic bag and store at room temperature for 3–4 days or in the refrigerator for 7 days. This bread also freezes well. Wrap each loaf in plastic wrap, then place in a resealable plastic freezer bag and freeze for up to 4 months. Thaw at room temperature before warming to your liking.*

☺ **Add a Layer of Cream Cheese!** *Mix 8 ounces softened cream cheese with ⅓ cup sugar, 1 egg and 1 tablespoon flour. Pour half the batter in the pan, then add the cream cheese mixture in an even layer and top with the remaining batter. Bake as directed above.*

PAIRINGS: French Toast (page 43), French Toast Bake (page 44), Cinnamon Butter (page 68)

ZUCCHINI BREAD

🕐 PREP TIME: 10 MINUTES
⏳ COOK TIME: 50 MINUTES
⏳ COOL TIME: 20 MINUTES
♡ MAKES: 2 LOAVES

✓ FREEZER FRIENDLY

✓ MAKE AHEAD

✓ DAIRY-FREE

INGREDIENTS

3 cups all-purpose flour

1 tablespoon ground cinnamon

1 teaspoon salt

1 teaspoon baking powder

1 teaspoon baking soda

3 large eggs

1 cup vegetable oil

1¼ cups granulated sugar

1 cup packed light brown sugar

1 tablespoon vanilla extract

2 cups grated zucchini (do not wring out)

½–1 cup chopped walnuts (optional)

 Scan me!

INSTRUCTIONS

1. Preheat the oven to 325 degrees F. Grease and flour two 5-x-9-inch loaf pans and set aside.

2. Sift flour, cinnamon, salt, baking powder and baking soda together into a medium bowl.

3. In a large bowl, beat eggs, oil, both sugars and vanilla together with a hand mixer. Add sifted ingredients to the wet ingredients and beat well (batter will be a little thick). Fold in zucchini and nuts until well combined. Pour batter evenly into the prepared pans.

4. Bake for 50–55 minutes, or until a toothpick inserted in the center comes out clean. Cool in the pans on a rack for 20 minutes, then remove from the pans and cool completely before serving.

⚙ **VARIATIONS**

➔ Add shredded coconut, mini chocolate chips or orange or lemon zest for added flavor.

➔ **MAKE IT MINI:** To make mini loaves, use four 3½-x-6-inch mini loaf pans. Bake for 35-40 minutes.

★ BONUS RECIPE

Zucchini Muffins

To make Zucchini Muffins, use the recipe above and divide the batter among the wells of two lined 12-cup muffin tins. Fill each well about two-thirds full and bake at 350 degrees F for 24–26 minutes. Makes 24 muffins.

👍 **RECIPE TIPS**

☺ **Make Ahead:** *Place cooled loaves in a large resealable plastic bag and store at room temperature for 3–4 days or in the refrigerator for 7 days. This bread also freezes well. Wrap each loaf in plastic wrap, then place in a resealable plastic freezer bag and freeze for up to 4 months. Thaw at room temperature before warming to your liking.*

PAIRINGS: Honey Butter (page 61), Cinnamon Butter (page 68), Pumpkin Bread (page 78), Banana Bread (page 81)

CHOCOLATE MUFFINS

◷ PREP TIME: 10 MINUTES
⏲ COOK TIME: 20 MINUTES
⏳ COOL TIME: 10 MINUTES
♡ MAKES: 24 MUFFINS

✓ **FREEZER FRIENDLY**

✓ **MAKE AHEAD**

INGREDIENTS

3 cups all-purpose flour

1 cup Dutch process cocoa powder (or unsweetened cocoa powder)

¾ cup sugar

1 tablespoon baking soda

½ teaspoon salt

2 cups milk

½ cup vegetable oil

3 large eggs

2 teaspoons vanilla extract

¾ cup semisweet chocolate chips, plus more for topping

½ cup milk chocolate chips, plus more for topping

Chocolate sprinkles for topping (optional)

Scan me!

INSTRUCTIONS

1. Preheat the oven to 350 degrees F. Prepare a 24-cup muffin tin or two 12-cup tins with liners or cooking spray. Set aside.

2. In a large bowl, combine flour, cocoa powder, sugar, baking soda and salt.

3. In a separate bowl, combine milk, oil, eggs and vanilla. Whisk until incorporated and egg yolks are broken. Fold in both chocolate chips.

4. Fold wet mixture into dry ingredients. Do not overmix, but make sure you do not have any dry spots.

5. Spoon batter into the prepared tins to fill about three-quarters of the way full. Sprinkle on additional chocolate chips and chocolate sprinkles (if desired)

6. Bake for 20–22 minutes, or until an inserted toothpick comes out clean.

7. Cool in tins for about 10 minutes before moving to a wire rack to cool completely.

★ **BONUS RECIPE**

Chocolate Bread

Prepare the Chocolate Muffins batter and spoon into two well-greased 5-x-9-inch loaf pans. Bake at 350 degrees F for 38–42 minutes. Let cool in the pans before moving to a wire rack.

👍 RECIPE TIPS

☺ **Make Ahead:** *Place cooled muffins in a large resealable plastic bag and store at room temperature for 3–4 days or in the refrigerator for 7 days. These muffins also freeze well. Place muffins in a single layer in a resealable plastic freezer bag and freeze for up to 3 months.*

☺ **Baking Time:** *Because each oven seems to bake a little differently, it can be easy to overbake muffins. We would suggest checking your muffins about 5 minutes before the end of the baking time. Insert a toothpick into the center of a muffin. If it comes out clean, your muffins are done; otherwise, cook for another few minutes.*

ALSO TRY: Blueberry Muffins (page 77), Zucchini Muffins (page 79)

BANANA BREAD

🕐 PREP TIME: **10 MINUTES**

⏱ COOK TIME: **55 MINUTES**

♡ MAKES: **1 LOAF**

✓ **FREEZER FRIENDLY**

✓ **MAKE AHEAD**

INGREDIENTS

DOUGH:

1½ cups all-purpose flour

1 teaspoon baking powder

1 teaspoon baking soda

½ teaspoon salt

3 large overripe bananas, mashed

½ cup granulated sugar

½ cup packed light brown sugar

1 egg

4 tablespoons unsalted butter, melted

CINNAMON-SUGAR MIXTURE (OPTIONAL):

1 tablespoon sugar

½ teaspoon ground cinnamon

Scan me!

INSTRUCTIONS

1. Preheat the oven to 325 degrees F. Lightly grease a 5-x-9-inch loaf pan with cooking spray and set aside.

2. To make the dough, sift flour, baking powder, baking soda and salt together into a medium bowl. Set aside.

3. In a separate bowl, mix together bananas, both sugars, egg and melted butter.

4. Fold in flour mixture and stir until smooth. Scoop batter into the prepared pan.

5. To make the cinnamon-sugar mixture, mix sugar and cinnamon together in a small bowl. Sprinkle over the batter.

6. Bake for 55–60 minutes, until a toothpick inserted in the center comes out clean. (NOTE: If not adding cinnamon-sugar mixture, cover with aluminum foil for the last 20 minutes of baking.)

★ **BONUS RECIPE**

Banana Bread Muffins

To make Banana Bread Muffins, use the recipe above but divide the batter among the wells of a lined 12-cup muffin tin. Fill each well two-thirds full and bake at 325 degrees F for 16–18 minutes. Makes 12 muffins.

👍 **RECIPE TIPS**

☺ **Make Ahead:** *Place cooled loaf in a large resealable plastic bag and store at room temperature for 3–4 days or in the refrigerator for 7 days. This bread also freezes well. Wrap each loaf in plastic wrap, then place in a resealable plastic freezer bag and freeze for up to 4 months. Thaw at room temperature before warming to your liking.*

☺ **Need to Ripen Your Bananas Quickly?** *Just place bananas in their peels on a baking sheet and bake at 400 degrees F for about 5 minutes, or until they are browned.*

PAIRINGS: French Toast (page 43), French Toast Bake (page 44), Cinnamon Butter (page 68)

APPETIZERS

"Charcuterie—because a generation raised on Lunchables is trying to be hip."

If you are like us, you would argue that the appetizers are the best part of a meal! It may be because they are served first, when you are starving, but it may be because they are simply delicious. Whether bite-sized, fried or dippable, appetizers are just plain fun, and there is no denying that the starter is very often the star of a meal!

HELPFUL TIPS + INFORMATION

How Much to Serve?

BEFORE A DINNER: We suggest setting appetizers out about an hour before the main meal will be served. Plan for each guest to be able to have 3–5 pieces or servings total.

FOR AN APPETIZER-ONLY PARTY: For a two-hour event, plan to serve 10–12 pieces or servings per person. Add about 5 more pieces per person for every additional hour.

DIPS: If you are offering both sweet and savory types, then plan for guests to have 2 ounces (¼ cup) of each dip per person. If you are only serving one type, then plan for guests to have about 3 ounces (⅓ cup) per person.

HOW MANY VARIETIES? Plan to provide 2–3 different appetizer dishes for 10 or fewer guests. Add another dish to the menu for every 5–8 more people.

CHIPS AND SALSA: Plan to serve 1 quart of salsa and 1 pound of chips for every 10 people.

Dip Tips

⊘ **CHOOSING YOUR DIPS:** Make sure that the dips are complementary to the other flavors being served as appetizers and to whatever is being served for dinner. For example, a bean dip would be best served with tortilla chips and tacos, not with meatballs and pasta.

⊘ **KEEPING DIP WARM:** The easiest way to keep dip warm is to use a small slow cooker on the warm setting. A 1½-quart slow cooker is perfect for keeping dip warm throughout.

⊘ **KEEPING DIP COLD:** If you are serving a cold dip inside at room temperature, it should be fine for a couple of hours. However, if you are serving it in a warmer environment, like an outdoor barbecue, you'll want to keep it on ice. You can place ice inside a bowl or on a tray, then place a smaller bowl of dip on top of the ice.

⊘ **WHAT TO DIP:** For savory dips, provide crackers, various vegetables, pretzels, baguette/bread slices or chips for dipping. For sweet dips, try sliced fruits, cookies, cubed cake, marshmallows or pretzels.

SPINACH ARTICHOKE DIP

⏱ PREP TIME: 10 MINUTES

⏳ COOK TIME: 25 MINUTES

♡ SERVES: 16

✓ FEED A CROWD

✓ MAKE AHEAD

✓ SLOW COOKER

✓ GLUTEN-FREE

INGREDIENTS

1 (12-ounce) box frozen chopped spinach, thawed

1 (14-ounce) can artichoke hearts, drained and chopped

2 cups shredded Parmesan cheese

1 (8-ounce) package cream cheese, softened

⅔ cup sour cream

⅓ cup mayonnaise

2 teaspoons minced garlic

Scan me!

INSTRUCTIONS

1. Preheat the oven to 375 degrees F.

2. In a medium bowl, mix spinach, artichoke hearts and Parmesan.

3. In a separate bowl, mix cream cheese, sour cream, mayonnaise and garlic. Add to spinach mixture and mix until well combined.

4. Pour into an 8-x-8-inch baking dish and bake for 25 minutes.

5. Serve immediately with chips, crackers or vegetables for dipping.

👍 RECIPE TIPS

☺ **Make Ahead:** *Make the dip as instructed through Step 4. Cover and store in the refrigerator for up to 24 hours before baking.*

☺ **You Can Use Fresh Spinach Too!** *Just chop up 1½–2 cups fresh raw spinach and throw it into the recipe. The spinach will cook down while the artichoke dip is baking in the oven.*

☺ **Slow Cooker Directions:** *Combine all ingredients in a slow cooker and cook on high for 1–2 hours or low for 3–4 hours. Use the warm setting to keep it warm while serving.*

PAIRINGS: French Bread (page 63), Bacon-Wrapped Smokies (page 92), Homemade Tortilla Chips (page 151)

BUFFALO CHICKEN DIP

PREP TIME: **5 MINUTES**

COOK TIME: **20 MINUTES**

SERVES: **10**

✓ PREPPED IN 5

✓ QUICK & EASY

✓ FEED A CROWD

✓ MAKE AHEAD

✓ **SLOW COOKER**

✓ GLUTEN-FREE

INGREDIENTS

2 cups shredded cooked chicken

1 (8-ounce) package cream cheese, softened

1 cup buffalo sauce

1 cup ranch dressing

1½ cups shredded cheddar cheese, divided

2-3 tablespoons blue cheese crumbles

Scan me!

INSTRUCTIONS

1. Preheat the oven to 350 degrees F. Grease a 9-x-9-inch baking dish and set aside.

2. In a medium bowl, mix chicken, cream cheese, buffalo sauce, ranch dressing and 1 cup of the cheddar cheese until well combined.

3. Pour into the prepared baking dish.

4. Sprinkle with remaining ½ cup cheddar and the blue cheese.

5. Bake for 20 minutes. Serve immediately with bread or tortilla chips.

🗘 RECIPE TIPS

☺ **Make Ahead:** *Make the dip as instructed through Step 4. Cover and store in the refrigerator for up to 24 hours before baking.*

☺ **Slow Cooker Directions:** *Mix chicken, cream cheese, buffalo sauce, ranch dressing and 1 cup of the cheddar cheese in a bowl, then pour into the slow cooker. Cover and cook on low for 1–2 hours, or until dip is hot and bubbly. Sprinkle remaining cheddar cheese and the blue cheese crumbles on top and cook for 30 minutes more, until cheddar cheese has melted.*

PAIRINGS: French Bread (page 63), Spinach Artichoke Dip (page 85), Homemade Tortilla Chips (page 151),

7-LAYER DIP

QUICK & EASY

FEED A CROWD

MAKE AHEAD

GLUTEN-FREE

INGREDIENTS

1 cup sour cream

1 cup mayonnaise

1 (1-ounce) package taco seasoning

2–3 (9-ounce) cans Frito Lay bean dip

½–1 cup guacamole (store-bought or homemade; see page 88)

1 cup shredded cheese (cheddar or Mexican blend)

½ cup diced olives

½ cup chopped tomatoes

¼ cup chopped green onions (or cilantro)

Scan me!

INSTRUCTIONS

1. In a medium bowl, mix sour cream, mayonnaise and taco seasoning until well combined. Set aside.

2. Spread ingredients one at a time into a 9-x-13-inch baking dish as follows:

    1st layer—bean dip
    2nd layer—guacamole
    3rd layer—mayonnaise–sour cream mixture
    4th layer—cheese
    5th layer—olives
    6th layer—tomatoes
    7th layer—green onions

3. Refrigerate for at least 1 hour before serving.

ALSO TRY: Guacamole (page 88), Queso Blanco (page 90), Homemade Salsa (page 153)

👍 RECIPE TIPS

☺ **Make Ahead:** *The first five layers can be made up to 24 hours in advance and stored, covered with plastic wrap, in the refrigerator. Wait to add chopped tomatoes and green onions until right before serving.*

GUACAMOLE

PREP TIME: 10 MINUTES

SERVES: 6

- QUICK & EASY
- ON THE TABLE IN 20
- FEED A CROWD
- MAKE AHEAD
- DAIRY-FREE
- GLUTEN-FREE

INGREDIENTS

5 avocados, peeled, pitted and cubed
2 tablespoons lime juice, plus more for topping
⅓ teaspoon kosher salt
½ teaspoon ground cumin
¼ teaspoon cayenne pepper
2 Roma tomatoes, seeded and diced
½ onion, chopped (optional)
2 tablespoons chopped fresh cilantro
1 tablespoon seeded and chopped jalapeño pepper
1 teaspoon minced garlic

Scan me!

INSTRUCTIONS

1. In a large bowl, combine avocado and lime juice and mix until coated.

2. Add salt, cumin and cayenne and mash avocado mixture using a potato masher or the back of a spoon.

3. Fold in tomatoes, onions, cilantro, jalapeño and garlic.

4. Add additional lime juice over the top to help keep guacamole from browning. Serve with tortilla chips.

PAIRINGS: Chimichangas (page 185), Flautas (page 187), Chicken Tacos (page 188), Tostadas (page 190)

👍 RECIPE TIPS

☺ **Make Ahead:** *To store guacamole, place it in a bowl and pour a thin layer of lime juice on top of the guacamole. Cover with plastic wrap and push the plastic down to touch the guacamole. This will prevent air pockets and will keep the guacamole from browning. Store in the refrigerator for 3–4 days.*

CREAM CHEESE BEAN DIP

⏱ PREP TIME: **5 MINUTES**

⏳ COOK TIME: **25 MINUTES**

♡ SERVES: **8**

✓ PREPPED IN 5

✓ QUICK & EASY

✓ FEED A CROWD

✓ MAKE AHEAD

✓ SLOW COOKER

✓ GLUTEN-FREE

INGREDIENTS

1 (16-ounce) can refried beans

1 cup sour cream

4 ounces cream cheese, softened

1 (1-ounce) package taco seasoning

¼ cup salsa (store-bought or homemade; see page 153)

1 cup shredded Mexican cheese

Scan me!

INSTRUCTIONS

1. Preheat the oven to 350 degrees F.

2. In a medium bowl, mix beans, sour cream and cream cheese until well combined. Add taco seasoning and salsa and stir to combine.

3. Pour into an 8-x-8-inch baking dish and top with shredded cheese. Bake for 25 minutes.

4. Serve hot with tortilla chips.

ALSO TRY: 7-Layer Dip (page 87), Homemade Salsa (page 153), Pico de Gallo (page 152), Creamy Refried Beans (page 190)

👍 **RECIPE TIPS**

☺ **Make Ahead:** *Mix all ingredients together except the shredded cheese and place in the baking dish. Cover and refrigerate for up to 3 days. Add shredded cheese right before baking.*

☺ **Slow Cooker Directions:** *Mix all the ingredients together except the shredded cheese. Spoon half of the bean dip into the slow cooker and cover with half of the cheese, then add the rest of the bean dip and top with the remaining cheese. Cook on low for 2–3 hours, or until the dip is heated through and the cheese is melted.*

QUESO BLANCO

⏱ **PREP TIME:** 5 MINUTES

⧖ **COOK TIME:** 10 MINUTES

♡ **SERVES:** 10

⊘ PREPPED IN 5

⊘ QUICK & EASY

⊘ ON THE TABLE IN 20

⊘ FEED A CROWD

⊘ MAKE AHEAD

INGREDIENTS

3 tablespoons unsalted butter

2 tablespoons all-purpose flour

1½ cups whole milk

1 (4-ounce) can diced green chiles

1 teaspoon garlic salt

½ teaspoon onion powder

¼ teaspoon chili powder

¼ teaspoon ground cumin (optional)

1 cup shredded white sharp cheddar cheese

2 tablespoons chopped fresh cilantro

2 tablespoons chopped tomatoes

INSTRUCTIONS

1. Melt butter in a medium pot over medium-low heat. Whisk in flour until bubbly.

2. Add milk and stir until well combined. Add green chiles, garlic salt, onion powder, chili powder and cumin.

3. Add cheese and mix until smooth. Add cilantro and tomatoes right before serving and mix well. Serve warm with tortilla chips or vegetables for dipping.

Scan me!

👍 RECIPE TIPS

☺ **Make Ahead:** *This recipe only takes 10 minutes to make, but if you want to make it a little early, prepare the recipe up through adding the cheese, then transfer to a small slow cooker and keep on the warm setting for a few hours before serving. Add chopped cilantro and tomatoes right before serving.*

⚙ VARIATIONS

⊕ Add some heat by including some minced jalapeños or more chili powder.

⊕ Swap out the cheddar for your favorite cheese or a Mexican blend of shredded cheese.

⊕ Add cooked ground beef or chorizo to make it more hearty.

PAIRINGS: Homemade Tortilla Chips (page 151), Chimichangas (page 185), Flautas (page 187), Chicken Tacos (page 188),

PIZZA DIP

PREP TIME: 5 MINUTES
COOK TIME: 25 MINUTES
SERVES: 12

✓ PREPPED IN 5
✓ QUICK & EASY
✓ FEED A CROWD
✓ MAKE AHEAD
✓ GLUTEN-FREE

INGREDIENTS

2 (8-ounce) packages cream cheese, softened

½ cup sour cream

1 teaspoon dried oregano

1 teaspoon pepper

½ teaspoon salt

1 (14-ounce) jar pizza sauce

2 cups shredded mozzarella cheese

PIZZA TOPPINGS: pepperoni, cooked sausage, ham, bacon, etc.

Scan me!

INSTRUCTIONS

1. Preheat the oven to 350 degrees F.

2. In a medium bowl, combine cream cheese, sour cream, oregano, pepper and salt. Mix until smooth and pour into a 9-x-13-inch baking dish.

3. Spread pizza sauce over cream cheese mixture. Top with mozzarella and any other desired toppings and bake for 23–25 minutes, or until bubbly.

4. Serve with crackers, breadsticks or pita chips.

👍 RECIPE TIPS

☺ **Make Ahead:** *Assemble all the ingredients in the pan as directed, but do not bake. Instead, cover and place in the refrigerator for up to 24 hours. When you are ready to bake, let the dip sit on the counter for about 20 minutes before throwing it in the oven.*

☺ **Topping Suggestions:**

Margherita: Sliced tomatoes, fresh mozzarella, basil.

Hawaiian: Ham/Canadian bacon and pineapple.

Barbecue Chicken: Use barbecue sauce instead of pizza sauce and add grilled chicken, onions and cilantro.

PAIRINGS: French Bread (page 63), Easy Garlic Knots (page 66), Homemade Tortilla Chips (page 151)

BACON-WRAPPED SMOKIES

PREP TIME: **10 MINUTES**
COOK TIME: **30 MINUTES**
SERVES: **12**

- FREEZER FRIENDLY
- FEED A CROWD
- MAKE AHEAD
- DAIRY-FREE
- GLUTEN-FREE

INGREDIENTS

2 (12-ounce) packages Hillshire Farm Beef Lit'l Smokies

1 pound bacon, cold, slices cut into thirds

½–¾ cup packed light brown sugar

Scan me!

INSTRUCTIONS

1. Preheat the oven to 325 degrees F. Line a baking sheet with aluminum foil and set aside.

2. Wrap each smokie with a piece of cold bacon. Secure bacon in place with a toothpick.

3. Place smokies on prepared baking sheet.

4. Sprinkle brown sugar over smokies.

5. Bake for 30–40 minutes, or until bacon is cooked as you prefer.

👍 RECIPE TIPS

☺ **Make Ahead:** *These smokies can be prepared through Step 4 up to 24 hours in advance. Simply cover and place in the refrigerator until ready to bake. Increase the bake time if needed to cook bacon through.*

⚙ VARIATIONS

→ Add ¼ teaspoon cayenne pepper (or more or less, to taste) to the brown sugar for a sweet-and-spicy kick.

→ Baste with barbecue sauce after baking, then broil for an additional 3-4 minutes until the smokies are sticky.

→ Add a small slice of pineapple or jalapeño pepper to each smokie before wrapping in bacon and sprinkling on the brown sugar.

PAIRINGS: Deviled Eggs (page 93) , Buffalo Wings (page 96), Fried Pickles (page 97)

DEVILED EGGS

⏱ **PREP TIME:** 20 MINUTES

⧗ **COOK TIME:** 15 MINUTES

♡ **SERVES:** 4

✓ **MAKE AHEAD**

✓ **GLUTEN-FREE**

INGREDIENTS

6 eggs

6 tablespoons mayonnaise

1 teaspoon mustard

salt and pepper to taste

paprika, for topping

Scan me!

INSTRUCTIONS

1. Fill a medium pot with enough water to cover eggs and bring to a boil over medium-high heat. Once water is boiling, gently lower eggs into the water using a strainer ladle. Turn the heat down to a simmer, and simmer eggs for 15 minutes.

2. Once done, transfer eggs to an ice bath for 5 minutes.

3. Remove eggs from water and tap on the counter to crack. Remove shells and rinse eggs.

4. Carefully cut each egg lengthwise, remove the yolk, and transfer yolks to a small bowl. Set egg whites aside.

5. Add mayonnaise and mustard to yolks and whip with a fork. Add salt and pepper. When ready to serve, spoon mixture into the hole of each egg white and sprinkle with paprika.

👍 **RECIPE TIPS**

☺ **Make Ahead:** *If you need to make these ahead of time, it is best to keep the egg filling separate from the whites until you are ready to serve them. Wrap the egg whites tightly in plastic wrap, and put the yolk mixture in a resealable plastic bag and squeeze all the air out. You can store the egg yolk mixture and egg whites separately in the refrigerator for up to 2 days. Unshelled hard-boiled eggs will last in the refrigerator for 1 week.*

☺ **Fancy Filling:** *To make your deviled eggs look a bit more fancy, use a piping bag with a large star tip to pipe the yolk mixture into each egg before dusting with paprika. You can also simply cut a hole at the corner of a resealable plastic bag to pipe the yolk mixture for a smooth, swirled yolk topping.*

PAIRINGS: Spinach Artichoke Dip (page 85), Bacon-Wrapped Smokies (page 92), Charcuterie Board (page 101)

BRUSCHETTA

⏱ **PREP TIME:** 5 MINUTES
⧖ **COOK TIME:** 5 MINUTES
♡ **SERVES:** 12

INGREDIENTS

8 Roma (plum) tomatoes, seeded and diced
⅓ cup chopped fresh basil
4-5 teaspoons minced garlic
1 tablespoon balsamic vinegar
1 teaspoon olive oil
1 teaspoon dried oregano
¼ teaspoon kosher salt
¼ teaspoon pepper
1 loaf French bread, Italian bread or baguette
4 tablespoons unsalted butter, softened
¼ cup grated Parmesan cheese, plus shaved
   Parmesan for topping (optional)

Scan me!

INSTRUCTIONS

1. Preheat the broiler (set to high if there is an option for that).

2. Combine tomatoes, basil and garlic in a medium bowl.

3. Mix in balsamic vinegar, olive oil, oregano, salt and pepper.

4. Slice bread ½–¾ inch thick. Spread butter onto each slice and sprinkle with grated Parmesan.

5. Place on a baking sheet and broil for 2–5 minutes, or until toasted. You can also toast buttered bread slices, sprinkled with cheese, in a skillet over medium-low heat.

6. Add tomato topping to toasted bread slices and sprinkle with shaved Parmesan before serving, if desired.

👍 **RECIPE TIPS**

☺ **Make Ahead:** *Add all of the ingredients except for the fresh basil and place in a covered bowl in the refrigerator for 24 hours. Right before broiling bread, add the basil to the other bruschetta ingredients.*

PAIRINGS: Baked Salmon (page 173), Roast Chicken (page 174), White Sauce Pasta (page 192)

MOZZARELLA STICKS

🕐 PREP TIME: 10 MINUTES
⏳ FREEZE TIME: 20 MINUTES
⏳ COOK TIME: 10 MINUTES
♡ MAKES: 24 STICKS

QUICK & EASY

FEED A CROWD

MAKE AHEAD

INGREDIENTS

12 string cheese sticks
½ cup all-purpose flour
⅛ teaspoon paprika
⅛ teaspoon seasoned salt
1½ cups panko breadcrumbs
1 tablespoon dried parsley
1 teaspoon dried oregano
2 eggs
¼ cup milk
vegetable oil, for frying

Scan me!

INSTRUCTIONS

1. Unwrap cheese sticks and cut them in half crosswise.

2. Combine flour, paprika and salt in a gallon-sized resealable plastic bag. In a second bag, mix panko, parsley and oregano. In a bowl, beat eggs and milk together.

3. Add 5 or 6 cheese sticks to the bowl with eggs and milk and toss around to coat. Transfer sticks to the flour bag and shake around, then return them to the milk bowl, making sure to coat every side. Finally, add sticks to the panko bag and toss to coat. Place panko-coated sticks on a baking sheet. Repeat to coat all the remaining cheese sticks.

4. Place the baking sheet in the freezer for 20–30 minutes. This will ensure that the cheese does not ooze out of the coating while frying.

5. Heat a few inches of vegetable oil in a large frying pan to 350–375 degrees F.

6. Working in batches, fry sticks in the oil until golden brown on all sides, 30–60 seconds.

7. Drain on a paper towel–lined plate. Serve immediately with marinara sauce or ranch dressing.

👍 RECIPE TIPS

☺ **Make Ahead:** *Bread your cheese sticks ahead of time and pop them in the freezer. Once they are frozen, transfer them to an airtight container or resealable plastic freezer bag. Store for up to 1 month before frying as instructed above.*

PAIRINGS: Bruschetta (page 94), Homemade Ranch (page 98), Fried Zucchini (page 98)

BUFFALO WINGS

⏱ **PREP TIME:** 10 MINUTES

⌛ **COOK TIME:** 15 MINUTES

♡ **SERVES:** 4–6

✓ **FEED A CROWD**

INGREDIENTS

vegetable oil, for frying
1-2 cups all-purpose flour
24 chicken wings, thawed if frozen
1 (12-ounce) bottle hot sauce
½ cup unsalted butter
1 tablespoon Worcestershire sauce

Scan me!

INSTRUCTIONS

1. Fill a heavy pot with 2–3 inches oil and heat over medium-high heat to 350–375 degrees F.

2. While oil is heating, place flour in a shallow dish and dredge wings in the flour, making sure to coat all sides of the wings.

3. Working in batches, add wings to hot oil and cook until golden brown, 5–7 minutes. Drain on a paper towel–lined plate.

4. While frying wings, combine hot sauce, butter and Worcestershire sauce in a saucepan over medium heat and cook until combined and heated through.

5. Toss fried wings in sauce, making sure to coat all sides. Serve warm with ranch dressing.

★ **BONUS RECIPE**

BONELESS BUFFALO WINGS

Use 3 skinless, boneless chicken breasts cut into 1-inch chunks in place of the wings. Mix 1 cup milk and 1 egg in a small bowl. Dip chicken chunks in egg mixture, then dredge in flour. Repeat this process so chicken pieces are double coated. Refrigerate for 20 minutes, then fry and coat in sauce as instructed in Steps 3–5 above. Serves 4.

🔥 **RECIPE TIPS**

☺ **Feed a Crowd:** *This is a great recipe to double or triple and make for parties or get-togethers. Just make your Homemade Ranch (page 98) beforehand and make sure the wings are thawed.*

PAIRINGS: Buffalo Chicken Dip (page 86), Pizza Dip (page 91), Homemade Ranch (page 98),

FRIED PICKLES

⏱ PREP TIME: 15 MINUTES
⌛ COOK TIME: 10 MINUTES
♡ SERVES: 6

✓ **DAIRY-FREE**

INGREDIENTS

vegetable oil, for frying
1 (16-ounce) jar dill pickle slices
½ cup all-purpose flour
2 teaspoons garlic salt
1 teaspoon Italian seasoning
¼ teaspoon pepper
¾ cup water
1½ cups panko breadcrumbs

Scan me!

INSTRUCTIONS

1. Fill a frying pan with ½ inch oil and heat over medium-high heat to 350–375 degrees F.

2. While oil is heating, drain pickles and place on paper towels. Pat dry to remove any excess juice.

3. Whisk flour, garlic salt, Italian seasoning and pepper together in a shallow bowl. Add water and mix until smooth.

4. Place breadcrumbs in a separate shallow dish.

5. Working in batches, add pickles to the batter and toss to coat. Then dip pickles in breadcrumbs, making sure to coat all sides.

6. Fry pickles in batches in the oil for 1–2 minutes on each side, or until golden brown. Repeat with the remaining pickles.

7. Serve immediately with ranch dressing.

PAIRINGS: Bacon-Wrapped Smokies (page 92), Buffalo Wings (page 96), Homemade Ranch (page 98), Dill Dip (page 101)

👍 **RECIPE TIPS**

☺ **Air Fryer Directions:** *Preheat the fryer to 425 degrees F. Bread the pickles as directed, then place in a single layer in the fryer basket and cook for 7–9 minutes. They should be golden brown and crispy. Flip the pickles and cook for an additional 7 minutes on the other side.*

⚙ **VARIATIONS**

Feel free to change up the seasonings in the batter for a different flavor, such as adding some paprika or chili powder to make it a little spicy.

FRIED ZUCCHINI

⏱ PREP TIME: **15 MINUTES**

⏳ COOK TIME: **10 MINUTES**

♡ SERVES: **6**

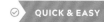
✓ **QUICK & EASY**

INGREDIENTS

vegetable oil, for frying

2–3 cups milk

3 cups all-purpose flour

2 cups panko breadcrumbs (plain or Italian)

2 zucchinis, sliced at an angle (about ¼ inch thick)

Scan me!

INSTRUCTIONS

1. Fill a frying pan with ¼–½ inch oil and heat over medium heat to 350–375 degrees F.

2. While oil is heating, place milk in a medium bowl, flour in a gallon-sized resealable plastic bag and breadcrumbs in a separate gallon-sized resealable plastic bag.

3. Working in batches, add zucchini slices to milk, then transfer to the bag of flour. Shake around to coat all sides, then return slices to the milk, making sure to coat all sides with milk. Transfer slices to the breadcrumb bag and shake around to coat.

4. Fry zucchini in batches in the hot oil for 1–2 minutes on each side, or until golden brown, and place on a paper towel–lined plate to drain.

5. Repeat the process until all the slices are breaded and fried. Serve warm with dip.

★ **BONUS RECIPE**

Homemade Ranch

In a large bowl, whisk together ½ cup sour cream, ½ cup buttermilk, ¼ cup mayonnaise, 1–2 teaspoons lemon juice, 1 teaspoon garlic salt with parsley, ½ teaspoon dried chives, ½ teaspoon dried parsley, ½ teaspoon dried dill weed, ¼ teaspoon onion powder and ¼ teaspoon pepper. Refrigerate for 30 minutes before serving.

👍 **RECIPE TIPS**

☺ **Air Fryer Directions:** *Preheat your air fryer to 390 degrees F. Prepare zucchini according to the directions above, then place a single layer of zucchini slices in the air fryer. Cook for 5–7 minutes, or until crispy. Flip and cook on the other side, if needed.*

PAIRINGS: Homemade Ranch (left), Dill Dip (page 101), Garlic Prime Rib (page 162), Fettuccine Alfredo (page 198)

FRIED EGG ROLLS

⏱ PREP TIME: 10 MINUTES
⏳ COOK TIME: 10 MINUTES
♡ SERVES: 16–20

- ON THE TABLE IN 20
- FREEZER FRIENDLY
- FEED A CROWD
- MAKE AHEAD
- DAIRY-FREE

INGREDIENTS

3 tablespoons olive oil
1 (16-ounce) package tricolor coleslaw mix
3 chicken breasts, cooked and shredded
salt and pepper to taste
1 (16-ounce) package egg roll wrappers
vegetable oil, for frying

Scan me!

INSTRUCTIONS

1. In a large saucepan, heat olive oil over medium heat. Add coleslaw and sauté until limp.

2. Add chicken and sauté for 2–3 minutes, until well mixed. Season with salt and pepper and turn off the heat.

3. Place an egg roll wrapper in front of you, angled so it looks like a diamond. Add ¼–⅓ cup chicken mixture horizontally across the middle of your egg roll wrapper. Fold in the left and right sides of the wrapper, then roll up from the bottom to enclose the filling. Add a little water to the edges of the wrapper to seal so it sticks.

4. Fill a medium frying pan with ¾ inch oil and heat over medium-high heat to 350–375 degrees F.

5. Working in batches, fry egg rolls in the hot oil until golden brown on both sides. Serve warm with your dipping sauce of choice.

⌁ RECIPE TIPS

☺ **Make Ahead:** *Assemble the egg rolls up to 24 hours in advance and store covered in the refrigerator until ready to fry.*

⚙ VARIATIONS

- ⊕ **BREAKFAST EGG ROLLS:** Fill with Scrambled Eggs (page 37), bacon and cheese.
- ⊕ **AVOCADO EGG ROLLS:** Fill with avocado, cheese and bacon.
- ⊕ **SOUTHWEST EGG ROLLS:** Fill with chicken, spices, corn and beans.
- ⊕ **CHERRY CHEESECAKE EGG ROLLS:** Fill with cherry pie filling and cream cheese.
- ⊕ **APPLE PIE EGG ROLLS:** Fill with apple pie filling and ground cinnamon.

PAIRINGS: Fried Rice (page 147), General Tso's Chicken (page 180), Sweet and Sour Sauce (page 181), Teriyaki Chicken (page 182)

SLOW COOKER MEATBALLS

🕐 PREP TIME: 5 MINUTES
⏳ COOK TIME: 4 HOURS
♡ MAKES: 50 MEATBALLS

✓ PREPPED IN 5
✓ FREEZER FRIENDLY
✓ FEED A CROWD
✓ MAKE AHEAD
✓ SLOW COOKER
✓ DAIRY-FREE

INGREDIENTS

1 (14-ounce) bottle ketchup

1½ cups cold water

1 cup packed light brown sugar

1 cup chili sauce

1 cup red currant jelly (or grape or huckleberry jelly)

juice of 2 lemons

½ teaspoon ground ginger

1 (32-ounce) bag frozen meatballs

Scan me!

INSTRUCTIONS

1. Combine ketchup, cold water, brown sugar, chili sauce, jelly, lemon juice and ginger in your slow cooker. Add frozen meatballs and stir so meatballs are coated in sauce.

2. Cook on high for 4 hours or on low for 6–8 hours.

👍 **RECIPE TIPS**

☺ **Make Ahead:** *These will keep in the slow cooker on the warm setting for several hours or can be made ahead and stored in the refrigerator. To store, allow meatballs to cool, then transfer to an airtight container. They'll keep in the refrigerator for 3–4 days. Reheat in the microwave or in a medium pot over low heat.*

⭐ BONUS RECIPE

Homemade Meatballs

Our homemade meatballs work great for this recipe! To make them, preheat the oven to 450 degrees F. Line a large, rimmed baking sheet with aluminum foil and spray with nonstick cooking spray. In a large bowl, combine 2 pounds ground beef (we use 80 percent lean), 2 eggs, 1 cup milk, ½ cup plain breadcrumbs (or Italian-style breadcrumbs), 2 tablespoons grated Parmesan cheese, 2–3 teaspoons salt, 2 teaspoons garlic powder, 1 teaspoon onion powder and ½ teaspoon pepper. Mix with your hands until just combined (do not overmix). Using a cookie scoop or your hands, divide meat mixture into 1½-inch meatballs. Bake for 10–14 minutes, or until the internal temperature is 160 degrees F. These meatballs can be used fresh, or frozen for up to 3 months for the recipe above.

PAIRINGS: Spinach Artichoke Dip (page 85), Mashed Potatoes (page 145), White Sauce Pasta (page 192)

CHARCUTERIE BOARD

🕐 **PREP TIME:** 20 MINUTES

♡ **SERVES:** 12

ON THE TABLE IN 20

FEED A CROWD

MAKE AHEAD

EQUIPMENT

Large wooden cutting board

Toothpicks or serving prongs

INGREDIENTS

2 dips (such as Homemade Ranch [page 98], Cream Cheese Fruit Dip [page 273] or hummus)

12 slices each assorted deli meats (such as pepperoni, prosciutto or salami)

2 cups cheese cubes or 12 slices each assorted cheeses (such as Colby Jack, provolone or Swiss)

½–1 cup soft cheese (such as cream cheese or goat cheese)

1 cup each assorted crackers, chips or pretzels

1 cup each assorted chopped or diced vegetables (such as baby carrots, broccoli, cucumbers or snap peas)

1 cup each assorted chopped or diced fruit (such as apples, blackberries or strawberries)

½ cup each assorted nuts (such as almonds or pistachios)

Scan me!

INSTRUCTIONS

1. Place dips in small bowls on opposite sides of the board.

2. Fold or roll the deli meats and place around the board.

3. Add the different cheeses on opposite sides from each other.

4. Place the different types of crackers and pretzels around the board.

5. Finally, fill in any empty spots with the vegetables, fruit and nuts.

6. Be sure to set out serving prongs or toothpicks near the tray.

★ BONUS RECIPE

Dill Dip

In a medium bowl, mix 1 cup mayonnaise, 1 cup sour cream, 2 teaspoons Worcestershire sauce, 2 teaspoons lemon juice, 1½ tablespoons dried dill weed, 1 tablespoon dried parsley, ½ tablespoon onion powder, ½ teaspoon salt and a dash of pepper. Refrigerate until ready to serve.

👌 RECIPE TIPS

☺ **Make Ahead:** *Depending on the size of your board, you may want to prepare the items ahead of time. Most items can be prepared and stored separately until you're ready to arrange your tray.*

☺ **Choose the Right Balance:** *As you are choosing items, be mindful of textures as well as colors. You want there to be beautiful pops of color throughout the board. The amount of each ingredient can be adjusted according to the size of your board.*

PAIRINGS: Homemade Ranch (page 98), Dill Dip (page 101), Cream Cheese Fruit Dip (page 273), Caramel Dip (page 274)

SALADS

"Knowledge is knowing a tomato is a fruit. Wisdom is not putting it into a fruit salad." —Brian O'Driscoll

Why do salads get so much flak? They may be viewed as the obligatory "healthy" item on a menu, but oftentimes, a salad is actually the perfect addition to round out any spread. Invited to a barbecue? Bring a salad! Invited to a pizza night? Bring a salad! Invited to a block party? Bring a salad! They definitely come in clutch more than we give them credit for.

HELPFUL TIPS + INFORMATION

How Much to Serve?

AS A SIDE DISH: For pasta salad, serve ½–1 cup per person; for green or vegetable-based salads, serve 1–1½ cups per person.

AS A MAIN DISH: For pasta salad, serve 1½–2 cups per person; for green or vegetable-based salads, serve 2–2½ cups per person.

Green Salad Tips

⊘ **PREP YOUR PRODUCE:** When preparing salads with produce, wash all vegetables and fruits under cool running tap water. This includes produce with a peel, skin, or rind that will be removed, because bacteria from the outside could find its way inside when it is being peeled. For leafy vegetables like cabbage or lettuce, remove the outer leaf before rinsing. To make things easier, you could use a colander or salad spinner to rinse.

⊘ **ADD PROTEIN:** Adding grilled chicken or beef to a salad is an easy way to make it more filling and turn it into a main dish rather than a side. You can also add shrimp, bacon bits, canned beans, hard-boiled eggs or chickpeas.

⊘ **KEEP IT BITE-SIZED:** Aside from a wedge salad, you should never have to use a knife to cut your salad. Cut all greens and mix-ins into bite-sized pieces before assembling the salad.

⊘ **KEEP IT COOL:** Set your salad platter or bowls on a tray of ice to help keep salads cool while sitting out. Set out only as much as can be eaten within 30 minutes, and keep the rest refrigerated. Refill the salad bowl as needed.

⊘ **MAKE IT AHEAD:** Most green salads can be prepped up to 4 hours in advance, but always store the dressing separately and toss with the salad just before serving.

Pasta Salad Tips

⊘ **SHAPE:** Choose shapes that can be stabbed, rather than twirled, with a fork. Elbow macaroni, rotini, rotelle (wagon wheel), fusilli, farfalle (bow tie), shell, or even ditalini are all great choices!

⊘ **COOKING:** Do not under- or overcook pasta. Bring water to a boil in a large pot, add the pasta along with a bit of salt. The time you boil the pasta is determined by what type of pasta you use. Check the package for timing. Ideally, you want it al dente.

⊘ **MAKE IT AHEAD:** Pasta salads lend themselves well to being prepped in advance, though depending on the recipe, you may want to wait to add the dressing until just before serving. See the Make Ahead tips in each recipe for details.

Salad Dressing Tips

⊘ **CHOOSE YOUR OIL WISELY:** The better the quality of oil, the better the dressing will be. Our favorites include a good-quality extra-virgin olive oil, sunflower oil and canola oil.

⊘ **MAKE IT HEALTHY:** Make creamy dressings healthier by using low-fat or Greek yogurt instead of sour cream, and low-fat milk instead of whole milk or heavy cream. You can also use honey instead of sugar for a healthier sweetener.

⊘ **MAKE IT AHEAD:** Most dressings can be stored in a mason jar or other airtight container with a lid in the refrigerator for up to 1 week. Stir or shake the jar, especially for a vinaigrette, before using.

FRUIT SALAD

⏱ PREP TIME: **15 MINUTES**

⧖ COOK TIME: **5 MINUTES**

⧖ CHILL TIME: **1 HOUR**

♡ SERVES: **10**

✓ FEED A CROWD

✓ MAKE AHEAD

✓ DAIRY-FREE

✓ GLUTEN-FREE

INGREDIENTS

¼ cup packed light brown sugar

¼ cup pineapple juice

2 tablespoons orange juice

1 teaspoon vanilla extract

2 cups green grapes

2 cups red grapes

1–2 cups cubed pineapple

1 cup sliced strawberries

1 cup blackberries

1 cup sliced kiwi

Scan me!

INSTRUCTIONS

1. Bring brown sugar, pineapple juice and orange juice to a boil in a small pot over medium-high heat, then reduce the heat and simmer for 5 minutes. Add vanilla and let cool.

2. Combine all fruit in a large bowl. Pour dressing over fruit, toss to coat and chill for at least 1 hour before serving.

PAIRINGS: Potato Salad (page 112), Pasta Salad (page 114), Classic Burgers (page 160), Baby Back Ribs (page 168)

👍 RECIPE TIPS

☺ **Make Ahead:** *Combine the fruit up to 1 day in advance and store in the refrigerator overnight or until you're ready to serve it. Add dressing and return to the refrigerator to chill 1 hour before serving.*

⚙ VARIATIONS

Add a little extra sweetness by mixing some mini marshmallows or toasted coconut into your fruit salad.

CAESAR SALAD

🕐 PREP TIME: **10 MINUTES**

♡ SERVES: **2–4**

✓ **QUICK & EASY**

✓ **ON THE TABLE IN 20**

✓ **MAKE AHEAD**

INGREDIENTS

DRESSING:

2 tablespoons lemon juice

2 teaspoons Worcestershire sauce

2 teaspoons minced garlic

½ teaspoon anchovy paste

1 cup mayonnaise

1 tablespoon olive oil

½ cup grated Parmesan cheese

¼ teaspoon pepper

¼ teaspoon salt

SALAD:

6 cups chopped romaine or other salad greens

2 chicken breasts, seasoned to taste, cooked and cubed

¼ cup shaved Parmesan cheese

1 cup croutons

Scan me!

INSTRUCTIONS

1. To make the dressing, in a medium bowl, whisk together lemon juice, Worcestershire sauce, garlic and anchovy paste. Add mayonnaise, olive oil, Parmesan, salt and pepper and whisk until combined. Store in the refrigerator until ready to toss with your salad.

2. To make the salad, place romaine in a salad bowl, then layer the chicken and half of the Parmesan on top. Add croutons and toss with desired amount of dressing.

3. Garnish with remaining Parmesan.

★ **BONUS RECIPE**

Homemade Croutons

Make homemade croutons to go with this recipe: Preheat the oven to 375 degrees F. In a large bowl, combine ¼ cup olive oil, 3 tablespoons melted unsalted butter, 1 tablespoon Italian seasoning, 1 teaspoon garlic salt and ½ teaspoon pepper. Cut ½ loaf of French bread into ¾–1-inch cubes and toss them in the liquid until evenly coated. Bake for 10 minutes, then turn and bake on the other side for an additional 8–10 minutes. Turn the oven setting to broil (set to high if there is an option for that), then broil for one minute, being careful to watch and make sure they do not burn. Enjoy with any salad of your choice.

👍 **RECIPE TIPS**

☺ **Make Ahead:** *We recommend cooking and cutting up the chicken in advance. The dressing can also be made in advance and stored in a jar with a lid in the refrigerator for up to 3 days before serving.*

☺ **Don't Like Anchovies?** *Feel free to omit the anchovy paste from the dressing. It will have a slightly different flavor, but it will still taste great.*

PAIRINGS: French Bread (page 63), Easy Garlic Knots (page 66), Marinated Steak (page 161), Roast Chicken (page 174)

STRAWBERRY SALAD

⏱ PREP TIME: **10 MINUTES**
♡ SERVES: **4**

✓ QUICK & EASY
✓ ON THE TABLE IN 20
✓ MAKE AHEAD
✓ GLUTEN-FREE

INGREDIENTS

SALAD:

6 cups chopped romaine lettuce

2 large chicken breasts, seasoned to taste, cooked and sliced

1 apple, thinly sliced

½ cup Craisins

½ cup shredded mozzarella cheese

½ cup candied pecans

sliced strawberries, for topping

STRAWBERRY VINAIGRETTE:

1 cup strawberries, tops cut off

2 tablespoons apple cider vinegar

2 tablespoons olive oil

¼ teaspoon salt

¼ teaspoon pepper

INSTRUCTIONS

1. To make the salad, place romaine in a salad bowl and top with chicken, apple slices, Craisins, cheese, pecans and strawberries.

2. To make the vinaigrette, combine all ingredients in a blender and blend until smooth. Add dressing to salad right before serving.

Scan me!

👍 RECIPE TIPS

☺ **Make Ahead:** *Do not add the dressing until you are ready to serve it. You may also want to wait to slice and add the strawberries so they do not get mushy. The rest of the salad can be assembled ahead and stored, covered, in the refrigerator for up to 24 hours.*

☺ **Candied Pecans:** *You can buy candied pecans, or you can make your own. To make them, set a small nonstick cooking pan over medium heat and add ¾ cup chopped pecans, 1½ tablespoons brown sugar and ½ tablespoon butter. Stir constantly until the sugar and butter melt together. Continue stirring for 2-3 more minutes as it caramelizes. Spread pecans in a single layer on a plate to cool.*

PAIRINGS: Slow Cooker Brisket (page 163), Parmesan-Crusted Pork Chops (page 167), Baby Back Ribs (page 168), Baked Salmon (page 173)

SOUTHWEST SALAD

⏱ **PREP TIME: 15 MINUTES**
♡ **SERVES: 6**

INGREDIENTS

CILANTRO RANCH DRESSING:

⅓–½ cup milk
1 packet (3 tablespoons) ranch dip or dressing mix
1 cup mayonnaise
1 cup sour cream
1 bunch cilantro
1 teaspoon minced garlic
1-3 teaspoons diced jalapeño peppers

SALAD:

1 head romaine lettuce, chopped
1 large orange bell pepper, chopped
1 (15.25-ounce) can black beans, rinsed and drained
1 pint cherry tomatoes, halved or quartered
2 cups corn
1 avocado, sliced or cubed
2 chicken breasts, seasoned to taste, cooked and
     cubed
diced green onions (optional)
chopped fresh cilantro (optional)

Scan me!

INSTRUCTIONS

1. For dressing, combine all ingredients
   in a blender, beginning with ⅓ cup milk. Blend until smooth.
   Add more milk as needed until it is the consistency you like.
   Refrigerate dressing until ready to serve.

2. Place all salad ingredients in a bowl and stir to combine.

3. Drizzle with dressing before serving.

👍 **RECIPE TIPS**

☺ **Make Ahead:** *You can prepare the salad ingredients 1–2 days ahead of time, except for the avocados, which cannot be cut until right before serving. Store the ingredients in separate airtight containers in the refrigerator. When you are ready to serve, cut the avocados and toss the salad ingredients together up to 30 minutes before serving.*

☺ **Storing Leftovers:** *How long leftover salad will stay fresh depends on whether it has been tossed in the dressing or not. If you think you may have leftover salad, I recommend serving the dressing on the side so your leftovers will last longer.*

PAIRINGS: Guacamole (page 88), Homemade Salsa (page 153), Chimichangas (page 185), Chicken Tacos (page 188)

ASIAN RAMEN SALAD

🕐 PREP TIME: **15 MINUTES**
♡ SERVES: **12–14**

✓ **QUICK & EASY**
✓ **ON THE TABLE IN 20**
✓ **FEED A CROWD**
✓ **MAKE AHEAD**

INGREDIENTS

3 (3-ounce) packages chicken ramen noodles
½ cup unsalted butter
1½ cups sliced almonds
½ cup olive oil
¼ cup white vinegar (or salad vinegar)
⅓ cup sugar
2 (16-ounce) bags tricolor coleslaw mix

Scan me!

INSTRUCTIONS

1. Open ramen packages and set seasoning packets aside. Place un-cooked noodles in a large plastic bag and break up using your hands or the bottom of a cup.

2. Melt butter in a skillet over medium-high heat. Add noodles and almonds and cook, stirring, for 3–4 minutes, until toasted and lightly browned. Spread onto a baking sheet and let cool.

3. In a medium container with a lid mix oil, vinegar, sugar and contents of ramen seasoning packets. Close the lid tight and shake well. Set aside.

4. When ready to serve, place coleslaw in a large bowl. Top with noodle mixture and dressing. Mix and serve immediately.

👍 RECIPE TIPS

☺ **Change It Up:** *Give your salad additional protein, color and flavor by adding shredded cooked chicken, mandarin oranges, edamame, sliced green onions, shredded carrots, sunflower seeds, sesame seeds, tofu, shrimp or roasted chickpeas.*

☺ **Low-Sodium Version:** *To make this salad a bit healthier, you can skip adding in the seasoning packets, which contain lots of added sodium. You can also use 1–2 tablespoons low-sodium soy sauce in place of the seasoning packets.*

☺ **To Avoid Soggy Noodles:** *Mix the noodles with the other ingredients right before serving. The longer the salad is stored, the softer the noodles will get.*

☺ **Make Ahead:** *Prepare dressing by putting ingredients in a container or mason jar and store in the refrigerator. When ready to serve, place coleslaw in a large bowl. Top with noodle mixture and the prepared dressing. Mix and serve immediately.*

PAIRINGS: Fried Egg Rolls (page 99), Sweet and Sour Chicken (page 181), Teriyaki Chicken (page 182)

BROCCOLI SALAD

⏱ **PREP TIME:** 10 MINUTES
⧗ **CHILL TIME:** 2 HOURS
♡ **SERVES:** 8–10

✓ FEED A CROWD

✓ MAKE AHEAD

✓ GLUTEN-FREE

INGREDIENTS

1 cup mayonnaise

3 tablespoons sugar

2 tablespoons white wine vinegar

7 cups chopped broccoli florets

½ cup Craisins

½ cup shelled sunflower seeds (raw or roasted)

8 slices bacon, cooked and crumbled

Scan me!

INSTRUCTIONS

1. In a large bowl, combine mayonnaise, sugar and vinegar and mix well.

2. Add broccoli and Craisins and stir to coat.

3. Cover and chill in the refrigerator for at least 2 hours or up to 24 hours.

4. Before serving, stir in sunflower seeds and bacon.

★ BONUS RECIPE

Cauliflower Broccoli Salad

Make the same dressing above and substitute half the broccoli with cauliflower florets. Add 1 cup cubed cheese along with sunflower seeds and crumbled bacon.

👍 RECIPE TIPS

☺ **Make Ahead:** *Broccoli salad can be prepared a day ahead of time without losing its texture. Just be sure to leave out the bacon and sunflower seeds until you are ready to serve, or they might get a little soggy. If you need to prepare it 2–3 days in advance, combine all the salad ingredients except the dressing; wait to add the dressing until you are ready to serve. Once the dressing has been added to the salad, it will only last 1–2 more days in the refrigerator.*

☺ **Additions:** *Add cubed cheddar cheese or other fruits and veggies, like cauliflower florets, chopped kale, shredded carrots, chopped celery or apple chunks.*

⚙ VARIATIONS

Swap out the sunflower seeds for pine nuts, chopped pecans, cashews or almonds.
Use raisins or fresh red grapes instead of Craisins.

PAIRINGS: Potato Salad (page 112), Pasta Salad (page 114), Chicken Salad (page 115)

POTATO SALAD

🕐 **PREP TIME:** 10 MINUTES

⧖ **COOK TIME:** 45 MINUTES

♡ **SERVES:** 12

✓ **FEED A CROWD**

✓ **MAKE AHEAD**

✓ **GLUTEN-FREE**

INGREDIENTS

5 pounds potatoes, washed

6–7 eggs

1 (2.25-ounce) can black olives, diced

3–4 baby dill pickles, diced

¼ cup pickle juice

2 cups mayonnaise

1 tablespoon mustard

salt and pepper to taste

MIX-INS (OPTIONAL): paprika, chopped celery, bacon bits, Dijon mustard

Scan me!

INSTRUCTIONS

1. Place potatoes in a large pot, cover with water and bring to a rolling boil over high heat. Boil potatoes for 40–45 minutes or until tender (a fork should easily pierce a potato).

2. While potatoes are cooking, fill a medium pot with enough water to cover eggs and bring to a boil over medium-high heat. Gently lower eggs into the water using a strainer ladle. Turn the heat down and simmer for 15 minutes. Once done, transfer eggs to an ice bath for 5 minutes, then peel and set aside.

3. Let potatoes cool, then peel off skins and cube potatoes into ¾-inch pieces. It is okay if they are soft or fall apart. Place in a large bowl.

4. Cube eggs and add to bowl.

5. Add olives, pickles and pickle juice and mix.

6. Add mayonnaise, mustard, salt and pepper and mix well (add more or less mayonnaise depending on what you like).

7. Stir in any other desired mix-ins and refrigerate until ready to serve.

PAIRINGS: Fruit Salad (page 105), Broccoli Salad (page 111), Classic Burgers (page 160), Slow Cooker Brisket (page 163), Baby Back Ribs (page 168)

👍 **RECIPE TIPS**

☺ **Make Ahead:** *This salad is best made ahead. We like to make this the day before and let it refrigerate for 18–24 hours, but this is not required.*

☺ **Texture:** *Different types of potatoes create different textures. If you want them to stay firm and hold their shape, use waxy potatoes like Yukon Gold or red potatoes. If you want the potatoes to slightly mash when you mix the salad, use starchy potatoes like russets (this is what we prefer).*

MACARONI SALAD

⏱ PREP TIME: **10 MINUTES**

⏳ COOK TIME: **10 MINUTES**

♡ SERVES: **16**

✓ QUICK & EASY

✓ ON THE TABLE IN 20

✓ FEED A CROWD

✓ MAKE AHEAD

INGREDIENTS

24 ounces (6 cups) macaroni

1½ cups cubed ham

1 (12-ounce) bag frozen peas, thawed

1½ cups mayonnaise

1 cup milk

½ cup ranch dressing

salt and pepper to taste

paprika to taste

MIX-INS (OPTIONAL): diced boiled egg, diced
   bell peppers, cheese cubes

INSTRUCTIONS

1. Cook macaroni in salted water according
   to package directions. Drain and rinse.

2. In a large bowl, combine cooked macaroni, ham and peas.

3. In a separate bowl, mix the mayonnaise, milk and ranch dressing.

4. Add dressing to the pasta and mix until coated.

5. Season with salt, pepper and paprika. Stir in any additional desired
   mix-ins and refrigerate until ready to serve.

Scan me!

👍 RECIPE TIPS

☺ **Make Ahead:** *Macaroni salad can be made
24 hours ahead of time. Mix most of the
dressing in before storing in an airtight
container in the refrigerator, but reserve a
little dressing to add right before serving, to
freshen up the salad in case it is a little dry.*

☺ **Try a Different Pasta:** *Anything that is
bite-sized and has grooves works well,
such as shells, wagon wheels, bow ties,
penne or rotini.*

☺ **Perfect for Parties:** *We use this recipe for
many get-togethers, like holidays and
baby showers. It makes a lot, so be sure
to halve it if you're looking to serve closer
to 8 people.*

PAIRINGS: Potato Salad (page 112), Chicken Salad (page 115), Classic
Burgers (page 160), Pigs in a Blanket (page 166)

PASTA SALAD

⊙ **PREP TIME:** 15 MINUTES

⧖ **COOK TIME:** 12 MINUTES

⧖ **CHILL TIME:** 2 HOURS

♡ **SERVES:** 8

⊘ FEED A CROWD

⊘ MAKE AHEAD

INGREDIENTS

16 ounces (4 cups) colored rotini pasta (fusilli, farfalle, and penne work, too), cooked

½ cup diced black olives

½ cup cubed Colby Jack cheese

½ cup mini pepperoni slices

¾–1 cup Italian dressing

MIX-INS (OPTIONAL): chopped cucumbers, halved cherry tomatoes, chopped peppers, ham cubes, pepperoncini, artichoke hearts

Scan me!

INSTRUCTIONS

1. Cook pasta as directed on the package. Drain and rinse with cold water.

2. In a large bowl, combine cool pasta, olives, cheese and pepperoni.

3. Pour at least half of Italian dressing into the pasta salad and mix well.

4. Add any desired mix-ins to the pasta salad and mix well.

5. Refrigerate for at least 2 hours. Stir in additional dressing to taste before serving.

PAIRINGS: Fruit Salad (page 105), Macaroni Salad (page 113), Chicken Salad (page 115), Pigs in a Blanket (page 166)

👍 **RECIPE TIPS**

☺ **Make Ahead:** *This pasta salad is best when eaten right after you put on the additional dressing after chilling. If you want to make it ahead of time, combine all ingredients except the dressing in a large bowl, cover and refrigerate. Toss with the dressing right before serving.*

CHICKEN SALAD

PREP TIME: **15 MINUTES**

CHILL TIME: **1 HOUR**

SERVES: **8**

FEED A CROWD

MAKE AHEAD

GLUTEN-FREE

INGREDIENTS

6 chicken breasts, cooked and cubed (rotisserie chicken and shredded chicken work, too)

1½ cups chopped celery

½ cup heavy cream

1 cup mayonnaise

2 tablespoons lemon juice

1 teaspoon salt

½ teaspoon pepper

½ cup sliced almonds

2 teaspoons chopped fresh parsley

Scan me!

INSTRUCTIONS

1. In a large bowl, combine chicken and celery.

2. In another bowl, whip cream by hand until thickened. Add mayonnaise, lemon juice, salt and pepper. Whisk together until smooth.

3. Pour dressing over chicken and celery. Add almonds and mix until combined.

4. Refrigerate for at least 1 hour. Sprinkle with parsley before serving.

PAIRINGS: Heavenly Rolls (page 68), Macaroni Salad (page 113), Pasta Salad (page 114)

👍 RECIPE TIPS

☺ **Make Ahead:** *The components can be made up to 2 days ahead of time. Store chicken, celery, almonds and parsley in one bowl and dressing in a separate container in the refrigerator. Combine dressing with other ingredients before serving.*

☺ **Additional Add-Ins:** *Here are a few more ingredient add-ins to try: pesto, sliced grapes, raisins, dried cranberries, chopped apples, walnuts, cashews, pecans, water chestnuts, green onions, bell peppers and curry powder.*

SOUPS

"Soup is like duct tape. It fixes everything."

When we are cold, we want soup. When we are sick, we want soup. When we are feeling sad, we want to snuggle in a blanket, watch Hallmark movies and eat soup. Right?! There is just something so comforting about soup, which means it's hard not to love. It was a challenge narrowing down our favorite soups for this section because we love so many, but these are some of our absolute favorites, and we can guarantee that you will find each of the recipes to be soup-erb!

HELPFUL TIPS + INFORMATION

How Much to Serve?

AS A SIDE DISH: The average soup serving is ¾–1 cup. A soup cup can usually hold 8 ounces, or 1 cup.

AS A MAIN DISH: The average soup serving is about 1½ cups or 12 ounces, which is the size of a typical soup bowl.

Soup Ingredients

⊘ **PREPPING VEGETABLES:** Make sure you cut your veggies all to roughly the same size, so they will cook at the same rate.

⊘ **TO SAVE TIME:** Buy fresh or frozen chopped vegetables at the supermarket rather than cutting up your own.

⊘ **BROTH VS. STOCK:** Broth and stock are the building blocks for soup. They are both available with a base of beef, chicken or vegetables, and in organic, gluten-free and vegan varieties. Broth is thinner, has fewer calories and has less fat than stock. Stock (aka bone broth) has slightly more calories, fat and protein, but also has a significantly higher quantity of vitamins and minerals. They can be used interchangeably, so pick the one that best fits your dietary needs.

Cooking and Serving

⊘ **LOW AND SLOW:** Don't cheat on cooking time. Simmering soups over low heat brings out the flavors. When cooking soups that contain dairy products, make sure to heat them slowly and don't allow them to come to a boil, which could cause the ingredients to separate.

⊘ **SLOW COOKER MATH:** The high setting on a slow cooker is about 300°F. Low is about 200°F. One hour on high equals about two hours on low.

⊘ **TO BUMP UP THE FLAVOR:** Opt for using more flavorful chicken or beef stock instead of broth. If a soup recipe calls for cooked meat, using seasoned cooked meat really lifts the entire soup.

⊘ **TO THICKEN SOUP:** If your soup seems too thin, there are a couple of ways to thicken it:

⊘ **WITH FLOUR:** Put 1–2 tablespoons flour per cup of soup in a separate heatproof bowl and add a cup of hot liquid from the soup. Mix the two until smooth, then pour the flour mixture back into the soup.

⊘ **WITH CORNSTARCH:** Put 2 tablespoons cornstarch per cup of soup in a separate bowl and mix with a little cold water until it is very smooth. Gradually stir the mixture into the hot soup until blended.

⊘ **KEEP IT WARM:** To keep soup warm for serving at a dinner party, use a slow cooker on the warm setting or a chafing dish.

TOMATO BASIL SOUP

⏱ PREP TIME: 5 MINUTES
⌛ COOK TIME: 50 MINUTES
♡ SERVES: 10

✓ **FEED A CROWD**

✓ **SLOW COOKER**

✓ GLUTEN-FREE

INGREDIENTS

4 teaspoons minced garlic

1 (28-ounce) can diced tomatoes, drained and liquid reserved

2 tablespoons basil puree (or chopped fresh basil)

½ teaspoon dried thyme

2 cups full-sodium chicken broth

garlic salt with parsley flakes to taste

pepper to taste

½ cup heavy cream, room temperature

TOPPINGS: croutons, grated Parmesan cheese, chopped fresh basil

Scan me!

INSTRUCTIONS

1. Place garlic in a large pot over medium heat, and cook, stirring, until fragrant.

2. Add tomatoes, basil and thyme and cook, stirring occasionally, for 10 minutes.

3. Add broth, then measure out 1 cup reserved tomato liquid and add to broth. Stir and lower heat to medium-low. Cook, uncovered, for 35–40 minutes, stirring occasionally.

4. Season with garlic salt and pepper to taste.

5. In small batches, puree soup in a blender until it is the consistency you prefer.

6. Return soup to the pot over low heat, stir in heavy cream and mix well.

7. Adjust seasoning with more garlic salt and pepper if needed, and garnish with croutons, basil and Parmesan cheese.

BONUS RECIPE

Grilled Cheese

Heat a skillet over medium heat. Butter one side of two slices of bread (or spread with mayo) and lay one slice butter side down on the skillet. Add 1 slice cheddar and 1 slice provolone to bread, then top with the other piece of bread, butter side up. Cook until golden brown on both sides and the cheese is melted, about 2 minutes per side.

👍 **RECIPE TIPS**

☺ **Slow Cooker Directions:** *Cook garlic, tomatoes, basil and thyme as directed in Steps 1 and 2 above. Transfer to a slow cooker and add broth and tomato liquid. Cover and cook on low for 6–7 hours or high for 2–3 hours. Puree soup in small batches, then return to the slow cooker and add heavy cream, garlic salt and pepper. Stir until creamy and serve.*

PAIRINGS: Cheesy Garlic Bread (page 67), Homemade Croutons (page 106), Grilled Cheese (left)

CHICKEN NOODLE SOUP

⏱ PREP TIME: 10 MINUTES

⏳ COOK TIME: 30 MINUTES

♡ SERVES: 8

INGREDIENTS

1 tablespoon unsalted butter

1 cup thinly sliced carrots

½ cup chopped celery

1 tablespoon minced garlic

4 (14.5-ounce) cans full-sodium chicken broth

1 (14.5-ounce) can vegetable broth

2 chicken breasts, seasoned to taste, cooked and chopped

1 teaspoon dried basil

½ teaspoon dried oregano

salt and pepper to taste

1½ cups medium egg noodles

Scan me!

INSTRUCTIONS

1. Melt butter in a large pot over medium heat. Add carrots and celery and cook, stirring, until just tender, about 5 minutes. Add garlic and cook for 1 minute more.

2. Add broths, chicken, basil, oregano and salt and pepper to taste and bring to a boil.

3. Reduce heat to a simmer, add egg noodles and simmer for 20 minutes. Serve warm.

PAIRINGS: French Bread (page 63), Easy Homemade Biscuits (page 65), Easy Garlic Knots (page 66), Grilled Cheese (page 119)

👍 **RECIPE TIPS**

☺ **Slow Cooker Directions:** *Combine all ingredients except the noodles in the slow cooker. Cover and cook on low for 6–7 hours or on high for 2–3 hours. Add noodles and cook an additional 30–40 minutes on low or 20 minutes on high, or until the noodles are tender.*

SLOW COOKER CHEESY POTATO SOUP

⏱ PREP TIME: **5 MINUTES**
⧖ COOK TIME: **3 HOURS**
♡ SERVES: **8**

✓ PREPPED IN 5
✓ MAKE AHEAD
✓ SLOW COOKER

INGREDIENTS

4 tablespoons unsalted butter

1 (32-ounce) package frozen diced hash browns, thawed

2 (10.5-ounce) cans cream of chicken soup

1 (10.5-ounce) can cream of celery soup

3 cups half-and-half (or heavy cream), plus more as needed

additional mix-ins (optional): 1 (14.75-ounce) can creamed corn or 2 cups chopped ham

1½ cups shredded cheddar cheese, divided

salt and pepper to taste

TOPPINGS: sour cream, bacon crumbles, chopped chives or green onions (optional)

Scan me!

INSTRUCTIONS

1. Set a slow cooker to high. Add butter to the slow cooker and let melt. Add hash browns, cream of chicken and celery soups and half-and-half (or heavy cream) and mix to combine. Stir in any other desired mix-ins, then cover and cook on high for 3–4 hours.

2. Add 1 cup cheese and salt and pepper to taste and stir to mix. Add more half-and-half if needed to reach the consistency you prefer.

3. Sprinkle with the remaining ½ cup cheese along with any other desired toppings before serving.

PAIRINGS: Bacon (page 37), Bread Bowls (page 64), Brown Sugar Ham (page 172)

👍 RECIPE TIPS

☺ **Stove Top Directions:** *Melt butter in a large pot over medium-high heat, then add hash browns, cream of chicken soup, cream of celery soup and half-and-half. Bring to a boil, then reduce the heat to low and cook for 30–40 minutes, or until potatoes are tender. Add cheese, salt and pepper before serving.*

☺ **Make Ahead:** *This soup can easily be made ahead of time and stored covered in an airtight container in the refrigerator for up to 3 days. To reheat, just microwave or heat soup over medium heat in a pot. You may need to add more half-and-half when reheating to make it a more smooth consistency.*

BROCCOLI CHEESE SOUP

FEED A CROWD

INGREDIENTS

2 (14.5-ounce) cans low-sodium chicken broth (or vegetable broth)

2 small heads broccoli, diced small

3 tablespoons unsalted butter

⅓ cup all-purpose flour

3½ cups milk, plus more as needed

4 cups shredded cheddar cheese, plus more for topping (optional)

1 teaspoon salt

½ teaspoon garlic pepper

6 slices bacon, cooked and chopped

Scan me!

INSTRUCTIONS

1. In a large pot, add broth and bring to a boil over medium-high heat. Reduce the heat to medium-low.

2. Add broccoli, cover and simmer for 10 minutes.

3. Meanwhile, melt butter in a large saucepan over medium-low heat. Whisk in flour and cook for another minute, until golden brown. Whisk in milk, turn the heat to medium and cook, stirring, for 5 minutes, or until the sauce thickens.

4. Add cheese and stir until it is all melted. Add salt and garlic pepper. Pour cheese sauce into the soup pot and stir until well combined.

5. Add more milk if you like a thinner consistency, and season with additional salt and garlic pepper to taste.

6. Top with bacon pieces and extra cheese, if desired, and serve warm.

★ BONUS RECIPE

Loaded Broccoli Cheese Potato Soup

Follow the recipe above, but after adding broth, add 4 medium potatoes (peeled and cubed), 2–3 large carrots (diced) and 1 teaspoon onion powder. Bring to a boil over medium-high heat then reduce the heat to medium-low, cover and simmer for about 10 minutes. Continue with Step 2, adding the broccoli and simmering for 10 more minutes and so on.

👍 RECIPE TIPS

☺ **Adjust the Texture:** *Use heavy cream or half-and-half instead of milk for a creamier soup. For a lighter texture, thin it out with extra broth or water.*

PAIRINGS: Bread Bowls (page 64), Easy Garlic Knots (page 66), Bacon (page 37)

SLOW COOKER BEEF STEW

- ⏱ **PREP TIME:** 5 MINUTES
- ⧗ **COOK TIME:** 6 HOURS
- ♡ **SERVES:** 8

✓ **PREPPED IN 5**
✓ **FREEZER FRIENDLY**
✓ **MAKE AHEAD**
✓ **SLOW COOKER**
✓ **DAIRY-FREE**

INGREDIENTS

3 pounds chuck roast or other stew meat, cubed
8 Yukon Gold potatoes, cubed
6 medium carrots, sliced
2 (10.5-ounce) cans golden mushroom soup
2–3 cups water (or beef broth)
1 (2-ounce) package onion soup mix
garlic salt to taste (optional)
pepper to taste (optional)
chopped fresh parsley (optional)

Scan me!

INSTRUCTIONS

1. Combine all ingredients in a slow cooker and stir to combine.

2. Cook on low for approximately 6 hours, then serve. Season with garlic salt, pepper and parsley as desired.

PAIRINGS: French Bread (page 63), Cornbread Muffins (page 71), Caesar Salad (page 106)

👍 RECIPE TIPS

☺ **Stove Top Directions:** *Cook meat with 2 tablespoons vegetable oil in a large pot over medium-high heat until well browned. Add mushroom soup, onion soup mix and water or beef broth. Bring to a boil, then lower the heat and simmer, uncovered, for 1 hour. Add potatoes and carrots and simmer for 1 more hour, or until vegetables are fork-tender. Season with salt and pepper.*

☺ **For Added Flavor:** *If you like, you can sear your meat in a pan on each side before cubing it and adding to the slow cooker. This will give it a nice flavor and a crisper outside.*

☺ **Make Ahead:** *Beef stew is a great soup for freezing. Place completely cooled soup into freezer bags or storage containers. Keep in the freezer for up to 6 months. When ready to use, thaw overnight in the refrigerator, then reheat on the stovetop.*

CHICKEN DUMPLING SOUP

PREP TIME: 5 MINUTES
COOK TIME: 25 MINUTES
SERVES: 6

PREPPED IN 5

QUICK & EASY

SLOW COOKER

INGREDIENTS

4 cups chicken broth

1 (10.5-ounce) can cream of chicken soup

1½–2 cups shredded cooked chicken

1 (16.3-ounce) can refrigerated biscuits, cut into fourths or eighths (or 1 recipe Easy Homemade Biscuit dough, page 65, cut into your desired size dumplings)

1 (8.75-ounce) can corn

3 medium carrots, sliced

TOPPING: chopped fresh parsley

Scan me!

INSTRUCTIONS

1. In a large pot, combine broth, cream of chicken soup and chicken and bring to a boil. Reduce heat to low, cover and simmer for 5 minutes.

2. Add biscuit pieces, corn and carrots. Cover and simmer for 15–20 minutes, stirring occasionally to keep biscuits from sticking together.

3. Serve topped with parsley.

PAIRINGS: Easy Homemade Biscuits (page 65), Green Bean Casserole (page 137), Roasted Vegetables (page 140)

👍 **RECIPE TIPS**

☺ **Slow Cooker Directions:** *Combine broth, soup and chicken in the slow cooker and cook for 2–3 hours on low. Add all remaining ingredients except the parsley and cook for 1–2 hours more. Be sure to keep the lid on as much as possible. Top with parsley and serve.*

SLOW COOKER SPINACH TORTELLINI SOUP

PREP TIME: **5 MINUTES**
COOK TIME: **3 HOURS**
SERVES: **6**

PREPPED IN 5
MAKE AHEAD
SLOW COOKER

INGREDIENTS

6 cups low-sodium chicken broth

2 (14.5-ounce) cans Italian-style diced tomatoes

1 (11-ounce) bag fresh spinach

1 (8-ounce) package cream cheese, cut into 1-inch cubes

1 teaspoon ground cumin

1 teaspoon dried oregano

1 teaspoon garlic salt

pepper to taste

1 (18–20-ounce) package three-cheese tortellini

Scan me!

INSTRUCTIONS

1. Place the chicken broth, tomatoes, spinach, cream cheese, cumin, oregano, garlic salt and pepper to taste in the slow cooker.

2. Cover and cook on high for 2–3 hours, stirring occasionally.

3. Add tortellini and continue cooking on high for 1 additional hour. Serve warm.

🖐 RECIPE TIPS

☺ **Stove Top Directions:** *Combine broth, tomatoes, spinach and seasonings in a large pot over medium-low heat and bring to a light simmer (this will take about 10 minutes). Add cream cheese and tortellini and allow tortellini to cook through while the cream cheese melts, 8–10 minutes. Once tortellini is cooked and cream cheese has melted, stir the soup to combine before serving.*

☺ **Make Ahead:** *This soup can be made ahead and stored in an airtight container in the refrigerator for 3–4 days. Be aware that the pasta may continue to absorb the liquid. Reheat in the microwave or the stovetop.*

PAIRINGS: Heavenly Rolls (page 68), Cornbread (page 71), Bruschetta (page 94)

BEST CHILI SOUP

 ⊘ **SLOW COOKER**

 ⊘ **DAIRY-FREE**

 ⊘ **GLUTEN-FREE**

INGREDIENTS

1 pound ground beef

1½ tablespoons sugar

2 tablespoons ground cumin

1 tablespoon garlic powder

1 tablespoon chili powder

1 teaspoon garlic salt

½ teaspoon paprika

pepper to taste

2 (8-ounce) cans tomato sauce

1 (15.5-ounce) can red kidney beans, drained

1 (14.5-ounce) can diced tomatoes

1½ cups beef broth

TOPPINGS: sour cream, shredded cheese, chopped green onions (optional)

Scan me!

INSTRUCTIONS

1. In a large pot, cook ground beef over medium heat, stirring to break up meat, until browned and cooked through. Drain fat.

2. Add sugar, cumin, garlic powder, chili powder, garlic salt, paprika and pepper and stir to mix.

3. Add tomato sauce, kidney beans, tomatoes and beef broth. Bring to a simmer and cook uncovered for 25–30 minutes.

4. Season with more garlic salt and pepper, if desired, and add any preferred toppings before serving.

👍 **RECIPE TIPS**

☺ **Slow Cooker Directions:** *Cook the meat and drain the fat as described in Step 1 above, then combine all ingredients in a slow cooker and cook on low for 3–4 hours.*

PAIRINGS: Quesadilla (page 70), Cornbread (page 71), Street Corn (page 150)

WHITE CHICKEN CHILI

○ PREP TIME: 5 MINUTES

⧖ COOK TIME: 20 MINUTES

♡ SERVES: 8

⊘ PREPPED IN 5

⊘ QUICK & EASY

⊘ SLOW COOKER

⊘ GLUTEN-FREE

INGREDIENTS

4 cups chicken broth

3–4 (15.5-ounce) cans great northern beans, drained and rinsed

2 cups shredded cooked chicken

1–2 (4-ounce) cans diced green chiles

1 teaspoon ground cumin

½ teaspoon garlic powder

½ teaspoon dried oregano

dash of pepper

2 cups shredded Monterey Jack (or Mexican blend) cheese

1 cup sour cream

Scan me!

INSTRUCTIONS

1. In a large pot, combine broth, beans, chicken, chiles, cumin, garlic powder, oregano and pepper over medium-low heat. Simmer for 20–30 minutes, or until soup is heated through.

2. Right before serving, add cheese and sour cream and stir until cheese is melted and ingredients are mixed.

PAIRINGS: Flour Tortillas (page 70), Cornbread (page 71), Homemade Tortilla Chips (page 151)

👍 **RECIPE TIPS**

☺ **Slow Cooker Directions:** *Combine all ingredients except cheese and sour cream in the slow cooker and cook on low for 2 hours. Add cheese and sour cream and cook for an additional 30–60 minutes, or until cheese is melted. Stir together and serve warm.*

SLOW COOKER CHICKEN TORTILLA SOUP

⏱ PREP TIME: 10 MINUTES
⏳ COOK TIME: 3 HOURS
♡ SERVES: 6

FREEZER FRIENDLY

SLOW COOKER

GLUTEN-FREE

INGREDIENTS

6 cups chicken stock (or chicken broth)

2 cups shredded cooked chicken

1–2 (14.5-ounce) cans diced tomatoes, drained

1 (14.5-ounce) can corn, drained

1 (15.25-ounce) can black beans, drained and rinsed

1 (4-ounce) can diced green chiles

½ cup chopped onion (optional)

2 teaspoons minced garlic

1½ teaspoons salt

¾ teaspoon pepper

½ teaspoon ground cumin

¼ teaspoon chili powder

TOPPINGS: corn tortilla strips (store-bought or homemade; see below), sour cream, shredded Monterey Jack cheese, chopped avocado, chopped fresh cilantro (optional)

Scan me!

INSTRUCTIONS

1. In a slow cooker, combine all ingredients except the toppings.

2. Cook on low for 8 hours or on high for 3–4 hours.

3. Add cheese, tortilla strips and other favorite toppings right before serving.

👍 RECIPE TIPS

☺ **Stove Top Directions:** *In a large pot, combine all ingredients except the toppings over medium-low heat. Simmer for 20–30 minutes, or until soup is heated through. Ladle into bowls and add cheese, tortilla strips and other favorite toppings.*

⚙ VARIATIONS

This slow cooker chicken tortilla soup is more on the brothy side. For a different texture, during the last 30 minutes of cooking in the slow cooker, just add ⅔ cup heavy cream and ⅓ cup sour cream to make the soup nice and creamy!

★ BONUS RECIPE

Corn Tortilla Strips

To make homemade corn tortilla strips, slice corn tortillas with a pizza cutter into thin strips. Heat vegetable oil over medium-high heat and flash fry strips in the oil until golden and crispy, 30–60 seconds. Or, toss strips in a bowl with 2 tablespoons vegetable oil and spread in a single layer on a baking sheet. Bake in the oven at 425 degrees F for 8–10 minutes, turning halfway through.

PAIRINGS: Flour Tortillas (page 70), Cornbread (page 71), Homemade Tortilla Chips (page 151)

SLOW COOKER GREEN CHILE CHICKEN ENCHILADA SOUP

PREP TIME: **10 MINUTES**
COOK TIME: **4 HOURS**
SERVES: **6**

INGREDIENTS

4 chicken breasts, cooked and shredded
2 (14.5-ounce) cans chicken broth
2 (15-ounce) cans mild green enchilada sauce
2 (4-ounce) cans diced green chiles
⅔ cup water
1½ tablespoons ground cumin
1 tablespoon chili powder
1 teaspoon onion powder
1 teaspoon garlic powder
⅔ cup corn (thawed if frozen)
⅔ cup instant rice
1 (8-ounce) package cream cheese, cubed and
  softened
salt and pepper to taste
TOPPINGS: shredded Monterey Jack cheese,
  chopped fresh cilantro

Scan me!

INSTRUCTIONS

1. Combine chicken, broth, enchilada sauce, green chiles, water, cumin, chili powder, onion powder and garlic powder in a slow cooker. Cover and cook on high for 3½ hours.

2. Add corn, rice and cream cheese. Stir and cook on high for 30 minutes more.

3. Add salt and pepper and top with cheese and cilantro before serving.

PAIRINGS: Guacamole (page 88), Queso Blanco (page 90), Homemade Tortilla Chips (page 151)

👍 RECIPE TIPS

☺ **Stove Top Directions:** *In a large pot, combine chicken, broth, enchilada sauce, green chiles, water, cumin, chili powder, onion powder and garlic powder and bring to a boil. Add corn, rice and cream cheese, reduce the heat and simmer for 25 minutes. Mix well so all cream cheese chunks are gone, then add salt and pepper. Serve garnished with cheese and cilantro.*

TACO SOUP

🕐 PREP TIME: 5 MINUTES

⏳ COOK TIME: 15 MINUTES

♡ SERVES: 8

PREPPED IN 5

QUICK & EASY

ON THE TABLE IN 20

FREEZER FRIENDLY

FEED A CROWD

MAKE AHEAD

SLOW COOKER

DAIRY-FREE

INGREDIENTS

3 (15-ounce) cans chili with beans

1 (15-ounce) can black beans, drained and rinsed

1 (15-ounce) can tomato sauce

1 (15-ounce) can diced tomatoes

1 (15-ounce) can corn

1 (4-ounce) can diced green chiles

3 tablespoons (1 packet) ranch dressing mix

3 tablespoons (1 packet) taco salad seasoning

1½ cups low-sodium beef broth

½ cup water

TOPPINGS: sour cream, tortilla strips, shredded cheese, chopped green onions, chopped fresh cilantro (optional)

Scan me!

INSTRUCTIONS

1. Combine all ingredients in a large pot and bring to a boil.

2. Reduce the heat and simmer for 15 minutes.

3. Serve warm with your desired toppings.

👍 RECIPE TIPS

☺ **Make Ahead:** *You can easily make this soup 1–2 days ahead of time. Store it in an airtight container in the refrigerator. When ready to serve, reheat on the stove or in a crockpot until warm.*

☺ **Slow Cooker Instructions:** *Combine all ingredients in a slow cooker and cook on high for 2–3 hours or low for 6–7 hours.*

☺ **Freezing Instructions:** *This soup makes a great freezer meal. Simply mix all the ingredients and pour into a freezer-safe container. To cook, remove from the freezer and place in the slow cooker for 4 hours on high or for 8 hours on low. You can also thaw overnight in the fridge and heat in a pot on the stove until warm.*

PAIRINGS: Quesadilla (page 70), Cornbread (page 71), Homemade Tortilla Chips (page 151), Corn Tortilla Strips (page 128)

EGG DROP SOUP

⏱ **PREP TIME:** 10 MINUTES
⧗ **COOK TIME:** 10 MINUTES
♡ **SERVES:** 4

✓ **QUICK & EASY**
✓ **ON THE TABLE IN 20**
✓ **DAIRY-FREE**

INGREDIENTS

4 cups chicken broth, divided
2 tablespoons chopped fresh chives
½ teaspoon salt
⅛ teaspoon ground ginger
1½ tablespoons cornstarch
2 eggs
1 egg yolk
fried wonton strips

Scan me!

INSTRUCTIONS

1. In a large saucepan, combine 3¼ cups chicken broth, chives, salt and ginger and bring to a rolling boil.

2. In a small bowl, stir together remaining ¾ cup broth and the cornstarch and mix until smooth. Set aside.

3. In another small bowl, whisk the eggs and egg yolk together using a fork.

4. Drizzle egg mixture a little at a time from the fork into the boiling broth mixture (egg should cook immediately).

5. Once all the eggs have been dropped, stir in the cornstarch mixture gradually until the soup is the desired consistency.

6. Top with fried wonton strips and serve warm.

PAIRINGS: Fried Egg Rolls (page 99), Fried Rice (page 147), Sweet and Sour Chicken (page 181), Teriyaki Chicken (page 182)

👍 **RECIPE TIPS**

☺ **Homemade Wonton Strips:** *You can make your own wonton strips rather than using store-bought; they're great for this soup as well as in salads, like our Asian Ramen Salad (page 110). To make them, cut wonton wrappers into thin strips and fry in vegetable oil over medium-high heat for 1–2 minutes, until golden brown.*

SIDES

"I am just so thankful for all the different ways to eat potatoes."

It's true—potatoes are the best! In fact, aren't side dishes the best in general? In our humble opinion, the sides are the true stars of every Thanksgiving feast. We love to change up our sides to complement whatever type of main-dish cuisine we're serving. Our family loves each and every one of the recipes included in this section, and we think you will, too!

HELPFUL TIPS + INFORMATION

How Much to Serve?

POTATO DISHES: Plan on ¾ cup per person. Two medium-sized russet potatoes will serve 2–3 people, 3–4 potatoes will serve 5 people, 8 potatoes will serve 10 people and 15–16 potatoes will serve 20 people.

RICE DISHES: ½ cup per person

PASTA SIDES: ½ cup per person

VEGETABLE DISHES: 1 cup per person

Picking Sides

- **ADD VARIETY:** Sides should complement your meal and provide contrasting flavors and textures. Serve both hot and cold sides together, and try not to repeat ingredients. If you are serving pork as the main dish, then don't choose sides that also contain pork.

- **PLAN AHEAD:** When choosing sides for a large party or a holiday, pick dishes that use different cooking methods (oven, stovetop, slow cooker, etc.) to make things easier in the kitchen.

Ingredient Prep

- You can save time the day of by prepping many ingredients individually in advance:

  - Wash and chop veggies 1–2 days ahead and store them in separate containers in the refrigerator.

  - Wash and chop raw potatoes and store in a bowl of water in the refrigerator for up to 24 hours. Drain and pat dry before using.

  - Make dressings and sauces ahead and store in separate containers in the refrigerator; add right before mixing and serving.

  - Cook pasta a day ahead, drain, and toss lightly in olive oil before storing in an airtight container in the refrigerator.

  - If you want to cut fruits ahead of time that brown quickly, such as apples or bananas, use a squeeze of lemon juice or lime juice to keep them from browning. Mix 1 cup water and 1 tablespoon citrus juice in a bowl and submerge fruit for a few minutes, then remove and store in an airtight container in the refrigerator.

GREEN BEAN BUNDLES

PREP TIME: **10 MINUTES**
COOK TIME: **20 MINUTES**
SERVES: **6**

QUICK & EASY

MAKE AHEAD

GLUTEN-FREE

INGREDIENTS

2 pounds fresh green beans
6 strips bacon
4 tablespoons unsalted butter, melted
3 tablespoons light brown sugar
garlic salt to taste

Scan me!

INSTRUCTIONS

1. Steam green beans until tender (see Recipe Tips).

2. Preheat the oven to 350 degrees F. Lightly grease a baking sheet and set aside.

3. Gather 6–10 green beans into a bundle and wrap with 1 piece of bacon. Secure bacon with a toothpick. Repeat to make 6 bundles.

4. Place bundles on the prepared baking sheet (or a wire rack over an aluminum foil–lined baking sheet). Sprinkle with melted butter, brown sugar and garlic salt.

5. Bake for 18–20 minutes. For extra crispiness, broil for 1 minute, then flip bundles and broil for 1 minute on the other side.

★ BONUS RECIPE

Asparagus Bundles

This same recipe can be made with asparagus. Just wrap up 6–8 pieces of asparagus with 1 slice of bacon and cook for the same amount of time.

👍 RECIPE TIPS

☺ **Make Ahead:** *To save a bit of time the day of your dinner, you can prep these bundles through Step 4 the night before, cover and store in the refrigerator.*

☺ **To Steam Green Beans:** *Put green beans in a microwave-safe bowl and cover with water. Cook on high for 3 minutes, or until green beans are tender.*

PAIRINGS: Heavenly Rolls (page 68), Mashed Potatoes (page 145), Garlic Prime Rib (page 162), Roast Turkey (page 175)

BROWN SUGAR– GLAZED CARROTS

⏲ PREP TIME: 5 MINUTES
⧗ COOK TIME: 15 MINUTES
♡ SERVES: 4

✓ PREPPED IN 5
✓ QUICK & EASY
✓ ON THE TABLE IN 20
✓ GLUTEN-FREE

INGREDIENTS

1 (16-ounce) bag baby carrots
½ cup water
2 tablespoons unsalted butter
2 tablespoons packed light brown sugar
salt and pepper to taste

Scan me!

INSTRUCTIONS

1. Combine carrots, water, butter and brown sugar in a pan over medium-high heat and bring to a boil.

2. Cover and reduce the heat to cook on low for approximately 6 minutes.

3. Keeping covered, turn the heat back to high and cook, stirring occasionally, until all the water is evaporated and carrots are tender, another 5–6 minutes.

4. Remove from the heat and sprinkle with salt and pepper.

PAIRINGS: Twice-Baked Potatoes (page 144), Marinated Steak (page 161), Meatloaf (page 164), Roast Turkey (page 175)

⚙ VARIATIONS

⊕ For some extra flavor and texture, add ⅓ cup pine nuts or chopped toasted walnuts or pecans after simmering for the first 6 minutes.

⊕ **OVEN DIRECTIONS:** Place baby carrots in a buttered casserole dish and sprinkle with salt and pepper. Sprinkle with brown sugar and drizzle on melted butter. Cover and bake at 350 degrees F for 1 hour.

GREEN BEAN CASSEROLE

🕐 **PREP TIME:** 5 MINUTES

⏳ **COOK TIME:** 25 MINUTES

♡ **SERVES:** 10

✓ PREPPED IN 5

✓ FEED A CROWD

✓ MAKE AHEAD

✓ SLOW COOKER

INGREDIENTS

3 (14.5-ounce) cans French-style green beans, drained

1 (10.5-ounce) can condensed cream of chicken soup

1 (10.5-ounce) can condensed cream of mushroom soup

¼ cup milk

salt and pepper to taste

1 (2.8-ounce) can crispy fried onions

Scan me!

INSTRUCTIONS

1. Preheat the oven to 350 degrees F. Lightly grease a 9-x-13-inch baking dish and set aside.

2. In a large bowl, mix green beans, soups, milk, salt and pepper and pour into the prepared pan.

3. Bake for 18–20 minutes. Top with onions and bake for 5 minutes more.

👍 RECIPE TIPS

☺ **Make Ahead:** *Assemble your green bean casserole as described in Step 2 up to 48 hours in advance and keep it covered in the refrigerator. Be sure to wait to add the fried onions until the last 5 minutes of baking, otherwise they will get soggy.*

☺ **Slow Cooker Directions:** *Lightly spray the slow cooker with cooking spray. Combine green beans, soups, milk, salt and pepper in the slow cooker. Cook on low for 2–3 hours, or on high for 1 hour. Meanwhile, bake fried onions in a 350 degree F oven for 5 minutes. Transfer green beans to a serving dish and sprinkle with fried onions.*

☺ **To Use Fresh Green Beans:** *Use 3–4 cups trimmed, halved green beans instead of the canned beans. Fresh green beans are more crispy, but if you like the softer texture found in canned green beans, you can blanch them for 7–8 minutes. If using a slow cooker, cooking time may be longer with fresh green beans.*

PAIRINGS: Creamed Corn (page 138), Mashed Potatoes (page 145), Garlic Prime Rib (page 162), Roast Chicken (page 174), Roast Turkey (page 175)

CREAMED CORN

⏱ PREP TIME: 5 MINUTES
⏳ COOK TIME: 15 MINUTES
♡ SERVES: 6

✓ PREPPED IN 5

✓ QUICK & EASY

✓ ON THE TABLE IN 20

INGREDIENTS

½ cup whole milk

1 tablespoon all-purpose flour

1 (12-ounce) package frozen corn kernels, thawed

½ cup heavy cream

1 tablespoon salted butter

1 tablespoon sugar

1 teaspoon minced garlic

garlic salt to taste (optional)

¼ teaspoon pepper

2 tablespoons grated Parmesan cheese

TOPPING: chopped fresh parsley (optional)

Scan me!

INSTRUCTIONS

1. In a small bowl, whisk together milk and flour. Set aside.

2. In a large skillet, combine corn, cream, butter, sugar, minced garlic, garlic salt and pepper over medium heat.

3. Stir milk mixture into corn mixture right away. Cook, stirring occasionally, until thickened and corn is cooked through, about 10 minutes.

4. Remove from the heat and stir in Parmesan until melted. Add more garlic salt to taste, if needed. Serve warm, sprinkled with parsley.

PAIRINGS: Brown Sugar–Glazed Carrots (page 136), Slow Cooker Brisket (page 163), Baby Back Ribs (page 168), Pulled Pork (page 171)

👍 **RECIPE TIPS**

☺ **Can You Use Canned or Fresh Corn?**

Of course! Follow the recipe as directed, but cook for less time. Since both canned (be sure to drain canned corn) and fresh corn will be at room temperature, you will not need as much time for the corn to cook through.

BAKED POTATOES

PREP TIME: **15 MINUTES**

COOK TIME: **1 HOUR**

SERVES: **4**

✓ MAKE AHEAD

✓ GLUTEN-FREE

INGREDIENTS

4 medium russet potatoes

2-3 tablespoons olive oil

kosher salt to taste

Scan me!

INSTRUCTIONS

1. Preheat the oven to 350 degrees F.

2. Wash potatoes with a stiff brush and cold water, then pat dry. Use a fork to poke 8–12 deep holes all over the surface of each potato to let the moisture escape during cooking.

3. In a large bowl, lightly coat potatoes with oil and salt. Then place potatoes in the oven directly on the middle rack (or on an aluminum foil–lined baking sheet).

4. Bake for 1 hour, until the skin is crisp and the flesh feels soft.

5. Let potatoes cool a bit until you can handle them. Create a dotted line from end to end of each potato with your fork, then crack potatoes open by squeezing the ends toward each other. Serve with any desired toppings (see Recipe Tips).

👍 RECIPE TIPS

☺ **Topping Ideas:** *The possibilities are almost endless when it comes to loaded baked potatoes! Here are some of the best toppings to try: Best Chili Soup (page 126), Homemade Salsa (page 153), Pulled Pork (page 171) and chopped bacon, chopped green onions, chopped fresh chives, chopped broccoli, shredded cheddar cheese and crumbled gorgonzola or blue cheese.*

☺ **Make Ahead:** *After baking your potatoes, choose from three different methods to keep them warm:*

- **Use cooking foil:** *Remove potatoes from the oven and immediately wrap each baked potato in a foil wrapper, carefully, to prevent all heat or steam from escaping.*

- **Use a slow cooker:** *After wrapping each of the baked potatoes in foil, place them into the slow cooker and keep them warm until ready to serve.*

- **Use portable warm containers:** *This is a prefered method to keep potatoes warm when bringing potatoes from another destination. Wrap potatoes in foil, keep in warm coolers or containers and cover with towels or blankets to trap all heat.*

PAIRINGS: Best Chili Soup (page 126), Baby Back Ribs (page 168), Roast Chicken (page 174), Creamy Swiss Chicken (page 177)

ROASTED VEGETABLES

⏱ **PREP TIME:** 10 MINUTES
⏳ **COOK TIME:** 25 MINUTES
♡ **SERVES:** 6

✓ **QUICK & EASY**
✓ **GLUTEN-FREE**

INGREDIENTS

1½ cups chopped red bell peppers

1½ cups baby carrots

1½ cups brussels sprouts

1½ cups cubed Yukon Gold potatoes

1½ cups cubed butternut squash

3 tablespoons olive oil

1 tablespoon garlic salt with parsley flakes

1 tablespoon Italian seasoning

¼ cup grated Parmesan cheese

Scan me!

INSTRUCTIONS

1. Preheat the oven to 425 degrees F. Line a baking sheet with aluminum foil and spray with nonstick cooking spray. Set aside.

2. Place all veggies in a bowl and add olive oil, garlic salt and Italian seasoning. Toss to coat.

3. Place veggies on a prepared baking sheet and sprinkle with Parmesan cheese. Bake for 25–30 minutes, flipping over halfway through.

PAIRINGS: Creamed Corn (page 138), Marinated Steak (page 161), Garlic Prime Rib (page 162), Parmesan-Crusted Pork Chops (page 167)

☝ RECIPE TIPS

☺ **Want to Add Other Veggies?** *Try these vegetables that also take 25–30 minutes to cook: acorn squash, pumpkin, yams or onions. Not all veggies take this long to cook, so if you want to add vegetables such as broccoli, zucchini, yellow squash and asparagus, be sure to take them out earlier so they don't burn.*

PARMESAN SWEET POTATO CUBES

⏱ **PREP TIME:** 10 MINUTES

⏳ **COOK TIME:** 20 MINUTES

♡ **SERVES:** 6

✓ **QUICK & EASY**

✓ **GLUTEN-FREE**

INGREDIENTS

2 tablespoons unsalted butter, melted

1 tablespoon olive oil

¼ cup grated Parmesan cheese

2 teaspoons minced garlic

½ teaspoon garlic salt

½ teaspoon Italian seasoning

2 sweet potatoes, cut into 1-inch cubes

TOPPING: dried parsley (optional)

Scan me!

INSTRUCTIONS

1. Preheat the oven to 400 degrees F. Line a baking sheet with aluminum foil and spray with nonstick cooking spray. Set aside.

2. Place butter, oil, Parmesan, garlic, garlic salt and Italian seasoning in a large resealable plastic bag and mix well.

3. Add sweet potatoes and shake until well coated.

4. Place coated sweet potatoes on the prepared baking sheet and spread out evenly. Bake for 18–22 minutes.

5. Serve warm, sprinkled with parsley.

PAIRINGS: Creamed Corn (page 138), Roasted Vegetables (page 140), Marinated Steak (page 161), Garlic Prime Rib (page 162)

👍 **RECIPE TIPS**

☺ **Crispy Sweet Potato Cubes:** *These cubes end up soft, with just a little bit of crispness. To make them extra crispy, be sure to flip cubes halfway through and broil for the last minute or two of cooking time.*

HOMEMADE MAC AND CHEESE

⏱ **PREP TIME:** 15 MINUTES
⧗ **COOK TIME:** 25 MINUTES
♡ **SERVES:** 10

✓ **FEED A CROWD**

✓ **MAKE AHEAD**

✓ **SLOW COOKER**

INGREDIENTS

1 (16-ounce) package elbow macaroni
½ cup plus 2 tablespoons salted butter, divided
½ cup all-purpose flour
1 tablespoon garlic salt
pepper to taste
4 cups milk
6 cups shredded sharp cheddar cheese
½ cup panko breadcrumbs

Scan me!

INSTRUCTIONS

1. Preheat the oven to 325 degrees F. Lightly grease a 9-x-13-inch baking dish and set aside.

2. Boil pasta according to package directions.

3. Meanwhile, in a large saucepan, melt ½ cup butter over medium heat. Whisk in flour and cook for 2–3 minutes. Add garlic salt and pepper. Slowly pour in milk, whisking until smooth. Heat to a low boil and cook, stirring occasionally, until thickened, 4–5 minutes. Remove from the heat.

4. Drain pasta and transfer to the prepared pan. Sprinkle cheese over pasta. Pour thickened cream sauce over pasta and cheese. Let sit until the cheese has melted, then stir together.

5. Melt remaining 2 tablespoons butter in a small skillet over medium heat. Add breadcrumbs, and cook, stirring constantly, until golden brown, 3–5 minutes. Sprinkle over the mac and cheese.

6. Bake for 15 minutes. Serve warm.

⚙ **VARIATIONS**

Change up the cheese for extra flavor. A popular blend is equal parts mozzarella, cheddar and American. Other cheeses that are good to use in mac and cheese include Parmesan, white cheddar, Gruyère, Colby Jack and Gorgonzola.

👍 **RECIPE TIPS**

☺ **Make Ahead:** *Prepare the mac and cheese as directed above, but do not add the buttered breadcrumbs. Cover and refrigerate for up to 24 hours. Before baking, make breadcrumbs, sprinkle on top and bake per recipe directions.*

☺ **Slow Cooker Directions:** *Follow Steps 2 and 3, then pour hot pasta into a greased slow cooker. Sprinkle cheese over pasta, followed by thickened cream sauce, and stir together. Cook on low for 2 hours, stirring occasionally. Make breadcrumbs as directed in Step 4 and pour over macaroni. Let warm for 5 minutes before serving.*

PAIRINGS: Easy Garlic Knots (page 66), Fried Zucchini (page 98), Brown Sugar Ham (page 172), Roast Chicken (page 174)

TWICE-BAKED POTATOES

PREP TIME: 10 MINUTES

COOK TIME: 1 HOUR 20 MINUTES

COOL TIME: 10 MINUTES

SERVES: 10

✓ MAKE AHEAD

✓ GLUTEN-FREE

INGREDIENTS

6–8 russet potatoes

3 tablespoons vegetable oil

1 tablespoon grated Parmesan cheese

½ teaspoon salt

dash of pepper

¼ teaspoon garlic powder

¼ teaspoon paprika

2 cups sour cream

2 cups shredded cheddar cheese, divided

4–6 slices cooked bacon, crumbled

TOPPING: chopped fresh chives

Scan me!

PAIRINGS: Roasted Vegetables (page 140), Parmesan-Crusted Pork Chops (page 167), Baked Salmon (page 173)

INSTRUCTIONS

1. Preheat the oven to 400 degrees F. Line a baking sheet with aluminum foil and set aside.

2. Wash potatoes with a stiff brush and cold water, then pat dry. Pierce each potato with a fork about 8–12 times. Place potatoes on the baking sheet and bake for 1 hour.

3. Let potatoes cool for 10–15 minutes.

4. Meanwhile, in a small bowl, combine oil, Parmesan, salt, pepper, garlic powder and paprika. Mix well.

5. Cut potatoes in half. Spoon out most of the insides and place in a large bowl, reserving potato skins.

6. Brush oil-Parmesan mixture over the tops and bottoms of each potato skin.

7. Lightly mash potato insides and mix in sour cream (you can use more or less to your liking), about 1 cup cheddar, bacon pieces and more salt and pepper to taste. Mix well.

8. Spoon mixture back into potato skins and discard any excess skins. Sprinkle potatoes with remaining 1 cup cheddar.

9. Place back on the baking sheet and bake for 16–18 more minutes. Sprinkle with chives before serving

☺ RECIPE TIPS

☺ **Make Ahead:** *Follow the recipe as written through Step 8. Place the filled potatoes in a covered container and store in the refrigerator for up to 24 hours. When you are ready to bake, place the potatoes on a baking sheet and bake at 400 degrees F for 15–20 minutes, or until hot and the cheese is bubbly.*

⚙ VARIATIONS

Instead of bacon pieces, try rotisserie or buffalo chicken, diced ham or cooked sausage.

MASHED POTATOES

INGREDIENTS

5 pounds russet potatoes, peeled and cut into cubes

4 ounces cream cheese

½ cup salted butter, softened

½ cup heavy cream

1½ teaspoons garlic salt with parsley flakes

salt and pepper to taste

Scan me!

INSTRUCTIONS

1. Place potatoes into a large pot and add enough water to cover. Bring water to a boil, then lower the heat and simmer for 20–25 minutes, or until potatoes are fork-tender. Drain the water.

2. Transfer potatoes to a large bowl and add cream cheese, butter, cream and garlic salt.

3. Use a potato masher to mash potatoes and combine ingredients together until they are the consistency you prefer.

4. Season with more salt and pepper, if desired.

★ BONUS RECIPE

Mashed Potato Gravy

Combine 2 cups beef stock (or broth) and 1–2 cubes beef bouillon in a microwave-safe bowl and heat in the microwave for 1 minute. Stir and repeat until the bouillon is dissolved. In a saucepan over medium-high heat, melt 2 tablespoons unsalted butter. Add ¼ cup all-purpose flour, ½ teaspoon dried sage and ¼ teaspoon dried thyme and cook for 1 minute. Slowly whisk in the stock until smooth. Bring to a boil, then reduce to a simmer. Continue to cook and whisk until gravy is smooth, about 1 minute. Season with salt and pepper to taste.

👍 RECIPE TIPS

☺ **Make Ahead:** *Here is an easy trick to keep your potatoes warm until ready to serve: Butter your slow cooker and add a few tablespoons of heavy cream to it. Set the slow cooker to low and transfer potatoes to it to keep warm for up to 4 hours. Stir before serving.*

PAIRINGS: Heavenly Rolls (page 68), Parmesan Sweet Potato Cubes (page 141), Marinated Steak (page 161), Roast Turkey (page 175)

FUNERAL POTATOES

⏱ PREP TIME: **20 MINUTES**

⧗ COOK TIME: **45 MINUTES**

♡ SERVES: **16**

✓ FEED A CROWD

✓ MAKE AHEAD

✓ GLUTEN-FREE

INGREDIENTS

1 (32-ounce) package frozen diced hash browns
  (or shredded potatoes)

2 cups sour cream

1 (10.5-ounce) can cream of chicken soup

¾ cup unsalted butter, melted, divided

2 cups shredded cheddar cheese

1 teaspoon salt

1 teaspoon onion powder (optional)

2–3 cups cornflakes, crushed

Scan me!

INSTRUCTIONS

1. Preheat the oven to 350 degrees F. Lightly grease a 9-x-13-inch baking dish and set aside.

2. Place hash browns in a colander and let sit until fully thawed and drained.

3. Meanwhile, in a large bowl, combine sour cream, soup and ½ cup melted butter and mix well.

4. Add cheese, salt and onion powder and mix until well combined.

5. Add potatoes to cheese mixture and stir until combined. Place in the prepared dish.

6. Combine cornflakes and remaining ¼ cup melted butter in a large resealable plastic bag and shake until cereal is coated.

7. Sprinkle buttered cornflakes over potatoes.

8. Bake for 42–46 minutes. Serve warm.

PAIRINGS: Green Bean Casserole (page 137), Marinated Steak (page 161), Brown Sugar Ham (page 172), Roast Turkey (page 175)

👍 RECIPE TIPS

☺ **Make Ahead:** *Make potatoes as directed, but do not add the buttered cornflake topping. Cover and refrigerate for up to 24 hours. When ready to bake, add the buttered cornflake topping and bake as directed.*

⚙ VARIATIONS

TOPPINGS: We think cornflakes work the best, but you can also use panko breadcrumbs or even crushed Ritz crackers.

FRIED RICE

⏱ **PREP TIME:** 5 MINUTES
⏳ **COOK TIME:** 15 MINUTES
♡ **SERVES:** 6

✓ **PREPPED IN 5**
✓ **QUICK & EASY**
✓ **ON THE TABLE IN 20**

INGREDIENTS

3 tablespoons sesame oil

1 cup frozen peas and carrots, thawed

2 teaspoons minced garlic

2 eggs, lightly beaten

3 cups cooked brown rice (or cooked instant white rice)

¼ cup soy sauce

Scan me!

INSTRUCTIONS

1. Heat oil in a large skillet or wok over medium-high heat.

2. Add peas and carrots and minced garlic. Cook, stirring, until tender, 8–10 minutes.

3. Lower the heat to medium-low and push the mixture off to one side.

4. Pour eggs on the other side of the skillet and cook, stirring, until scrambled. Add rice and soy sauce. Mix everything together and cook until heated through.

👍 **RECIPE TIPS**

☺ **Pro Tip:** *Use cold rice because it instantly begins to fry when it hits the hot pan, leaving the rice with a crisp outside and a warm inside, whereas freshly cooked rice can become soggy.*

⚙ **VARIATIONS**

Add more of your favorite veggies in Step 2 along with the peas and carrots for added flavor. For added protein, you can also add any cooked meat or seafood, such as shrimp, pork, bacon, or chicken, when adding the rice and soy sauce.

PAIRINGS: Egg Drop Soup (page 131), General Tso's Chicken (page 180), Sweet and Sour Chicken (page 181), Teriyaki Chicken (page 182)

SPANISH RICE

⏱ **PREP TIME:** 5 MINUTES
⏲ **COOK TIME:** 40 MINUTES
♡ **SERVES:** 8

✓ **PREPPED IN 5**
✓ **FEED A CROWD**
✓ **SLOW COOKER**
✓ **DAIRY-FREE**
✓ **GLUTEN-FREE**

INGREDIENTS

2 tablespoons vegetable oil

2 cups long-grain white rice

1 cube chicken-flavored bouillon

4 cups water (or use 4 cups lower-sodium chicken broth and omit the bouillon)

1 (8-ounce) can tomato sauce

1 teaspoon minced garlic

1 teaspoon salt

1 teaspoon ground cumin

dash of garlic pepper

TOPPING: chopped fresh cilantro (optional)

Scan me!

INSTRUCTIONS

1. Heat oil in a large frying pan over medium heat.

2. Add rice and cook, stirring, until golden brown, about 5 minutes.

3. Combine bouillon and water in a microwave-safe container and microwave for 3 minutes.

4. When rice is browned, add bouillon mixture, tomato sauce, garlic, salt, cumin and garlic pepper to the pan.

5. Stir and cover the pan. Simmer for 30–40 minutes, stirring occasionally, or until cooked through and there is no liquid left. Fluff before serving and top with cilantro if desired.

👍 **RECIPE TIPS**

☺ **Slow Cooker Directions:** *Grease a slow cooker with cooking spray. Heat oil in a large frying pan over medium heat. Add rice and cook until golden brown, about 5 minutes. Remove rice from heat and add to the slow cooker. Pour in broth, tomato sauce, garlic, salt, cumin and garlic pepper and stir to combine. Cover and cook on high for 2½–3 hours, or until the liquid is gone. Add cilantro and serve warm.*

⚙ **VARIATIONS**

Try using Homemade Salsa (page 153) in place of the tomato sauce to add more flavor and even a bit more spice to this mild rice recipe.

PAIRINGS: Green Chile Chicken Enchiladas (page 183), Cheese Enchiladas (page 184), Chimichangas (page 185), Chicken Tacos (page 188), Tostadas (page 190)

CILANTRO-LIME RICE

⏱ **PREP TIME:** 5 MINUTES
⧖ **COOK TIME:** 25 MINUTES
♡ **SERVES:** 6

✓ PREPPED IN 5
✓ QUICK & EASY
✓ GLUTEN-FREE

INGREDIENTS

2 cups long-grain white rice
1 (4-ounce) can diced green chiles
1 bunch cilantro, chopped
2 tablespoons salted butter
garlic salt and pepper to taste
4 cups chicken broth
1 tablespoon lime juice

Scan me!

INSTRUCTIONS

1. Combine all ingredients in a large saucepan and bring to a boil over medium-high heat.

2. Cover, lower the heat and simmer, stirring occasionally, for 20–25 minutes, until rice is cooked.

3. Fluff and serve warm.

👍 RECIPE TIPS

☺ **What Kind of Rice Is Best?** *We prefer long-grain white rice, but you can also use basmati rice, jasmine rice, brown basmati rice or long-grain brown rice (add a few extra minutes of cooking time for brown rice).*

PAIRINGS: Sweet Pork (page 170), Green Chile Chicken Enchiladas (page 183), Cheese Enchiladas (page 184), Flautas (page 187), Chicken Tacos (page 188)

STREET CORN
(ESQUITES)

⏱ PREP TIME: 5 MINUTES

⧖ COOK TIME: 20 MINUTES

♡ SERVES: 6–8

✓ PREPPED IN 5

✓ QUICK & EASY

✓ FEED A CROWD

✓ SLOW COOKER

✓ GLUTEN-FREE

INGREDIENTS

⅓ cup Mexican crema (or sour cream)

¼ cup mayonnaise

2 teaspoons lime juice

garlic salt with parsley flakes to taste

2 (12-ounce) bags frozen corn

2 tablespoons salted butter

½ cup cotija cheese

chili powder to taste

fresh cilantro, for garnish

1 lime, cut into wedges, for garnish

Scan me!

INSTRUCTIONS

1. In a small bowl, combine crema, mayonnaise, lime juice and garlic salt. Set aside.

2. Bring a medium pot of water to a boil, then add corn and cover. Bring back to a simmer and cook for 4–5 minutes, or until corn is cooked through.

3. Drain water and transfer corn to a pan over high heat. Cook until a few pieces are a little charred, about 5 minutes, then add butter and crema mixture and cook until heated through.

4. Divide among serving cups or in a serving bowl and top with cotija, chili powder and cilantro. Serve warm with lime wedges on the side.

PAIRINGS: Quesadilla (page 70), Green Chile Chicken Enchiladas (page 183), Chimichangas (page 185), Chicken Tacos (page 188), Tostadas (page 190)

👌 RECIPE TIPS

☺ **To Use Fresh or Canned Corn:** *Just follow the directions above and cook corn for a lesser amount of time. If you really want to add an extra layer of flavor, grill corn on the cob, then cut the kernels off and continue from Step 3.*

HOMEMADE TORTILLA CHIPS

PREP TIME: 15 MINUTES
COOK TIME: 15 MINUTES
SERVES: 4

INGREDIENTS

8 corn tortillas

¾–1 cup vegetable oil

kosher salt (or other coarse salt) to taste

Scan me!

INSTRUCTIONS

1. Tortillas fry better when they are a little dried out. You can lay them out on paper towels or wax paper for a few hours before cutting, or dry them in the oven: Lay tortillas out in a single layer on a baking sheet and bake at 200 degrees F for 10 minutes.

2. Cut each tortilla into 6 triangle-shaped wedges.

3. Add enough oil to a large skillet to fill about ¼ inch high and heat over medium heat to about 350 degrees F. You can test the heat of the oil by adding a small piece of tortilla to it; if the oil is hot enough, the tortilla should sizzle.

4. Working in batches, fry tortilla triangles in the hot oil until color changes just slightly and pieces are crispy, 3–4 minutes. Place on a paper towel–lined plate when done.

5. Sprinkle chips with salt while warm.

♻ RECIPE TIPS

☺ **Baking Instructions:** *Place tortilla triangles in a large bowl and drizzle with 1 tablespoon vegetable oil. Toss until lightly coated. Spread triangles in a single layer on a parchment paper–lined baking sheet and sprinkle with salt. Bake at 350 degrees F for 10 minutes, then flip and bake for an additional 4–5 minutes. Remove from the oven and season with more salt.*

☺ **Make Ahead:** *Once tortilla chips are fried, store the cooled chips in an airtight container or a plastic sandwich bag. The chips will easily last for 3 days.*

PAIRINGS: Spinach Artichoke Dip (page 85), Pico de Gallo (page 152), Homemade Salsa (page 153), Sweet Salsa Verde (page 154), Black Bean and Corn Salsa (page 155)

PICO DE GALLO

🕐 **PREP TIME:** 10 MINUTES
♡ **SERVES:** 12

✓ QUICK & EASY

✓ ON THE TABLE IN 20

✓ FEED A CROWD

✓ MAKE AHEAD

✓ DAIRY-FREE

✓ GLUTEN-FREE

INGREDIENTS

4 Roma tomatoes, chopped

¼–½ red or purple onion, chopped

1 teaspoon minced garlic

¼–½ teaspoon garlic salt with parsley flakes

½ teaspoon lime juice

2 tablespoons chopped fresh cilantro

Scan me!

INSTRUCTIONS

1. Combine all ingredients except cilantro in a medium bowl and mix to combine.

2. Refrigerate until ready to serve and add chopped cilantro right before serving.

PAIRINGS: Homemade Tortilla Chips (page 151), Chimichangas (page 185), Chicken Tacos (page 188), Tostadas (page 190)

👍 **RECIPE TIPS**

☺ **Make Ahead:** *Store in an airtight container in the refrigerator for up to 3 days.*

HOMEMADE SALSA

🕐 PREP TIME: 10 MINUTES

♡ SERVES: 12

✓ QUICK & EASY

✓ ON THE TABLE IN 20

✓ FEED A CROWD

✓ MAKE AHEAD

✓ DAIRY-FREE

✓ GLUTEN-FREE

INGREDIENTS

1 (14.5-ounce) can diced tomatoes, drained

1 (10-ounce) can original Ro-Tel, drained

2–3 Roma tomatoes (seeded, if desired)

½ white onion (or 1 tablespoon onion powder)

1 medium handful fresh cilantro leaves

1 (4-ounce) can diced green chiles (optional)

1–2 tablespoons diced jalapeño pepper

1 teaspoon minced garlic

1 teaspoon sugar

1 teaspoon garlic salt with parsley flakes

1 teaspoon ground cumin

1 tablespoon lime juice

Scan me!

INSTRUCTIONS

1. Combine all ingredients in a blender
   and pulse until blended to the consistency you desire.

2. Add more salt or lime juice to taste, if needed.

🖐 RECIPE TIPS

☺ **Make Ahead:** *Store in an airtight container in the refrigerator for 4–6 days.*

☺ **Seeding Tomatoes:** *To prevent watery salsa, seed the tomatoes before adding to the blender.*

PAIRINGS: Flour Tortillas (page 70), Quesadilla (page 70), Homemade Tortilla Chips (page 151), Chicken Tacos (page 188), Tostadas (page 190)

SWEET SALSA VERDE

✓ PREPPED IN 5

✓ QUICK & EASY

✓ ON THE TABLE IN 20

✓ FEED A CROWD

✓ MAKE AHEAD

✓ DAIRY-FREE

✓ GLUTEN-FREE

INGREDIENTS

1 (28-ounce) can tomatillos (about 20), drained

½–⅔ cup sugar

1 small bunch fresh cilantro

2–3 tablespoons diced jalapeño pepper

 *Scan me!*

INSTRUCTIONS

1. Combine all ingredients in a blender and pulse until blended to the consistency you desire.

2. Add additional jalapeños for more spice, or add more sugar if you like it sweeter.

PAIRINGS: Flour Tortillas (page 70), Quesadilla (page 70), Homemade Tortilla Chips (page 151), Chicken Tacos (page 188), Tostadas (page 190)

👍 **RECIPE TIPS**

☺ **Make Ahead:** *Store in an airtight container in the refrigerator for 4–6 days.*

☺ **Seeding Tomatillos:** *To prevent watery salsa, seed the tomatillos before adding to the blender.*

BLACK BEAN AND CORN SALSA

(AKA COWBOY CAVIAR)

PREP TIME: **10 MINUTES**

SERVES: **16**

QUICK & EASY

ON THE TABLE IN 20

FEED A CROWD

MAKE AHEAD

DAIRY-FREE

GLUTEN-FREE

INGREDIENTS

1 (15.5-ounce) can black beans, drained and rinsed

1 (14.5-ounce) can corn, drained

6–8 Roma tomatoes, chopped

1 bunch fresh cilantro, chopped

¼ cup Italian dressing

2 tablespoons lime juice

2–3 avocados, cubed

½ teaspoon garlic salt

pepper to taste

Scan me!

INSTRUCTIONS

1. Combine beans, corn, tomatoes and cilantro in a medium bowl.

2. Add dressing and lime juice.

3. Stir in avocados and add garlic salt and pepper right before serving.

PAIRINGS: Homemade Tortilla Chips (page 151), Chimichangas (page 185), Flautas (page 187), Chicken Tacos (page 188)

👍 RECIPE TIPS

☺ **No Italian Dressing?** *When we don't have it on hand, we like to make our own by mixing ¼ cup olive oil, ¼ cup white wine vinegar, 1 tablespoon lime juice, 1 teaspoon sugar, ½ teaspoon garlic salt and a dash of pepper.*

☺ **Make Ahead:** *You can put together most of this salsa ahead of time and store in the refrigerator. We recommend adding the avocados, cilantro and dressing right before serving for the best results.*

MAIN DISHES

"Alexa, please make dinner."

What's for dinner? It's probably the most asked question of all time. Fortunately, it does not have to be hard to figure out. Menu planning will make dinnertime easier—see page 158 for some helpful suggestions and resources—but even if you haven't planned ahead, these dinner ideas are all simple and kid-friendly. From recipes that take just minutes to prep to others made in the slow cooker or oven, we hope that these dinner ideas will be loved by the entire family.

HELPFUL TIPS + INFORMATION

How Much to Serve?

PASTA: 2–3 ounces dry pasta per person

MEAT: 8–12 ounces per person

SOUP OR STEW: 5–6 ounces or 1½–2 cups per person

CASSEROLES: a 9-x-13-inch pan can typically serve 12–15 people.

Make-Ahead Dinner Tips

⊘ **PRECOOK MEAT:**

CHICKEN: For recipes that call for shredded cooked chicken, you can use a rotisserie chicken from the supermarket, or cook your own ahead of time. To make your own, place boneless, skinless chicken breasts in a slow cooker, drizzle with olive oil and season with salt and pepper. Cook on low for 8 hours or high for 4 hours. Shred while still warm. Place shredded chicken in a resealable plastic freezer bag and freeze for up to 3 months. Defrost in the refrigerator overnight before use.

BEEF: For shredded beef, we love to use our classic Pot Roast recipe (page 165). Shred while still warm and place in a resealable plastic freezer bag to freeze for up to 3 months. Defrost in the refrigerator overnight before use.

⊘ **USE THE SLOW COOKER:** Whether you're cooking for a large group or a smaller family dinner, utilizing the slow cooker can get dinner on the table in the evening quickly and easily. You can make everything from beef roast to lasagna in the slow cooker. Just look for the "Slow Cooker" tag throughout this chapter for recipe ideas.

⊘ **PREP AHEAD OF TIME:** Having prechopped veggies, preshredded chicken or meat thawing in the fridge will help your dinner preparation run more smoothly.

⊘ **STOCK YOUR FREEZER:** To easily get a stockpile of freezer meals, simply double a recipe you are already making and freeze half of it. Be sure to use a freezer-safe container, and follow the recipe's specific freezing instructions.

Using a Slow Cooker

⊘ Before adding everything to your slow cooker, be sure to take note of whether any ingredients should be saved to add at the end. Recipes will often specify to add dairy-based ingredients, tender vegetables, precooked pasta or rice, and fresh herbs toward the end of the cooking time.

⊘ Don't put frozen meat in the slow cooker—always thaw it first overnight in the refrigerator.

⊘ When cooking meat in a slow cooker, cheaper cuts work better than more expensive cuts. Trim off extra fat from the meat before cooking.

⊘ Browning meat before adding it to the slow cooker can help give a dish an extra layer of texture and flavor, but for most red meat you can skip browning to save some time. Ground beef, chicken and sausage should typically be browned.

⊘ For the most even cook, be sure not to overfill your slow cooker. The food should fill your insert halfway to two-thirds full. Most of the recipes here are designed for a 5–6-quart slow cooker.

⊘ For easy cleanup, use a slow cooker liner.

MEAT DISHES

"You have no idea what's at steak here!"

No main dish is more filling to eat or rewarding to prepare for others than a hearty meat-based dish. Here we have our favorite poultry, beef, fish and pork recipes. Cooking meats can be daunting, but these recipes have been tried and tested to come out great every time.

CLASSIC BURGERS

⏱ PREP TIME: 10 MINUTES

⏳ COOK TIME: 10 MINUTES

♡ SERVES: 4

✓ QUICK & EASY

✓ ON THE TABLE IN 20

✓ DAIRY-FREE

INGREDIENTS

1½ pounds ground beef (80 percent lean/
   20 percent fat; or ground chuck)
1 tablespoon Worcestershire sauce
1½ teaspoons minced garlic
½ teaspoon pepper
1½ teaspoons seasoned salt
4 brioche buns, toasted
TOPPINGS: lettuce, sliced tomatoes, sliced
   cheese, pickles, sliced onions, bacon and sliced
   avocado (optional)

Scan me!

INSTRUCTIONS

1. Preheat the grill to medium-high heat or to 375 degrees F.

2. In a large bowl, combine beef, Worcestershire sauce, garlic and pepper. Mix with your hands until just combined (do not overmix).

3. Divide mixture into fourths and shape into patties using your hands. The patties should be about ¾ inch thick. Use the back of a spoon to make an indent in the middle of each patty to keep it from puffing up too much in the middle while cooking. Sprinkle patties with seasoned salt.

4. Add burgers to the grill and cook for 3–3½ minutes per side, until the internal temperature reaches about 140 degrees F, for a medium burger.

5. Place each burger on a toasted bun and serve with your favorite toppings.

👍 RECIPE TIPS

☺ **Doneness Guide:** *Measuring the internal temperature is the best way to gauge your burger's doneness. Cook to:*

120 degrees F for rare (red/raw in the center)

130 degrees F for medium-rare (pink and warm)

140 degrees F for medium (totally pink, starting to dry out)

150 degrees F for medium-well (grayish pink, significantly drier)

160 degrees F for well-done (completely gray, very little moisture)

☺ **To Panfry:** *A cast-iron skillet works best for panfrying burgers. Heat ½ tablespoon olive oil in the pan over high heat. When you put the burgers in, they should immediately sizzle. Cook until browned, 3–5 minutes on each side.*

PAIRINGS: Fruit Salad (page 105), Potato Salad (page 112), Pasta Salad (page 114), Creamed Corn (page 138)

MARINATED STEAK

○ PREP TIME: **5 MINUTES**

⧗ MARINATING TIME: **4 HOURS**

⧗ COOK TIME: **15 MINUTES**

♡ SERVES: **2**

INGREDIENTS

1 cup Italian dressing

½ cup A.1. Original sauce

½ cup Worcestershire sauce

1 teaspoon lemon juice (optional)

1 pound steak of choice (flat-iron, skirt, top sirloin or flank steak)

Scan me!

INSTRUCTIONS

1. Combine dressing, A.1. sauce, Worcestershire sauce and lemon juice in a large resealable plastic bag or airtight container. Mix well.

2. Add steak to the marinade, making sure it is coated on all sides.

3. Place in the refrigerator to marinate for at least 4 hours or up to 36 hours.

4. When ready to cook, preheat the grill to 450–500 degrees F. Allow steaks to come to room temperature.

5. Place steaks on the grill and cook until browned and slightly charred (4–5 minutes). Flip steaks over and continue to grill to the desired doneness (see Recipe Tips; 5–7 minutes for medium).

6. Let meat rest for 5 minutes before serving. The steak will continue to cook a bit, and the juices will distribute.

👍 RECIPE TIPS

☺ **Grill Prep:** *Start with a clean grill and add a little vegetable or olive oil to the grate before heating.*

☺ **Doneness Guide:** *For steaks that are 1½ inches or thicker, use a meat thermometer. Start by charring them on both sides over high heat, then move them to low heat to finish cooking to the desired temperature:*

120 degrees F for rare (red/raw in the center)

130 degrees F for medium-rare (pink and warm)

140 degrees F for medium (totally pink, starting to dry out)

150 degrees F for medium-well (grayish pink, significantly drier)

160 degrees F for well-done (completely gray, very little moisture)

PAIRINGS: Fried Zucchini (page 98), Roasted Vegetables (page 140), Mashed Potatoes (page 145)

GARLIC PRIME RIB

PREP TIME: 5 MINUTES
REST TIME: 1 HOUR
COOK TIME: 2 HOURS 30 MINUTES
SERVES: 10

✓ PREPPED IN 5
✓ FEED A CROWD
✓ DAIRY-FREE
✓ GLUTEN-FREE

INGREDIENTS

1 (10-pound) prime rib roast
10 cloves garlic, minced
2 tablespoons olive oil
2 teaspoons salt
2 teaspoons pepper
2 teaspoons dried thyme

Scan me!

INSTRUCTIONS

1. Place the roast in a large roasting pan with the fatty side up.

2. In a small bowl, mix the garlic, olive oil, salt, pepper and thyme. Spread the mixture over the fatty layer of the roast.

3. Allow the roast to rest on the counter for 1–2 hours, until it comes to room temperature.

4. When ready to roast the prime rib, preheat your oven to 450–500 degrees F.

5. Cook prime rib for 15–20 minutes to sear, then reduce the oven temperature to 325 degrees F. Continue to roast until the internal temperature reaches 5–10 degrees less than your desired internal temperature, depending on desired doneness (see Recipe Tips).

6. Loosely tent aluminum foil over roast and allow to rest for 10 minutes before carving and serving. The internal temperature will continue to rise while resting, leaving you with a perfectly cooked prime rib roast.

👍 RECIPE TIPS

☺ **Doneness Guide:** *Roast prime rib according to the following guidelines, using a meat thermometer to check the internal temperature:*

For rare: Cook to 120–125 degrees F, 10–12 minutes per pound. The center will be bright red then fade to pink.

For medium: Cook to 140–145 degrees F, 13–14 minutes per pound. The center will have a band of pink and fade to brown toward the outer portion.

For medium-well: Cook to 150 degrees F, 14–15 minutes per pound. The center may have a light pink band, but meat will be mostly brown throughout.

☺ *Prime rib is a cut of meat that does not need to be marinated; adding herb seasoning to the outside is all you need. Here we use garlic and thyme, but you can also try rosemary, oregano, lemon zest, light brown sugar, sweet or smoked paprika and butter.*

PAIRINGS: Heavenly Rolls (page 68), Green Bean Bundles (page 135), Brown Sugar–Glazed Carrots (page 136), Twice-Baked Potatoes (page 144)

SLOW COOKER
BRISKET

⏱ PREP TIME: 5 MINUTES

⏳ COOK TIME: 8 HOURS

⏳ REST TIME: 10 MINUTES

♡ SERVES: 8

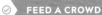 ✓ PREPPED IN 5

 ✓ FEED A CROWD

✓ MAKE AHEAD

✓ SLOW COOKER

 ✓ DAIRY-FREE

INGREDIENTS

1 (3-pound) flat-cut beef brisket

1 (1-ounce) envelope dry onion soup mix

1 tablespoon packed light brown sugar

2 teaspoons garlic powder

2 (12-ounce) bottles Heinz chili sauce

Scan me!

INSTRUCTIONS

1. Place brisket in the slow cooker. Sprinkle onion soup mix, brown sugar and garlic powder over top of brisket and massage gently into meat. Pour chili sauce over the top, covering meat completely.

2. Cook on low for 8–10 hours. Remove brisket from the slow cooker and let rest for 10–20 minutes, then slice against the grain. Pour sauce over brisket slices to serve.

👍 RECIPE TIPS

☺ **Make Ahead:** *This brisket can be served right away, but it's quite good the next day, too. Be sure to place brisket and the juices into an airtight container and store in the refrigerator for up to 4 days. You can also freeze it for up to 2 months. To reheat, let the meat defrost completely. Preheat the oven to 350 degrees F and double wrap the meat in aluminum foil. Bake for 20 minutes or until the internal temperature is 165 degrees F.*

☺ **Do Not Trim the Fat:** *The fat will help give the meat flavor and retain moisture during cooking. You can remove any fat after it has been cooked.*

PAIRINGS: Heavenly Rolls (page 68), Potato Salad (page 112), Roasted Vegetables (page 140), Homemade Mac and Cheese (page 142)

MEATLOAF

⏱ **PREP TIME:** 5 MINUTES
⏳ **COOK TIME:** 1 HOUR 10 MINUTES
♡ **SERVES:** 8

✓ **PREPPED IN 5**
✓ **FREEZER FRIENDLY**
✓ **FEED A CROWD**
✓ **MAKE AHEAD**
✓ **DAIRY-FREE**

INGREDIENTS

1 cup ketchup

⅔ cup packed light brown sugar

2 tablespoons lemon juice, divided

2 teaspoons dry mustard

4 bread slices

2 pounds lean ground beef (80 percent lean/
    20 percent fat)

¼ cup diced onion

1 egg, beaten

1 beef bouillon cube, crushed

Scan me!

INSTRUCTIONS

1. Preheat the oven to 350 degrees F.

2. In a small bowl, combine ketchup, brown sugar, 1 tablespoon lemon juice and dry mustard and mix until smooth. Set aside.

3. Pulse bread slices in a food processor until crumbled and uniform in size.

4. In a large bowl, combine ground beef, crumbled bread, onion, egg, bouillon cube and remaining 1 tablespoon lemon juice. Add half the ketchup mixture and mix until well combined. Form meat into a loaf and place in a lightly greased casserole dish.

5. Bake for 1 hour. Drain fat from the dish, then top with remaining ketchup mixture and bake for an additional 10 minutes.

PAIRINGS: Heavenly Rolls (page 68), Brown Sugar–Glazed Carrots (page 136), Creamed Corn (page 138), Mashed Potatoes (page 145)

👍 **RECIPE TIPS**

☺ **Make Ahead:** *Meatloaf can be mixed, shaped in its pan and frozen raw: After shaping, take it out of the pan, wrap tightly in aluminum foil and freeze for up to 3 months. Thaw, wrapped, in the refrigerator for 24 hours before baking as directed.*

POT ROAST

⏱ **PREP TIME: 5 MINUTES**
⧗ **COOK TIME: 7 HOURS**
♡ **SERVES: 6**

✓ **PREPPED IN 5**
✓ **FREEZER FRIENDLY**
✓ **SLOW COOKER**

INGREDIENTS

1 tablespoon brown gravy dry mix
1 tablespoon dry ranch mix
1 tablespoon Italian dressing dry mix
1 (2–3 pound) beef chuck roast
⅓ cup water

Scan me!

INSTRUCTIONS

1. In a small bowl, mix gravy and ranch and Italian dressing mixes together.

2. Place chuck roast in the slow cooker and pour water over roast. Sprinkle dry mix mixture all over the top.

3. Cook on low for 7–8 hours, or until meat is tender and easy to shred.

★ **BONUS RECIPE**

Pot Roast Gravy

After the pot roast has finished cooking, transfer ⅓–½ cup of the drippings from the slow cooker to a small pot on the stove over low heat. Add 1 tablespoon all-purpose flour and 1 tablespoon milk. Cook, stirring and adding a little more milk or flour as needed, until it's the consistency you like, 4–5 minutes. Top off with salt and pepper.

👍 **RECIPE TIPS**

☺ **In a Hurry?** *You can also cook this roast on high for 4 hours, but we prefer cooking it on low because the meat comes out more tender.*

☺ **Want to Add Vegetables?** *You can add any vegetables you would like, such as diced or baby carrots or diced potatoes, to the slow cooker along with the roast.*

☺ **Use Up Leftovers:** *Leftover roast makes a great filling for burritos, Cheese Enchiladas (page 184), Chimichangas (page 185), Flautas (page 187), Chicken Tacos (page 188) or Empanadas (page 189)*

PAIRINGS: Creamed Corn (page 138), Baked Potatoes (page 139), Roasted Vegetables (page 140), Mashed Potatoes (page 145)

PIGS IN A BLANKET

⏱ **PREP TIME:** 5 MINUTES

⏳ **COOK TIME:** 15 MINUTES

♡ **SERVES:** 8

✓ PREPPED IN 5

✓ QUICK & EASY

✓ ON THE TABLE IN 20

✓ FEED A CROWD

✓ MAKE AHEAD

✓ DAIRY-FREE

INGREDIENTS

1 (8-ounce) can refrigerated crescent rolls

8 hot dogs

1 egg, lightly beaten

1 tablespoon water

TOPPING: sesame seeds

 *Scan me!*

INSTRUCTIONS

1. Preheat the oven to 375 degrees F. Lightly grease a baking sheet and set aside.

2. Separate crescent dough into triangles.

3. Place a hot dog at the wide end of each triangle and roll up. Place on prepared baking sheet.

4. In a small bowl, combine egg and water. Brush egg wash over the tops of rolls. Sprinkle with sesame seeds and press gently into rolls.

5. Bake for 12–15 minutes, or until golden brown.

🖐 **RECIPE TIPS**

☺ **Make Ahead:** *Roll the crescent dough around the hot dogs and put them onto a baking sheet. Wrap with plastic wrap and store in the refrigerator for up to 24 hours. When you are ready to eat them, pop them in the oven to bake as directed!*

☺ **Want to Make Mini Pigs?** *Cut puff pastry or a full sheet of crescent roll dough into 1½-inch squares. Wrap little smokies or cut pieces of hot dog in the dough, brush with egg wash and bake as directed above.*

PAIRINGS: Caesar Salad (page 106), Broccoli Salad (page 111), Pasta Salad (page 114), Parmesan Sweet Potato Cubes (page 141)

PARMESAN-CRUSTED PORK CHOPS

⏱ **PREP TIME:** 10 MINUTES
⏲ **COOK TIME:** 30 MINUTES
♡ **SERVES:** 4

INGREDIENTS

⅓ cup grated Parmesan cheese

2–3 tablespoons Italian breadcrumbs

1 teaspoon dried parsley

½ teaspoon garlic powder

¼ teaspoon pepper

⅛ teaspoon paprika

4 boneless pork chops (about ¾ inch thick)

2 tablespoons olive oil

Scan me!

INSTRUCTIONS

1. Preheat the oven to 350 degrees F.

2. Mix Parmesan, breadcrumbs, parsley, garlic powder, pepper and paprika together in a shallow dish.

3. Dip pork chops in the mixture, making sure it sticks on both sides.

4. Heat oil in a pan over medium-high heat. Add pork chops and cook for 5 minutes on each side to sear.

5. Transfer pork chops to a glass baking dish large enough to hold them with 1 inch of room around each chop (or, for crispier chops, bake on a greased wire rack over a baking sheet).

6. Bake for 15–20 minutes, or until the internal temperature reaches 145 degrees F. Let rest for 5–10 minutes before serving.

👍 RECIPE TIPS

☺ **For Quicker Cleanup:** *To skip the searing step, preheat the oven to 350 degrees F and place pork chops in a baking dish. Spread 1 teaspoon butter over each pork chop and coat with breadcrumb and spice mixture. Bake as directed above.*

☺ **For a Thicker Crust:** *Whisk 1 egg with a little bit of milk. Dredge the chops in flour, then dip in the egg-milk mixture. Then continue on with Steps 2–5 as directed.*

PAIRINGS: Heavenly Rolls (page 68), Green Bean Bundles (page 135), Roasted Vegetables (page 140), Mashed Potatoes (page 145)

BABY BACK RIBS

🕐 PREP TIME: 10 MINUTES

⏳ CHILL TIME: 2 HOURS

⏳ COOK TIME: 2 HOURS 30 MINUTES

♡ SERVES: 8

✓ FEED A CROWD

✓ DAIRY-FREE

INGREDIENTS

DRY RUB:

¼ cup packed light brown sugar

1½ tablespoons paprika

1½ tablespoons black pepper

1 tablespoon kosher salt

1 teaspoon garlic powder

1 teaspoon onion powder

¼ teaspoon cayenne pepper

RIBS:

2 pounds pork baby back ribs

1 (18-ounce) bottle barbecue sauce, divided

Scan me!

INSTRUCTIONS

1. Make the dry rub: In a medium bowl, combine brown sugar, paprika, black pepper, salt, garlic powder, onion powder and cayenne.

2. Prepare the ribs by pulling off the clear membrane from the underside. Lightly massage dry rub into both sides of ribs and place on a large aluminum foil–lined baking sheet.

3. Brush 1½ cups barbecue sauce all over the ribs. Tear off enough aluminum foil to cover the ribs and spray foil with cooking spray. Wrap ribs tightly with the foil pieces and refrigerate for at least 2 hours, or ideally overnight.

4. When ready to bake, preheat the oven to 300 degrees F.

5. Bake ribs, still wrapped in the foil, for 2½ hours.

6. Unwrap the foil, brush ribs with remaining ¾ cup barbecue sauce and broil for about 5 minutes to caramelize the barbecue sauce.

PAIRINGS: Cornbread (page 71), Potato Salad (page 112), Macaroni Salad (page 113), Creamed Corn (page 138), Homemade Mac and Cheese (page 142)

👍 **RECIPE TIPS**

☺ **How to Choose Baby Back Ribs:** *When you are shopping for a good slab of ribs, look for an even layer of meat across the whole rack. Avoid racks with "shiners" (exposed bone). Read the package label and avoid enhanced cuts—"enhanced" means it has been pumped with water and salt.*

MONTE CRISTO SANDWICHES

PREP TIME: 5 MINUTES
COOK TIME: 10 MINUTES
SERVES: 6

PREPPED IN 5
QUICK & EASY
ON THE TABLE IN 20

INGREDIENTS

1½ cups all-purpose flour
1 tablespoon baking powder
¼ teaspoon salt
1 egg, beaten
1⅓ cups water
6 slices turkey
6 slices Swiss cheese
6 slices ham
12 slices white bread
vegetable oil, for frying
TOPPING: powdered sugar

Scan me!

INSTRUCTIONS

1. Sift flour, baking powder and salt together into a medium bowl.

2. In a separate bowl, mix egg and water. Add egg mixture to flour mixture and blend thoroughly.

3. Stack one slice each of turkey, cheese, and ham, in that order, onto bread and top each sandwich with a second slice of bread. Cut sandwiches in half and put a toothpick in each half to hold sandwiches together.

4. In a large pot, heat about 3 inches oil over medium-high heat to 360 degrees F.

5. Working in batches, dip each sandwich half in batter and fry in hot oil until golden, about 3 minutes on each side.

6. Drain on paper towels. Remove toothpicks and sprinkle sandwiches with powdered sugar just before serving.

👍 RECIPE TIPS

☺ **Serving Suggestion:** *Serve the sandwiches with your favorite store-bought jam for dipping, or make your own (see below).*

Raspberry Jam

BONUS RECIPE

Crush 6 cups raspberries in a large bowl with a potato masher. Add 5¼ cups sugar and mix well. Let stand for 10 minutes, stirring occasionally. Meanwhile, combine 1 (1.75-ounce) package Original Sure Jell Fruit Pectin and ¾ cup water in a small pot and bring to a boil over medium-high heat. Boil for 1–2 minutes, stirring constantly, then remove from the heat and stir into raspberries. Stir constantly until sugar is completely dissolved, about 3 minutes. Pour into clean glass jars or plastic containers, leaving ½-inch space at the top. Cover with lids and let stand at room temperature for 24 hours until set. Refrigerate for 2–3 weeks or freeze for up to 1 year. Makes 7 cups.

PAIRINGS: Fruit Salad (page 105), Caesar Salad (page 106), Macaroni Salad (page 113), Pasta Salad (page 114)

SWEET PORK

- ✓ **PREPPED IN 5**
- ✓ **FREEZER FRIENDLY**
- ✓ MAKE AHEAD
- ✓ **SLOW COOKER**
- ✓ **DAIRY-FREE**
- ✓ GLUTEN-FREE

INGREDIENTS

3 pounds pork sirloin roast

1 (16-ounce) bottle Dr Pepper

1 (28-ounce) can green enchilada sauce

¾ cup sugar

¾ cup packed light brown sugar

2 tablespoons minced garlic

2 tablespoons granulated garlic

1 teaspoon ground cumin

¾ teaspoon dry mustard

½ teaspoon chili powder

Scan me!

INSTRUCTIONS

1. Spray slow cooker with nonstick cooking spray.

2. Add pork and soda to the slow cooker. Cover and cook on high for 4 hours.

3. After 4 hours, combine all remaining ingredients in a large bowl and whisk to mix well.

4. Add this mixture to your slow cooker and cook for 2–3 hours more, until pork is falling apart as you try to remove it from the slow cooker.

5. Shred pork pieces with a fork, removing fat as you go, and place back in the sauce. Serve warm.

👍 RECIPE TIPS

☺ **Serving Suggestions:** *Serve this pork in tacos, burritos, enchiladas and wraps. Or make a salad bowl using Guacamole (page 88), Cilantro Ranch Dressing (page 109), Cilantro-Lime Rice (page 149), Homemade Salsa (page 153), Creamy Refried Beans (page 190) and chopped lettuce, chopped tomatoes and sour cream.*

☺ Make Ahead: *This recipe is perfect for leftovers! We always make extra and store it in the refrigerator or freezer so we have some on hand for tacos, burritos, enchiladas, tostadas and more. Store leftovers in an airtight container or resealable bag in the refrigerator for up to 4 days. To freeze, place it in an airtight, freezer-safe container or freezer bags and freeze for 2–3 months. When ready to use, let it thaw in the refrigerator overnight and reheat it in the microwave or in the oven.*

PAIRINGS: Flour Tortillas (page 70), Spanish Rice (page 148), Homemade Tortilla Chips (page 151)

PULLED PORK

PREPPED IN 5

FREEZER FRIENDLY

FEED A CROWD

MAKE AHEAD

SLOW COOKER

DAIRY-FREE

GLUTEN-FREE

INGREDIENTS

3–4 pounds pork butt

2 tablespoons kosher salt

⅓ cup liquid smoke

barbecue sauce (optional)

8 hamburger buns

TOPPINGS: coleslaw, pickles, onion rings (optional)

Scan me!

INSTRUCTIONS

1. Rub pork butt generously with salt.

2. Place pork in your slow cooker and pour liquid smoke over it.

3. Cook on low for 8–10 hours, or until pork shreds easily.

4. Shred pork with a fork, then stir in barbecue sauce if desired. Serve on hamburger buns with additional sauce and any desired toppings (coleslaw, pickles, onion rings, etc.).

👍 RECIPE TIPS

☺ **To Freeze:** *Freezing this pork is super easy, and a great way to save leftovers. Store individual servings in resealable plastic freezer bags. Make sure to seal the bags tightly so none of it will leak out. Frozen pulled pork will last 2–3 months in the freezer. Pull it out for a quick and easy meal when you do not have time to make dinner! Let it thaw at room temperature, then heat it up on the stove or in the microwave.*

☺ **Oven Directions:** *Preheat the oven to 350 degrees F. Rub liquid smoke and salt over the pork butt and wrap in aluminum foil. Place in a roasting pan and cook for 5 hours, or until the internal temperature is 145 degrees F. Shred and serve as directed above.*

PAIRINGS: Fruit Salad (page 105), Potato Salad (page 112), Pasta Salad (page 114), Broccoli Salad (page 111)

BROWN SUGAR HAM

⏱ PREP TIME: **10 MINUTES**
⏳ COOK TIME: **4–5 HOURS**
♡ SERVES: **14**

✓ FEED A CROWD
✓ SLOW COOKER
✓ DAIRY-FREE
✓ GLUTEN-FREE

INGREDIENTS

8 pounds bone-in, spiral-cut cured ham
2–2½ cups packed light brown sugar, divided
1 cup pineapple juice
¼ cup pure maple syrup (not artificially flavored pancake syrup) (optional)

Scan me!

INSTRUCTIONS

1. Spray your slow cooker with nonstick cooking spray. Place ham cut side down in the greased slow cooker.

2. Rub 1 cup brown sugar all over the ham, then pour pineapple juice and syrup over the top.

3. Cook on low for 3–4 hours.

4. Remove excess liquid from the slow cooker and transfer to a pot. Add remaining 1–1½ cups brown sugar to pot, using more sugar if you prefer a sweeter ham. Bring to a rolling boil, then remove from the heat and pour over the ham. Cook on warm for an additional 30–60 minutes.

5. Remove ham to a platter and spoon extra juices over ham slices. Garnish with fresh herbs before serving.

👍 RECIPE TIPS

☺ **Ham Cures:** *There are a few different types of ham, and while all of them are adaptable to this recipe, some might yield better results than others. Always look over the packaging when you are at the grocery store—it will specify exactly what type of ham it is.*

fresh ham: uncured, and always comes un-cooked. (NOTE: If you decide to use a fresh ham, you will have to fully cook it before putting in the slow cooker with the glaze.)

cured ham: brined or cured with a dry rub; sometimes sold ready to eat and other times requires cooking.

cooked and smoked: the same as cured ham, with the additional step of smoking.

PAIRINGS: Heavenly Rolls (page 68), Green Bean Casserole (page 137), Parmesan Sweet Potato Cubes (page 141), Mashed Potatoes (page 145)

BAKED SALMON

PREP TIME: 5 MINUTES
COOK TIME: 35 MINUTES
SERVES: 2

PREPPED IN 5

DAIRY-FREE

GLUTEN-FREE

INGREDIENTS

6 tablespoons olive oil

1 tablespoon lemon juice

1 tablespoon chopped fresh parsley

2 teaspoons minced garlic

1 teaspoon dried basil

1 teaspoon garlic salt with parsley flakes

1 teaspoon pepper

2 (6-ounce) salmon fillets

Scan me!

INSTRUCTIONS

1. Preheat the oven to 375 degrees F. Lightly grease a baking dish and set aside.

2. In a medium bowl mix olive oil, lemon juice, parsley, garlic, basil, garlic salt and pepper to create a marinade.

3. Place salmon fillets in prepared baking dish. Pour marinade over the salmon and turn to coat all sides, then place salmon skin side down.

4. Bake uncovered for 35 minutes, until salmon flakes easily with a fork. Serve immediately.

PAIRINGS: Roasted Vegetables (page 140), Twice-Baked Potatoes (page 144), Mashed Potatoes (page 145)

👍 RECIPE TIPS

☺ **Salmon Skin:** *Unless you are poaching salmon, you should always leave the skin on during cooking to protect the bottom of the salmon from overcooking. The skin will slide right off a cooked fillet.*

☺ **Doneness Guide:** *Perfectly cooked salmon will be opaque on the outside, and in the center, the meat should easily separate and look translucent pink. If the meat does not separate well and the fish looks completely translucent, the salmon is undercooked. Overcooked fish will flake and look opaque all the way through. Also, as the fish cooks it will begin to develop a white film on top; overcooked salmon will have a lot of this film.*

ROAST CHICKEN

⏱ **PREP TIME:** 10 MINUTES

⏳ **COOK TIME:** 1 HOUR 10 MINUTES

⏳ **REST TIME:** 10 MINUTES

♡ **SERVES:** 6

✓ **SLOW COOKER**

✓ GLUTEN-FREE

INGREDIENTS

1 (4–5 pound) whole chicken

salt and pepper to taste

1 large lemon, cut into quarters

3–4 sprigs fresh rosemary

2 tablespoons salted butter, softened

Scan me!

INSTRUCTIONS

1. Preheat the oven to 400 degrees F.

2. Prepare the chicken by patting it dry with paper towels and removing the giblets and/or gravy pouch.

3. Sprinkle chicken with salt and pepper. Place lemon and rosemary in the cavity. Tie chicken's legs together with kitchen twine. Spread butter over the top of the skin.

4. Place chicken in a roasting pan or a 9-x-13-inch baking dish. Bake for 60 minutes, then check the temperature in the thickest part of the thigh. Continue cooking, checking every 10 minutes, until it reaches 165 degrees F.

5. Remove chicken from the oven and let it sit 10–15 minutes before carving and serving.

👍 **RECIPE TIPS**

☺ **Slow Cooker Directions:** *Spray a slow cooker with cooking spray. Roll a piece of aluminum foil into a ring and place it around the bottom of the slow cooker as a rack for the chicken. Prepare chicken as directed in Steps 2 and 3 above, then place it on top of the aluminum foil ring. Cover and cook on high for 3–4 hours, until a thermometer inserted in the thigh registers 165 degrees F or higher. Move chicken to a sheet pan or baking dish and broil in the oven for 3–5 minutes, until the skin is browned. Let rest for 10 minutes before cutting and serving.*

☺ **Use It Up:** *Leftover chicken can be used to make White Chicken Chili (page 127), Slow Cooker Chicken Tortilla Soup (page 128), Chimichangas (page 185), Flautas (page 187) or Chicken Tacos (page 188).*

PAIRINGS: Roasted Vegetables (page 140), Twice-Baked Potatoes (page 144), Mashed Potatoes (page 145)

ROAST TURKEY

⏱ **PREP TIME:** 20 MINUTES

⧖ **COOK TIME:** 3 HOURS

⧖ **REST TIME:** 20 MINUTES

♡ **SERVES:** 12

INGREDIENTS

TURKEY:

1 (14–16 pound) turkey, thawed if frozen

¼ cup olive oil

1 teaspoon salt

½ teaspoon pepper

2 Granny Smith apples, cored and sliced

2–3 carrots, cut into 1-inch pieces

1 onion, cut into 1-inch pieces

5–6 stalks celery, cut into 1-inch pieces

GLAZE:

1 cup honey

½ cup unsalted butter, melted

2 teaspoons dried sage leaves

1 teaspoon ground thyme

1 teaspoon dried parsley

1 teaspoon dried basil

1 teaspoon salt

1 teaspoon pepper

Scan me!

INSTRUCTIONS

1. Preheat the oven to 425 degrees F. Set an elevated rack into the bottom of a roasting pan.

2. Make the turkey: Brush olive oil all over turkey and sprinkle with salt and pepper. Place about two-thirds of the vegetables and apples on the rack in the prepared roasting pan.

3. Place turkey on the rack and stuff remaining third of the vegetables and apples inside the turkey. If turkey's legs are not already tied together, tie them with kitchen twine.

4. Roast turkey uncovered in the oven for 30 minutes, then cover loosely with aluminum foil and reduce the heat to 375 degrees F. Roast for another 2–2½ hours, until a thermometer inserted into the thickest part of the thigh reads 165 degrees F.

5. Make the glaze: Whisk together all glaze ingredients in a medium bowl.

6. Brush glaze over turkey and return it to the oven, uncovered, for 15–20 minutes, until golden. Remove from the oven, discard the vegetables, and let turkey rest for 20 minutes before serving.

👍 RECIPE TIPS

☺ **What Size Turkey Should I Buy?** *Take a head count and plan to serve each person 1–1½ pounds of turkey—so for ten people, you'll need a 10–15-pound turkey. If you are hosting a large crowd, consider cooking two smaller turkeys to cut down on cooking time.*

☺ **Thawing Turkey:** *How long you'll need to thaw your turkey in the refrigerator depends on its size. Use the guide below and plan ahead!*

4 pounds: 1 day

8 pounds: 2 days

12 pounds: 3 days

16 pounds: 4 days

20 pounds: 5 days

PAIRINGS: Heavenly Rolls (page 68), Green Bean Casserole (page 137), Creamed Corn (page 138), Mashed Potatoes (page 145), Pumpkin Pie (page 235)

HAWAIIAN HAYSTACKS

🕐 PREP TIME: 5 MINUTES
⌛ COOK TIME: 1 HOUR
♡ SERVES: 4

✓ PREPPED IN 5

✓ SLOW COOKER

INGREDIENTS

1 (14.5-ounce) can chicken broth

1 (10.5-ounce) can cream of chicken soup

1 cup sour cream

2–3 chicken breasts, cooked and cubed

½ teaspoon salt

½ teaspoon pepper

3–4 cups steamed white rice (or instant rice cooked according to the package instructions)

TOPPINGS: slivered almonds, shredded cheese, chopped green onions, pineapple tidbits, chow mein noodles, chopped celery, Homemade Wonton Strips (page 131)

Scan me!

👍 RECIPE TIPS

☺ **Stove Top Directions:** *Combine broth and soup in a large saucepan over medium-low heat. Add sour cream, chicken, salt and pepper and mix. Cook, stirring occasionally, until heated through, about 10 minutes, then serve over rice.*

☺ **To Make with Uncooked Chicken:** *Add uncooked chicken cubes in Step 2, along with salt and pepper. Stir, cover and cook on high for 3–4 hours or on low for 6–8 hours.*

☺ **To Make Rice in the Slow Cooker:** *Coat the inside of your slow cooker with butter or cooking spray. Add 1 cup rice (Uncle Ben's converted white rice works best) and 1½ cups water (or chicken broth). Cover and cook on high for 2–3 hours, stirring every 20–30 minutes. Once the water has been absorbed and the rice is soft and fluffy, it's ready. Add salt and pepper to taste.*

INSTRUCTIONS

1. Combine broth, soup and sour cream in a slow cooker and stir to mix.

2. Add chicken cubes, salt and pepper and stir. Cover and cook on high for 1–2 hours or on low for 3–4 hours.

3. Serve chicken and gravy over rice. Top with desired toppings.

PAIRINGS: Macaroni Salad (page 113), Pasta Salad (page 114), Asian Ramen Salad (page 110), Mashed Potatoes (page 145)

CREAMY SWISS CHICKEN

PREP TIME: **5 MINUTES**

COOK TIME: **1 HOUR**

SERVES: **4**

INGREDIENTS

4 boneless, skinless chicken breasts

4 slices Swiss cheese (or mozzarella cheese)

½ cup mayonnaise

½ cup sour cream

¾ cup grated Parmesan cheese, divided

1 teaspoon garlic powder

½ teaspoon salt

½ teaspoon pepper

4 cups cooked rice, for serving (optional)

Scan me!

INSTRUCTIONS

1. Preheat the oven to 375 degrees F. Grease a 9-x-13-inch baking dish and set aside.

2. Pat chicken dry and place in prepared pan.

3. Place a slice of Swiss cheese on top of each chicken breast.

4. In a bowl, mix mayonnaise, sour cream, ½ cup Parmesan, garlic powder, salt and pepper. Spread mixture over chicken and sprinkle with remaining ¼ cup Parmesan.

5. Bake for 1 hour, until the internal temperature of chicken reaches 165 degrees F. Serve chicken on its own or over rice, if desired.

PAIRINGS: Heavenly Rolls (page 68), Asparagus Bundles (page 135), Roasted Vegetables (page 140)

👍 RECIPE TIPS

☺ **A Lighter Option:** *To cut back on calories, you can use light dairy products (light Swiss cheese, light mayo, light sour cream). The flavor is still delicious!*

CHICKEN NUGGETS

⏲ PREP TIME: **15 MINUTES**

⏳ COOK TIME: **15 MINUTES**

♡ SERVES: **4**

✓ **QUICK & EASY**

✓ **MAKE AHEAD**

INGREDIENTS

2 boneless, skinless chicken breasts

1 cup all-purpose flour

2 eggs

2 tablespoons water

1 cup plain breadcrumbs (or panko breadcrumbs)

½ cup Parmesan cheese

1 tablespoon Italian seasoning

1 teaspoon garlic salt

vegetable oil, for frying

Scan me!

INSTRUCTIONS

1. Cut chicken into bite-sized pieces (about 1–1½ inches).

2. Place flour in a medium bowl.

3. Combine eggs and water in a second bowl and beat together.

4. In a third bowl, combine breadcrumbs, Parmesan, Italian seasoning and garlic salt and mix together.

5. Fill a frying pan with about 2 inches of oil and heat over medium heat to 350 degrees F.

6. While oil is heating up, coat each chicken nugget with flour, then dip into the egg mixture. Finally, coat with the breadcrumb mixture.

7. When oil is ready, place one nugget into the oil to test. It should sizzle immediately. If it darkens too quickly without cooking on the inside, then the oil is too hot. Adjust the heat accordingly.

8. Fry nuggets in batches for 3–4 minutes on each side, then place on a wire rack or paper towel–lined plate to drain before serving.

PAIRINGS: Cilantro Ranch Dressing (page 109), Pasta Salad (page 114), Creamed Corn (page 138), Homemade Mac and Cheese (page 142)

👍 RECIPE TIPS

☺ **Make Ahead:** *You can bread the chicken as described in Step 6, then place the nuggets in a single layer, cover tightly with plastic wrap and store in the refrigerator for 1 day before frying.*

☺ **Oven Directions:** *Place breaded nuggets on a wire rack over an aluminum foil–lined baking sheet. Spray with olive oil spray and bake at 400 degrees F for 10 minutes. Flip, spray again and cook for an additional 8 minutes. Broil for a few minutes more to brown nuggets.*

CHICKEN POT PIE

FREEZER FRIENDLY

FEED A CROWD

MAKE AHEAD

INGREDIENTS

1 medium russet potato, peeled and cubed
2 chicken breasts, cubed
1 cup sliced carrots
1 cup frozen peas
½ cup corn
2 (9-inch) pie crusts, unbaked (Perfect Pie Crust, page 232)
2 tablespoons unsalted butter
½ cup all-purpose flour
1 teaspoon garlic salt
¼ teaspoon pepper
2 cups chicken broth
⅔ cup milk
1 egg

Scan me!

INSTRUCTIONS

1. Preheat the oven to 375 degrees F.

2. Place potatoes in a large pot and cover with water. Bring to a boil for 10 minutes, then add chicken, carrots, peas and corn and boil for 15 minutes more. Remove from the heat, drain the water and set aside.

3. Place bottom crust in a 9-inch pie plate and bake for 5 minutes.

4. While the crust is baking, cook butter in a saucepan over medium heat. Once butter is melted, stir in flour, garlic salt and pepper. Slowly whisk in chicken broth and milk and heat until thickened, 5–6 minutes.

5. Remove bottom crust from the oven and add chicken and veggies to the crust. Pour the broth mixture over the chicken and veggies.

6. Cover with the top pie crust, making sure to seal the edges. Cut slits on the top to allow steam to escape.

7. Create an egg wash by whisking egg with a little water. Brush egg wash on top of the pie crust.

8. Bake for 40–45 minutes, or until the top is golden brown.

9. Let rest for 10–15 minutes before cutting and serving.

PAIRINGS: Easy Homemade Biscuits (page 65), Heavenly Rolls (page 68), Caesar Salad (page 106), Creamy Swiss Chicken (page 177)

👍 **RECIPE TIPS**

☺ **To Freeze:** *Wrap chicken pot pie tightly with aluminum foil or plastic wrap and place in a large resealable plastic freezer bag. It will last for up to 4 months. When ready to bake, there is no need to thaw. Simply remove plastic, cover with foil and bake as directed, adding an additional 35–40 minutes to the baking time.*

GENERAL TSO'S CHICKEN

🕐 PREP TIME: 5 MINUTES

⏳ COOK TIME: 15 MINUTES

♡ SERVES: 4

✓ PREPPED IN 5

✓ QUICK & EASY

✓ ON THE TABLE IN 20

✓ FREEZER FRIENDLY

✓ DAIRY-FREE

INGREDIENTS

2 tablespoons sugar

2 tablespoons sweet chili sauce

1 tablespoon rice vinegar

¼ cup all-purpose flour

2 tablespoons cornstarch

1 tablespoon soy sauce

1 egg white

3 boneless, skinless chicken thighs, cut into bite-sized pieces

2 tablespoons vegetable oil

1 bunch broccoli florets, cut into bite-sized pieces (about 3 cups)

2 cups cooked white rice (or cooked noodles)

Scan me!

INSTRUCTIONS

1. Mix sugar, chili sauce and vinegar in a small bowl. Set aside.

2. In another bowl, mix flour and cornstarch. In a third bowl, beat soy sauce and egg white. Add chicken to the egg white mixture and toss to coat, then transfer coated chicken to the flour bowl and toss around.

3. Heat oil in a skillet over medium heat. Add floured chicken and cook, stirring occasionally, for 7–8 minutes, or until chicken is cooked and crispy.

4. Add broccoli to the skillet and cook, stirring often, until broccoli is softened, then add chili sauce mixture to the skillet and cook for 2–3 more minutes, making sure to coat the broccoli and chicken.

5. Serve over rice or noodles.

PAIRINGS: Fried Egg Rolls (page 99), Egg Drop Soup (page 131), Fried Rice (page 147)

👍 RECIPE TIPS

☺ **To Freeze:** *For longer storage, store in an airtight freezer-safe container for 3–4 months. Thaw in the refrigerator and reheat in a skillet. If you are in a hurry, you can also microwave the chicken.*

⚙ VARIATIONS

If you like a sweeter sauce, add ½–1 tablespoon sugar or honey. For a spicier dish add 5–6 whole dried chiles, or you can use red chili flakes. Add 2 teaspoons of hoisin sauce for an extra layer of flavoring. Top with sesame seeds.

SWEET AND SOUR CHICKEN

INGREDIENTS

¾–1 cup canola oil, for frying

½ cup cornstarch

3–4 chicken breasts (or chicken thighs), cut into 1-inch pieces

2 eggs, beaten

½ cup all-purpose flour, plus more if needed

1 red bell pepper, cut into 1-inch chunks

1 green bell pepper, cut into 1-inch chunks

1 cup pineapple chunks

SWEET AND SOUR SAUCE:

¾ cup water

⅓ cup pineapple juice

⅓ cup distilled white vinegar

⅓ cup soy sauce

⅓ cup ketchup

½ cup granulated sugar

¼ cup packed light brown sugar

⅛ teaspoon salt

3 tablespoons cornstarch mixed with ¼ cup water

Scan me!

INSTRUCTIONS

1. Prepare the sauce: In a medium pot combine water, pineapple juice, vinegar, soy sauce, ketchup, both sugars and salt over low heat. Cook, stirring occasionally, while frying chicken.

2. To prepare the chicken, heat 1–1½ inches of oil in a large frying pan over medium-high heat.

3. Place cornstarch in a large resealable plastic bag, then add chicken pieces. Shake until all the pieces are evenly coated.

4. Beat eggs in a small bowl. Place flour in a separate bowl. Dip each piece of chicken into egg, then into flour. Once coated, add to the hot oil.

5. Cook chicken for 2–3 minutes, flipping with metal tongs, until cooked through and crispy. Once crisp, place chicken on a paper towel–lined plate. Once all the pieces have been cooked, discard all but a few tablespoons of oil.

6. Add bell peppers and pineapple to the frying pan and cook for 1–2 minutes, or until peppers are crisp-tender.

7. Meanwhile, finish the sauce by adding cornstarch-water slurry. Mix and bring to a low boil, then cook, stirring, for about 2 minutes, until thickened.

8. Add the sauce to the pineapple and peppers. Add the chicken and stir to coat.

9. Cook until sauce is bubbling, 4–5 minutes more.

🖐 RECIPE TIPS

☺ **Chicken Cut:** *Boneless chicken thighs are a great alternative to chicken breast.*

☺ **Healthier:** *Make this a little healthier by skipping the coating and putting the cubed chicken directly into the pan to fry.*

⚙ VARIATIONS

Try adding some additional vegetables to your sweet and sour chicken or swapping out the bell peppers for onions, shredded carrots, broccoli florets or mushrooms.

PAIRINGS: Fried Egg Rolls (page 99), Asian Ramen Salad (page 110), Egg Drop Soup (page 131), Fried Rice (page 147)

TERIYAKI CHICKEN

🕐 **PREP TIME:** 10 MINUTES

⏳ **COOK TIME:** 20 MINUTES

♡ **SERVES:** 4

 DAIRY-FREE

INGREDIENTS

1 tablespoon olive oil

4–5 boneless, skinless chicken thighs, cubed

2 cups cooked rice, noodles and/or steamed vegetables (optional)

1-2 tablespoons sesame seeds (optional)

TERIYAKI SAUCE:

1 cup water

¼ cup low-sodium soy sauce (or tamari sauce)

2 tablespoons honey

1 tablespoon pineapple juice (optional)

⅓ cup packed light brown sugar

1 teaspoon minced garlic

¼ teaspoon ground ginger

2 tablespoons cornstarch mixed with ⅓ cup cold water

 Scan me!

INSTRUCTIONS

1. Heat oil in a large skillet over medium heat.

2. Add cubed chicken and cook, stirring, for 7–8 minutes, until no longer pink, browned and a little crisped.

3. Meanwhile, make teriyaki sauce: Combine water, soy sauce, honey, pineapple juice, brown sugar, garlic and ginger in a medium saucepan over medium heat.

4. Whisk cornstarch-water mixture until dissolved and add to the sauce.

5. Cook, stirring occasionally, for about 5 minutes, until sauce thickens. If the sauce becomes too thick, add more water to thin it out.

6. Add sauce to the skillet with the chicken and cook for about 5 minutes to thoroughly coat chicken. Serve topped with sesame seeds (if desired) and with rice, noodles and/or steamed veggies.

PAIRINGS: Fried Egg Rolls (page 99), Asian Ramen Salad (page 110), Egg Drop Soup (page 131), Fried Rice (page 147)

👍 **RECIPE TIPS**

☺ **Additions:** *Add some of your favorite veggies to the mix along with the chicken in Step 2. Broccoli florets, snap peas, bell peppers and asparagus are all great additions that add flavor and nutrition.*

GREEN CHILE CHICKEN ENCHILADAS

○ PREP TIME: 20 MINUTES
⊠ COOK TIME: 20 MINUTES
♡ SERVES: 8

INGREDIENTS

2 cups shredded cooked chicken

2 cups shredded Colby Jack cheese (or Mexican blend cheese), divided

1 (4-ounce) can chopped green chiles

salt and pepper to taste

1 (28-ounce) can Las Palmas green chile enchilada sauce

8 (6-inch) corn tortillas

1 cup sour cream

Scan me!

INSTRUCTIONS

1. Preheat the oven to 350 degrees F.

2. In a small bowl, combine chicken, 1 cup cheese, chiles, salt and pepper.

3. In a small skillet, bring enchilada sauce to a boil, then lower temperature and bring to a simmer.

4. Dip each tortilla into heated sauce for a few seconds to soften.

5. Place a tortilla in a 9-x-11-inch baking dish and spoon ⅓ cup of chicken mixture and 2 tablespoons sour cream down the center. (NOTE: The squeeze sour cream works great.)

6. Roll the tortilla and place seam side down.

7. Repeat with remaining tortillas. Pour enough sauce over to cover the enchiladas. Sprinkle with remaining 1 cup cheese.

8. Bake for 20 minutes, or until cheese is melted and bubbly.

⟳ RECIPE TIPS

☺ **Make Ahead:** *Make the enchiladas as instructed through Step 7, then cover with aluminum foil or plastic wrap and place in the refrigerator for up to 24 hours. When ready to serve, uncover and bake as instructed, adding a few additional minutes to the bake time.*

☺ **Substitutions:** *Swap the corn tortillas for similarly sized flour tortillas. You do not need to dip flour tortillas in sauce before rolling.*

PAIRINGS: Spanish Rice (page 148), Homemade Tortilla Chips (page 151), Homemade Salsa (page 153)

CHEESE ENCHILADAS

⏱ **PREP TIME:** 10 MINUTES
⏳ **COOK TIME:** 40 MINUTES
♡ **SERVES:** 8

✓ **FREEZER FRIENDLY**
✓ **FEED A CROWD**
✓ **MAKE AHEAD**

INGREDIENTS

2 tablespoons vegetable oil

¼ cup all-purpose flour

2–3 tablespoons Gebhardt chili powder

½ teaspoon garlic powder

½ teaspoon garlic salt with parsley flakes (or salt)

½ teaspoon ground cumin

¼ teaspoon dried oregano

2 cups full-sodium chicken broth

9 (6-inch) corn tortillas

4 cups shredded Mexican cheese, divided

2 cups cooked hamburger or cooked pork (optional)

Scan me!

INSTRUCTIONS

1. Heat oil in a large pot over medium heat. Add flour and cook, whisking together, for 1–2 minutes.

2. Add chili powder, garlic powder, garlic salt, cumin and oregano and mix until clumpy. Pour in chicken broth, whisking the entire time until there are no more clumps. Reduce heat to low and cook for 15–20 minutes, or until thickened.

3. Preheat the oven to 350 degrees F. Grease a 7-x-11-inch (or 9-x-13-inch) baking dish and set aside.

4. After the sauce has thickened, dip each tortilla in the sauce until soft and immediately put it into the prepared dish. Add ⅓ cup cheese and any meat you wish to add to the tortilla, roll it up and push it to the end of the pan.

5. Repeat with all the tortillas until your pan is full. Pour remaining sauce over the tortillas. Sprinkle the top with remaining 1 cup of cheese.

6. Bake for 20–25 minutes, or until cheese is melted and bubbly.

👍 RECIPE TIPS

☺ **Make Ahead:** *We often make these 24 hours in advance up through Step 5, but skip adding the last 1 cup cheese until ready to bake. Store in the refrigerator, covered tightly with aluminum foil or plastic wrap. When ready to serve, top with cheese and bake, adding a few additional minutes to the cooking time.*

☺ **To Freeze:** *Prepare as directed through Step 5, then place in a freezer-safe pan, cover tightly with aluminum foil and place in a large resealable plastic freezer bag. Store in the freezer for up to 2 months. Thaw overnight in the refrigerator before baking.*

☺ **Chili Powder:** *Our favorite is Gebhardt chili powder, which can be found at most stores and on Amazon.*

☺ **Make It Mild:** *For a milder version of the sauce (this does have a nip), reduce the amount of chili powder to 2 tablespoons and/or add 1 (8-ounce) can tomato sauce in Step 2.*

PAIRINGS: Spanish Rice (page 148), Cilantro-Lime Rice (page 149), Homemade Tortilla Chips (page 151), Homemade Salsa (page 153)

CHIMICHANGAS

INGREDIENTS

2 tablespoons vegetable oil

1 medium onion, chopped

2 teaspoons minced garlic

1 jalapeño pepper, seeded and diced

1½ teaspoons chili powder

1 teaspoon ground cumin

1 teaspoon salt

¼ teaspoon ground cinnamon

1 Roma tomato, chopped

2 tablespoons chopped fresh cilantro

2 cups shredded cooked chicken

¼ cup sour cream

6 (10-inch) flour tortillas, warmed

1 (16-ounce) can refried beans

1½ cups shredded Monterey Jack cheese (or Mexican blend cheese)

vegetable oil, for frying

TOPPINGS: shredded lettuce, chopped tomatoes, sour cream, chopped fresh cilantro, additional shredded cheese

Scan me!

INSTRUCTIONS

1. Heat oil in a medium skillet over medium heat. Add onion, garlic and jalapeño, and cook, stirring, until softened, 3–4 minutes. Add chili powder, cumin, salt and cinnamon and stir to combine. Add tomato and cilantro and cook for 2–3 minutes. Stir in the chicken and sour cream and cook until heated through.

2. To assemble the chimichangas, spread a few tablespoons of refried beans down the center of each tortilla. Top each tortilla with one-sixth of the chicken mixture and ¼ cup of cheese. Fold the sides of the tortilla toward the center, then roll tortilla up into a burrito shape.

3. Fill a heavy pot or deep fryer with 1–2 inches of oil and heat to 350 degrees F. Secure the chimichangas with toothpicks to prevent them from opening while frying. Fry chimichangas 1–2 at a time for 3–4 minutes, or until golden brown, flipping halfway through.

4. Serve the chimichangas hot with the toppings of your choice.

PAIRINGS: Spanish Rice (page 148), Cilantro-Lime Rice (page 149), Sweet Pork (page 170), Creamy Refried Beans (page 190)

🖒 RECIPE TIPS

☺ **Make Ahead:** *You can assemble the chimichangas ahead of time to cook later. Complete Steps 1 and 2 as directed above. Wrap each assembled chimichanga with plastic wrap and place them in an airtight container in the refrigerator for up to 24 hours.*

☺ **Baking Instructions:** *Brush each chimichanga with oil and place on a greased baking sheet. Bake at 450 degrees F for 8 minutes, then flip and bake for an additional 5–8 minutes, until golden brown.*

CREAM CHEESE AND CHICKEN TAQUITOS

⏱ **PREP TIME:** 5 MINUTES
⧗ **COOK TIME:** 25 MINUTES
♡ **SERVES:** 12

✓ PREPPED IN 5
✓ QUICK & EASY
✓ FEED A CROWD
✓ MAKE AHEAD
✓ GLUTEN-FREE

INGREDIENTS

vegetable or canola oil, for frying

3 cups shredded cooked chicken

6 ounces cream cheese, softened

1½ cups baby spinach, stems removed and chopped

1½ cups shredded Colby Jack cheese (or Mexican blend cheese)

⅓ cup salsa (store-bought or homemade, page 153)

⅓ cup sour cream

salt and pepper to taste

12 (6-inch) corn tortillas (or flour tortillas)

TOPPINGS: shredded lettuce, chopped tomatoes, sour cream, Pico de Gallo (page 152)

Scan me!

INSTRUCTIONS

1. Fill a saucepan with ½ inch of oil and heat over medium heat to 350 degrees F.

2. Meanwhile, in a large bowl mix together chicken, cream cheese, spinach, Colby Jack cheese, salsa and sour cream. Add salt and pepper.

3. Once oil is hot enough, add a few tablespoons of chicken–cream cheese mixture to the center of a tortilla and spread out. Roll tortilla up and use tongs to place it seam side down in hot oil. Cook until golden brown on both sides, 2–3 minutes per side. Set on paper towels to drain.

4. Repeat until all tortillas have been filled, rolled and fried.

5. Serve warm with your favorite toppings.

PAIRINGS: Guacamole (page 88), Spanish Rice (page 148), Cilantro-Lime Rice (page 149), Street Corn (page 150), Homemade Tortilla Chips (page 151), Homemade Salsa (page 153)

👍 RECIPE TIPS

☺ **Make Ahead:** *You can mix the filling as described in Step 2 up to 24 hours in advance. Cover and refrigerate until ready to use.*

☺ **Corn Tortillas Cracking?** *If your corn tortillas are cracking when you roll them, wrap a stack of corn tortillas in some damp paper towels and microwave for 15–30 seconds until warmed up. The reason many tortillas crack or break is because they are not warm enough.*

⚙ VARIATIONS

Change it up by using shredded beef or pork. You can also use a different salsa to change the flavor.

FLAUTAS

○ PREP TIME: 10 MINUTES

⧗ COOK TIME: 15 MINUTES

♡ SERVES: 12

INGREDIENTS

vegetable or canola oil, for frying

3 cups shredded cooked chicken (or beef)

1 cup shredded Mexican blend cheese

½ cup salsa (store-bought or homemade, page 153)

1 (4-ounce) can diced chiles

garlic salt with parsley flakes to taste

pepper to taste

12 (6-inch) flour tortillas (or corn tortillas for a gluten-free option)

salt to taste

TOPPINGS: shredded lettuce, chopped tomatoes, Sweet Salsa Verde (page 154), Guacamole (page 88), Cilantro Ranch Dressing (page 109)

Scan me!

INSTRUCTIONS

1. Fill a large saucepan with about ¾ inch oil. Heat over medium heat to 375 degrees F.

2. In a medium bowl, combine chicken, cheese, salsa, chiles, garlic salt and pepper.

3. Working with 4 tortillas at a time, spread a heaping spoonful of chicken filling along the middle of each tortilla. Roll the tortillas tightly around the filling and secure each one with a toothpick.

4. Using tongs, hold each flauta in hot oil until firm, then release to continue cooking. Cook until golden brown, about 2 minutes, then remove to a paper towel–lined plate and immediately season with salt.

5. Transfer flautas to an aluminum foil–lined baking sheet and keep warm in the oven while assembling and cooking the remaining tortillas. Serve warm with your favorite toppings.

PAIRINGS: Spanish Rice (page 148), Cilantro-Lime Rice (page 149), Street Corn (page 150), Black Bean and Corn Salsa (page 155)

👍 RECIPE TIPS

☺ **Make Ahead:** *We do not suggest making any fried foods ahead of time, but you can make the filling in advance. Store in an airtight container in the refrigerator for up to 48 hours.*

☺ **Baking Directions:** *Place the rolled flautas seam side down in a lightly greased 9-x-13-inch baking dish or on a metal baking sheet. Spray with olive oil cooking spray and bake at 350 degrees F for 20 minutes.*

CHICKEN TACOS

🕐 **PREP TIME:** 10 MINUTES

⧗ **COOK TIME:** 15 MINUTES

♡ **SERVES:** 8

✓ **QUICK & EASY**

✓ **FEED A CROWD**

✓ **GLUTEN-FREE**

INGREDIENTS

2 cups shredded cooked chicken

1 cup shredded Mexican blend cheese

1 (4-ounce) can green chiles

salt and pepper to taste

vegetable oil

8 (6-inch) corn tortillas

TOPPINGS: shredded lettuce, chopped tomatoes, shredded cheese, Homemade Salsa (page 153), Guacamole (page 88)

Scan me!

INSTRUCTIONS

1. In a medium bowl, combine chicken, cheese, chiles, salt and pepper, and mix.

2. Fill a large saucepan with about ¾ inch oil. Heat over medium heat to 375 degrees F.

3. Add ¼ cup of chicken mixture to the middle of a corn tortilla, then fold like a taco and grab with your tongs. Rock the taco back and forth in the oil until it can lay down without opening, then place into the oil on its side.

4. Cook for 2–3 minutes on each side. When both sides are cooked, remove from oil and place on a paper towel–lined plate to drain. Repeat with the remaining tortillas and filling.

5. Add your desired toppings to fill the tacos before serving.

PAIRINGS: Guacamole (page 88), Spanish Rice (page 148), Pico de Gallo (page 152), Homemade Salsa (page 153), Sweet Salsa Verde (page 154)

👍 **RECIPE TIPS**

☺ **If Your Corn Tortillas Are Cracking Easily:**
Flash fry them in the oil for a second or two on each side, then fill and refry. Or wrap a stack of corn tortillas in a damp paper towel and microwave for 15 seconds.

⚙ **VARIATIONS**

➔ **SOFT TACOS:** Combine the chicken, chiles, salt and pepper and heat in the microwave, then add the cheese. Serve with toppings in soft flour tortillas.

➔ **CHANGE THE MEAT:** Use ground beef, shredded beef, shredded pork or even diced potatoes to make other yummy taco alternatives.

EMPANADAS

PREP TIME: **10 MINUTES**
REST TIME: **4 HOURS**
COOK TIME: **10 MINUTES**
SERVES: **12**

FEED A CROWD
MAKE AHEAD
DAIRY-FREE

INGREDIENTS

DOUGH:

3 cups all-purpose flour
1 tablespoon baking powder
1 tablespoon salt
½ cup lard (or shortening)
1¼ cups warm water (110–115 degrees F)

FILLING:

2½ pounds roast beef, cooked and shredded
    (store-bought or homemade, page 165)
1–2 cups red enchilada sauce, to taste
½ cup sliced black olives
vegetable oil, for frying

Scan me!

INSTRUCTIONS

1. Prepare the dough: In a medium bowl, mix all ingredients for the dough together with a wooden spoon until well combined and a little sticky. Pinch away golf ball–sized pieces of dough and roll each one into a ball. Place dough balls on a glass or ceramic plate and cover with plastic wrap. Let rest at room temperature for 4–6 hours (we usually make ours in the morning to be ready for dinner).

2. Prepare the filling: In a medium bowl, combine meat, red enchilada sauce and sliced olives. Mix and set aside.

3. When dough is ready, fill a medium saucepan with ¾ inch oil. Heat over medium heat to 365 degrees F.

4. Roll out each dough ball on a floured surface into a 5–6-inch round.

5. Add ¼ cup of roast beef mixture to one side of each dough circle. Fold the other half over and pinch around the entire edge.

6. Working in batches, fry empanadas in oil for 2–3 minutes on each side until golden brown.

7. Transfer to a paper towel–lined plate to drain. Serve warm.

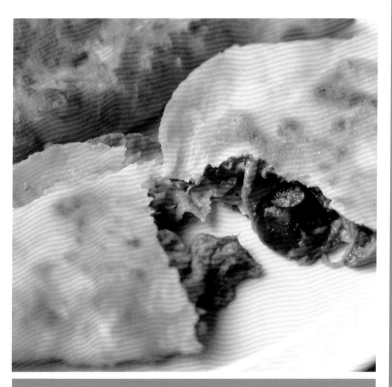

PAIRINGS: Spanish Rice (page 148), Cilantro-Lime Rice (page 149), Street Corn (page 150), Homemade Salsa (page 153), Chicken Tacos (page 188)

👍 **RECIPE TIPS**

☺ **Make Ahead:** *The filling can be made in advance. Store in an airtight container in the refrigerator for up to 48 hours.*

⚙ **VARIATIONS**

→ **PORK:** Use Pulled Pork (page 171) and mix with your favorite green chile sauce.

→ **CHICKEN:** Use the chicken mixture from our Flautas (page 187) in place of the beef.

TOSTADAS

PREP TIME: **10 MINUTES**
COOK TIME: **10 MINUTES**
SERVES: **8**

- QUICK & EASY
- ON THE TABLE IN 20
- FEED A CROWD
- MAKE AHEAD
- GLUTEN-FREE

INGREDIENTS

CREAMY REFRIED BEANS:

1 (30-ounce) can refried beans

¼ cup Crisco shortening

⅔ cup milk

1½ cups shredded Mexican blend or Colby Jack cheese

TOSTADAS:

½–1 cup vegetable oil

12 (6-inch) corn tortillas

salt to taste

TOPPINGS: shredded cooked chicken, beef or pork; shredded cheese, sour cream, chopped tomatoes

Scan me!

INSTRUCTIONS

1. Combine beans, shortening and milk in a pot over medium heat. Stir vigorously with a wire whisk until silky smooth. Add cheese and let melt, then remove from the heat and set aside.

2. Heat ½ inch oil in a medium saucepan over medium-high heat. Fry tortillas one at a time for 30–60 seconds on each side, until golden. Place on a paper towel–lined plate and sprinkle with salt.

3. When ready to serve, top each tortilla with beans, then add any desired toppings.

👍 RECIPE TIPS

☺ **Make Ahead:** *We like to make our tostada shells fresh, but you can make them up to 24 hours in advance. Just store in a resealable plastic bag to keep them crunchy until serving time. You can also prepare the beans ahead of time as directed in Step 1 and store in an airtight container in the refrigerator for 3–4 days. Warm them up right before serving on the stove top or in the microwave, adding additional milk, if needed, to make them smooth again.*

☺ **Feed a Crowd:** *This is a great meal idea to serve for a crowd. Lay out all your favorite tostada toppings, fry some tortillas, and let everyone assemble their own tostadas.*

PAIRINGS: Guacamole (page 88), Spanish Rice (page 148), Pico de Gallo (page 152), Homemade Salsa (page 153), Sweet Pork (page 170)

PASTA AND PIZZA

"The trouble with eating Italian food is that five or six days later, you're hungry again." —George Miller

Each Tuesday we have Italian food. That's not only because it's simple but also because it's loved by the entire family—even the picky kids. From pasta to pizza, we have so many memories of gathering in the kitchen to make these recipes as a family. They're definitely favorites, and we think they'll be favorites of yours as well.

WHITE SAUCE PASTA

🕐 PREP TIME: 5 MINUTES

⧗ COOK TIME: 20 MINUTES

♡ SERVES: 6

✓ PREPPED IN 5

✓ QUICK & EASY

INGREDIENTS

1 (16-ounce) package penne (about 4 cups)

3 tablespoons unsalted butter

2 teaspoons minced garlic

3 tablespoons all-purpose flour

1 cup milk

1 cup chicken broth

1 cup grated Parmesan cheese

2 teaspoons dried parsley

garlic salt with parsley flakes (or salt) to taste

pepper to taste

½ cup shredded mozzarella cheese or additional
    Parmesan cheese (optional)

Scan me!

INSTRUCTIONS

1. Cook pasta according to package directions. Drain and set aside.

2. Meanwhile, in a large saucepan, melt butter over medium heat. Add garlic and cook, stirring, for 1 minute.

3. Add flour and cook, stirring constantly, for 1 minute more.

4. Add milk and broth and cook, stirring constantly, until the sauce boils and thickens, about 5 minutes.

5. Add Parmesan, parsley, garlic salt and pepper. Continue stirring until the cheese has melted.

6. Add pasta to the sauce and stir to combine. Add mozzarella and stir until melted. Serve warm.

PAIRINGS: Easy Garlic Knots (page 66), Brown Sugar–Glazed Carrots (page 136), Roasted Vegetables (page 140)

⚙ VARIATIONS

Try adding cubed grilled chicken, chicken sausage, diced ham or shrimp for protein, or adding vegetables like halved cherry tomatoes or steamed asparagus, broccoli, bell peppers or mushrooms. You can also change up the flavoring with spices and herbs such as red chili flakes (for heat), dried Italian seasoning and fresh basil or parsley.

CHICKEN TETRAZZINI

⏱ **PREP TIME:** 15 MINUTES
⧗ **COOK TIME:** 40 MINUTES
♡ **SERVES:** 8

✓ **FEED A CROWD**
✓ **MAKE AHEAD**

INGREDIENTS

1 (16-ounce) package linguine (or fettuccine or spaghetti)

4 chicken breasts, cooked and diced (or turkey)

2 (10.5-ounce) cans cream of chicken soup

2 cups sour cream

½ cup unsalted butter, softened

1 cup chicken broth

1 teaspoon garlic salt with parsley flakes

½ teaspoon pepper

2 cups shredded mozzarella cheese

2 tablespoons grated Parmesan cheese

Scan me!

INSTRUCTIONS

1. Preheat the oven to 350 degrees F. Grease a 9-x-13-inch baking dish and set aside.

2. Cook linguine according to package directions. Drain and set aside.

3. Meanwhile, in a large bowl, combine chicken, soup, sour cream, butter, chicken broth, garlic salt and pepper. Mix well, then stir in cooked noodles.

4. Pour into prepared baking dish.

5. Sprinkle both cheeses on top and bake for 36–42 minutes, until cheeses are melted and bubbling.

PAIRINGS: Fried Zucchini (page 98), Asparagus Bundles (page 135), Roasted Vegetables (page 140),

---

☝ **RECIPE TIPS**

☺ **Make Ahead:** *Prepare the recipe as instructed through Step 4, then cover tightly with aluminum foil or plastic wrap and place in the refrigerator for up to 24 hours. When ready to cook, add the cheeses and bake as directed.*

⚙ **VARIATIONS**

Feel free to add your favorite vegetables such as peas, corn, broccoli florets, mushrooms or asparagus in Step 3.

BEEF GOULASH

PREP TIME: 10 MINUTES

COOK TIME: 45 MINUTES

SERVES: 8

FEED A CROWD

MAKE AHEAD

SLOW COOKER

INGREDIENTS

2 pounds ground beef (80 percent lean/
    20 percent fat)

1 tablespoon minced garlic

3 cups water (or beef broth)

2 (15-ounce) cans tomato sauce

2 (14.5-ounce) cans diced tomatoes

3 tablespoons soy sauce

2 tablespoons Italian seasoning

1 teaspoon seasoned salt

3 bay leaves

2 cups elbow macaroni (or penne or shell pasta)

TOPPING: 1 cup shredded cheddar cheese
    (optional)

Scan me!

INSTRUCTIONS

1. In a large skillet over medium-high heat, sauté ground beef until cooked, 8–10 minutes, then drain off excess fat.

2. Add garlic and sauté for 2–3 minutes. Add water, tomato sauce, diced tomatoes, soy sauce, Italian seasoning, seasoned salt and bay leaves. Stir, cover and cook for 15–20 minutes.

3. Add macaroni to the skillet, stir well and cover. Simmer for 15–20 minutes. Turn off the heat, remove the bay leaves, and add cheese right before serving.

PAIRINGS: Easy Garlic Knots (page 66), Baked Potatoes (page 139), Roasted Vegetables (page 140), Twice-Baked Potatoes (page 144)

👍 RECIPE TIPS

☺ **Make Ahead:** *Simply follow the recipe directions, but do not add the cheese. Cover and store in the refrigerator for up to 24 hours until ready to serve. Reheat in a large saucepan, adding a bit of water if needed to thin out the sauce. Cook until heated through, then add cheese.*

☺ **Slow Cooker Directions:** *Sauté ground beef in a skillet until cooked. Drain excess fat, add garlic and sauté for 2 minutes. Transfer beef to the slow cooker along with all remaining ingredients except the cheese. Cook on high for about 3 hours or on low for 6–7 hours. Add cheese 20–30 minutes before serving.*

EASY LASAGNA

⏲ PREP TIME: 40 MINUTES

⧗ COOK TIME: 25 MINUTES

⧗ REST TIME: 5 MINUTES

♡ SERVES: 9

✓ **FREEZER FRIENDLY**

✓ **FEED A CROWD**

INGREDIENTS

1 tablespoon vegetable oil

3–4 teaspoons minced garlic

2 tablespoons fresh basil

salt and pepper to taste

6 cups tomato sauce

1 pound ground beef

1 pound ground pork

1 (16-ounce) container sour cream

2 cups low-fat cottage cheese

1 cup shredded Parmesan cheese

2 cups shredded mozzarella cheese, more if needed

1 package no-boil lasagna noodles

shredded Parmesan cheese, to taste

Scan me!

INSTRUCTIONS

1. Preheat oven to 350 degrees F.

2. In a large pan over medium heat, saute garlic in vegetable oil for 2–3 minutes. Stir in basil, salt, dash of pepper and tomato sauce. Reduce heat to low, cover and simmer for 10 minutes.

3. In another pan over medium heat, cook beef and pork until browned and no longer pink, about 10 minutes. Drain fat.

4. Add meat to the tomato sauce mixture, cover and simmer for an additional 10 minutes.

5. Combine sour cream, cottage cheese and shredded Parmesan cheese in a bowl. Mix well and set aside.

6. In a 9x13 pan, spread 1 cup of the tomato sauce on the bottom. Layer lasagna noodles over the sauce and then spread another cup of tomato sauce on top of the noodles.

7. Add 1 cup of shredded mozzarella cheese on top of the tomato sauce and then add half of the sour cream/cottage cheese mixture on top of the mozzarella cheese.

8. Add another layer of lasagna noodles, followed by a cup of tomato sauce, the last cup of shredded mozzarella and then the rest of the sour cream/cottage cheese mixture.

9. Then add one more layer of noodles and the remainder of the tomato sauce.

10. Add shredded Parmesan cheese to the top and bake for 25–30 minutes. Let set for 5–10 minutes before serving.

PAIRINGS: Easy Garlic Knots (page 66), Cheesy Garlic Bread (page 67), Fried Zucchini (page 98), Caesar Salad (page 106)

👍 **RECIPE TIPS**

☺ **Texture Tip:** *For the best texture, be sure to use the right ingredients. A few things can cause too much moisture in lasagna. If you use a thin tomato sauce or nonfat sour cream and cottage cheese, the added water content in your ingredients will cause the lasagna to be too soupy.*

ITALIAN SAUSAGE PASTA

⏱ PREP TIME: 5 MINUTES
⏳ COOK TIME: 15 MINUTES
♡ SERVES: 5

⊘ PREPPED IN 5
⊘ QUICK & EASY
⊘ ON THE TABLE IN 20

INGREDIENTS

1 (16-ounce) package bow tie pasta

1 pound mild Italian sausage

½ cup chopped onion (optional)

1½ teaspoons minced garlic

½ teaspoon crushed red pepper flakes (optional)

2 (14.5-ounce) cans Italian stewed tomatoes, drained and chopped

1½ cups heavy cream

½ teaspoon salt

¼ teaspoon dried basil

1 cup shredded Parmesan cheese, divided

Scan me!

INSTRUCTIONS

1. Cook pasta according to package directions. Drain and set aside.

2. Meanwhile, in a large skillet over medium heat, cook sausage, onion, garlic and pepper flakes, stirring for 4–5 minutes or until meat is no longer pink. Drain excess fat.

3. Stir in tomatoes, cream, salt, basil and ½ cup Parmesan and bring to a boil.

4. Reduce heat and simmer, uncovered and stirring occasionally, for 6–8 minutes or until thickened.

5. Add pasta to sausage mixture and toss.

6. Garnish with remaining ½ cup Parmesan before serving.

PAIRINGS: Fried Zucchini (page 98), Caesar Salad (page 106)

⚙ VARIATIONS

Swap out the mild Italian sausage for chicken sausage, turkey sausage or spicy sausage, or substitute mozzarella or a blend of provolone, fontina, Romano and Asiago cheeses for the Parmesan. You can also add vegetables such as zucchini, bell peppers, mushrooms or spinach in Step 3.

CHEESY PASTA BAKE

○ **PREP TIME:** 5 MINUTES

⏳ **COOK TIME:** 30 MINUTES

♡ **SERVES:** 8

INGREDIENTS

12 ounces penne (about 3 cups)

3 cups whole milk

4 tablespoons unsalted butter

⅓ cup all-purpose flour

1 pinch ground nutmeg

coarse salt and freshly ground black pepper to taste

½ cup heavy cream

1 cup shredded Parmesan cheese, divided

1 cup shredded Swiss cheese, divided

2 tablespoons grated Parmesan cheese

Scan me!

INSTRUCTIONS

1. Preheat oven to 400 degrees F. Butter a 9-x-13-inch baking dish and set aside.

2. Cook pasta according to package directions until al dente, or slightly underdone. Drain and set aside.

3. While pasta is cooking, heat milk in a small saucepan over low heat to warm, but do not let it simmer.

4. In a large saucepan, melt butter over medium heat. Add flour and stir for 1–2 minutes, until mixture is golden. Slowly whisk in warm milk. Add nutmeg, salt and pepper. Cook, whisking often, until thickened, about 10 minutes, then remove from the heat.

5. Add cream, ½ cup shredded Parmesan and ½ cup Swiss cheese. Stir until cheese is melted.

6. Combine pasta with cheese sauce and pour into the prepared pan. Top with remaining ½ cup shredded Parmesan, ½ cup Swiss cheese and the grated Parmesan. Cover with aluminum foil and bake for 10–15 minutes.

7. Remove foil and continue baking until cheese is golden brown, about 5 minutes.

8. Remove from the oven and let cool for at least 5–10 minutes before serving.

🔥 RECIPE TIPS

☺ **Make Ahead:** *Assemble the pasta, cover tightly with aluminum foil and refrigerate for up to 24 hours. Let it sit at room temperature for a few minutes before baking.*

⚙ VARIATIONS

Crumbled bacon, diced cooked chicken, chopped chicken sausage and vegetables such as chopped broccoli or bell peppers make great additions.

PAIRINGS: Easy Garlic Knots (page 66), Cheesy Garlic Bread (page 67), Bruschetta (page 94), Caesar Salad (page 106)

FETTUCCINE ALFREDO

INGREDIENTS

1 (16-ounce) package fettuccine

2 tablespoons unsalted butter

2 teaspoons minced garlic

1 pint heavy cream

1 cup grated Parmesan cheese, plus more for serving

½ teaspoon garlic pepper

salt to taste

Scan me!

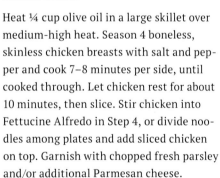

INSTRUCTIONS

1. Cook pasta according to package directions. Drain and set aside.

2. Meanwhile, heat butter in a large saucepan over medium-low heat to melt. Add minced garlic and sauté for 1–2 minutes.

3. Add cream and bring to a simmer. Add Parmesan and mix well. Cook, stirring, for 3–4 minutes, until the sauce begins to thicken.

4. Add cooked pasta to the sauce and toss to mix. Top with garlic pepper and salt, and sprinkle with more cheese if desired.

★ **BONUS RECIPE**

Chicken Alfredo

Heat ¼ cup olive oil in a large skillet over medium-high heat. Season 4 boneless, skinless chicken breasts with salt and pepper and cook 7–8 minutes per side, until cooked through. Let chicken rest for about 10 minutes, then slice. Stir chicken into Fettucine Alfredo in Step 4, or divide noodles among plates and add sliced chicken on top. Garnish with chopped fresh parsley and/or additional Parmesan cheese.

PAIRINGS: Easy Garlic Knots (page 66), Cheesy Garlic Bread (page 67), Fried Zucchini (page 98)

👍 **RECIPE TIPS**

☺ **Sauce Too Thin?** *Adding a bit more Parmesan cheese typically does the trick to thicken the sauce, but you can also add flour. To make it thicker and more cheesy, you can also add ½–1 cup shredded Parmesan or mozzarella cheese before serving.*

☺ **Sauce Too Thick?** *You can always add a little pasta cooking water or more heavy cream to thin the sauce.*

KID-FRIENDLY SPAGHETTI

◷ **PREP TIME:** 5 MINUTES

⧗ **COOK TIME:** 45 MINUTES

♡ **SERVES:** 8

> ⊘ **PREPPED IN 5**
>
> ⊘ **FEED A CROWD**

INGREDIENTS

1 pound ground beef (80 percent lean/20 percent fat)

2 cups hot water

2 cubes beef bouillon (or use 2 cups beef broth and omit hot water)

1 (8-ounce) can tomato sauce

1 (6-ounce) can tomato paste

2 teaspoons sugar

½ teaspoon dried basil

½ teaspoon dried oregano

Pinch of garlic powder

salt and pepper to taste (optional)

1 (16-ounce) package spaghetti

TOPPING: grated Parmesan cheese, for serving (optional)

Scan me!

INSTRUCTIONS

1. Cook ground beef in a large pan over medium heat, breaking into small pieces, until browned, 8–10 minutes. Drain excess fat.

2. Dissolve bouillon cubes in hot water and add to meat. Add tomato sauce, tomato paste, sugar, basil, oregano, garlic powder, salt and pepper. Simmer on low for 30 minutes.

3. A few minutes before sauce is done, cook spaghetti noodles according to package directions.

4. Drain spaghetti and add to the sauce, tossing to coat. Top with Parmesan.

> ⟳ **RECIPE TIPS**
>
> ☺ **Make It Meatless:** *For a vegetarian version, skip the ground beef, and add a tablespoon of olive oil to the pan before adding the other ingredients. You can also make meatballs on the side if some people want the option to add meat!*
>
> ☺ **Low-Carb Version:** *Try using zucchini noodles, rice noodles or spaghetti squash in lieu of traditional spaghetti noodles.*

Spaghetti Bake

⭐ **BONUS RECIPE**

Turn this into a casserole: Follow the recipe to Step 2, adding an extra 8-ounce can of tomato sauce, but only simmer for 10 minutes. Add 1 cup sour cream and 1 cup shredded mozzarella cheese and stir to combine. Cook and drain spaghetti, add to sauce and mix well. Preheat oven to 350 degrees F. Pour spaghetti mixture into a greased 11-x-14-inch baking dish and sprinkle with 1 cup shredded mozzarella cheese. Cover with aluminum foil and bake for 25 minutes, then remove the foil and bake for 5–10 minutes more, until cheese is melted.

PAIRINGS: Easy Garlic Knots (page 66), Fried Zucchini (page 98), Homemade Meatballs (page 100), Lemonade (page 282)

BEEF STROGANOFF

PREP TIME: 10 MINUTES
COOK TIME: 20 MINUTES
SERVES: 8

QUICK & EASY
FEED A CROWD
SLOW COOKER

INGREDIENTS

2 tablespoons canola oil

1½ pounds chuck roast or sirloin steak, sliced into bite-sized strips (or ground beef)

¼ cup all-purpose flour

½ teaspoon salt, plus more to taste

½ teaspoon pepper, plus more to taste

2 cups full-sodium beef broth

1–2 tablespoons Worcestershire sauce

3 cups (12 ounces) medium egg noodles

1 cup sour cream

¼ cup heavy cream

1–2 teaspoons garlic salt

TOPPING: chopped fresh parsley, for garnish (optional)

Scan me!

INSTRUCTIONS

1. Heat oil in a large saucepan over medium-high heat. Toss meat with flour, salt and pepper and cook in hot oil for about 2 minutes per side.

2. Add broth and Worcestershire sauce and simmer for 15 minutes.

3. Meanwhile, cook egg noodles according to package directions. Drain and set aside.

4. Add sour cream, heavy cream and garlic salt to meat mixture and stir.

5. Add noodles and toss to coat, or serve meat over noodles. Add more salt and pepper to taste if needed.

6. Sprinkle with parsley and serve warm.

PAIRINGS: Easy Garlic Knots (page 66), Fried Zucchini (page 98), Asparagus Bundles (page 135)

👍 RECIPE TIPS

☺ **Slow Cooker Directions:** *Cook meat as directed in Step 1. Add to slow cooker with broth and Worcestershire sauce and cook on low for 3–4 hours, stirring occasionally. Add sour cream and heavy cream and stir. Cook egg noodles according to package directions. Drain noodles and toss into meat sauce, or divide noodles among plates and pour sauce over the top. Garnish with parsley.*

BAKED ZITI

⏱ PREP TIME: 10 MINUTES
⏳ COOK TIME: 45 MINUTES
♡ SERVES: 10

✓ QUICK & EASY
✓ FEED A CROWD
✓ MAKE AHEAD

INGREDIENTS

1 (16-ounce) package ziti
½ pound ground beef (80 percent lean/20 percent fat)
½ pound mild Italian sausage
1 ½–2 cups marinara sauce (we love Rao's)
1 (14.5-ounce) can diced tomatoes
4 ounces cream cheese, softened
½ cup sour cream
1 teaspoon garlic salt with parsley flakes
1 teaspoon Italian seasoning
8 ounces fresh mozzarella cheese, sliced
1 cup shredded mozzarella cheese
fresh basil, for garnish

Scan me!

INSTRUCTIONS

1. Preheat the oven to 375 degrees F. Grease a 9-x-13-inch baking dish and set aside.

2. Cook pasta to al dente according to package directions. Drain and set aside.

3. Meanwhile, cook ground beef and Italian sausage in a large saucepan over medium heat, stirring and breaking up into small pieces, until no longer pink, 7–10 minutes. Drain fat and set saucepan aside.

4. In a large pot over medium heat, combine marinara sauce, tomatoes, cream cheese and sour cream and cook, stirring often, until well blended and cream cheese is melted.

5. Add cooked pasta and sauce to the saucepan with ground beef and mix well. Add garlic salt and Italian seasoning.

6. Pour into the prepared pan. Top with fresh mozzarella and shredded mozzarella.

7. Bake for 20 minutes, uncovered.

8. Let rest for at least 5 minutes before serving. Garnish with fresh basil.

👍 RECIPE TIPS

☺ **Make Ahead:** *Prepare as directed through Step 6, but do not add the cheeses. Cover and store in the refrigerator for up to 2 days before adding the cheese and baking.*

⚙ VARIATIONS

You can use all ground beef or all sausage instead of a combination of meat for the sauce, or even substitute the beef for ground turkey or chicken. And while this is called Baked Ziti, you can easily change the pasta to shells, wagon wheels, penne, bow ties or any other similar-sized pasta. Whatever shape you use, be sure to undercook it because it will finish cooking when it is baked in the oven.

PAIRINGS: Easy Garlic Knots (page 66), Cheesy Garlic Bread (page 67), Fried Zucchini (page 98), Roasted Vegetables (page 140)

PIZZA

- PREP TIME: 20 MINUTES
- RISE TIME: 30 MINUTES
- COOK TIME: 15 MINUTES
- SERVES: 8

- ✓ QUICK & EASY
- ✓ FREEZER FRIENDLY
- ✓ FEED A CROWD
- ✓ MAKE AHEAD

INGREDIENTS

PIZZA DOUGH:

3 cups warm water (110–115 degrees F)

3 tablespoons rapid rise yeast

2 tablespoons sugar

1 tablespoon salt

6 tablespoons vegetable oil

6–6½ cups all-purpose flour

1 tablespoon cornmeal

olive oil, for brushing

PIZZA TOPPINGS:

2 cups pizza sauce

6–8 cups shredded mozzarella cheese

2 teaspoons pizza seasoning (optional)

2 cups pepperoni (mix of regular and mini)

ADDITIONAL TOPPINGS: sausage crumbles, chopped peppers, chopped bacon (optional)

Scan me!

INSTRUCTIONS

1. Preheat the oven to 450 degrees F. Place a pizza stone or baking sheet in the oven to preheat as well.

2. In a large bowl, combine water, yeast and sugar and let sit for 5 minutes, or until bubbly.

3. Add salt and oil, then mix in flour 1 cup at a time with a wooden spoon until combined and dough is soft and slightly sticky. Knead for about 3 minutes (dough will be sticky and will stick to your hands).

4. Cover dough with a tea towel and let rise at room temperature for 30–45 minutes.

5. This dough makes four 12-inch pizza crusts. Divide dough into four pieces and roll each out on a floured surface to about ½ inch thick.

6. Sprinkle cornmeal onto a pizza peel and, working with one crust at a time, transfer rolled-out dough to the peel. Brush with olive oil and poke with a fork a few times to eliminate bubbling while baking.

7. At this point, there are a few different ways to cook the dough. The first is our favorite if you have a pizza stone:

   a. Use the peel to transfer crust to the preheated pizza stone and blind bake for 6–8 minutes. Remove from the oven, add sauce, cheese, pizza seasoning, pepperoni and any other desired toppings, and bake for 8–10 more minutes.

   b. If you don't have a pizza stone, use peel to transfer crust to the preheated baking sheet and blind bake for 6–8 minutes. Remove from the oven, add toppings and bake for 8–10 more minutes.

   c. To skip blind baking: While the dough is still on the peel, add sauce, cheese, pizza seasoning and other toppings. Transfer pizza to the preheated pizza stone or baking sheet and bake for 10–12 minutes.

8. Repeat with the remaining crusts and toppings.

★ **BONUS RECIPE**

White Pizza Sauce

Combine 1 cup heavy cream, ½ cup unsalted butter and 2 tablespoons cream cheese in a medium pot over medium heat. Mix and simmer for about 5 minutes, or until melted. Stir in ⅓ cup shredded Parmesan cheese and ½ teaspoon garlic powder. Reduce the heat to low and simmer for 15–20 minutes. Spread over your favorite dough and add toppings as desired, like shredded chicken and chopped spinach.

☺ **RECIPE TIPS**

☺ **Make Ahead:** *You can blind bake the pizza crusts and freeze them plain to be topped and baked later. Blind bake the plain crusts for 6–8 minutes as directed above. Let cool, then wrap in plastic wrap and then in aluminum foil. Freeze for up to 4 months. Thaw for 30 minutes before adding toppings and baking.*

PAIRINGS: Easy Garlic Knots (page 66), Cheesy Garlic Bread (page 67), Pizza Dip (page 91), Buffalo Wings (page 96)

DESSERTS

"Life is short. Eat dessert first." —Jacques Torres

If we had to pick which category in this cookbook is our favorite, it's probably no surprise that desserts would win. Our family and neighbors can definitely attest to the fact that we love baking yummy treats! In fact, we love desserts so much that almost weekly the kids have dessert-making competitions. We love that nothing brings a smile to someone's face like a plate of warm cookies, or some delicious bars or even an amazing cake. Here you will find some classic desserts done the right way, as well as some new desserts that will soon become your favorites. We dare you to try them all!

HELPFUL TIPS + INFORMATION

Ingredients and Equipment

PLAN AHEAD: Always use room-temperature ingredients. This is especially important when "room temperature" is specified in the recipe, such as for butter or milk.

FLOUR TYPES: Some dessert recipes specify using cake flour, but often it's a matter of preference. Cake flour will give a lighter, more airy cake, whereas all-purpose flour and bread flour have a higher gluten content and are designed to be a bit chewier and denser in comparison. If you are okay with this textural trade-off, in most recipes the flours can be swapped out in a one-to-one ratio.

POPCORN MATH: How many cups are in one bag of popcorn? One 3.2-ounce bag of microwave popcorn contains 5 tablespoons of unpopped kernels, which equals about 11 cups of popped corn. For the recipes in this chapter that call for popping one bag of plain microwave popcorn, you can also buy 11 cups of plain prepopped popcorn or pop 5 tablespoons of your own kernels.

COOKING CANDY: A candy thermometer makes candy making so much easier, but it is possible to make candy without a thermometer. For recipes that call for cooking candy to the "hardcrack" stage, once the syrup starts boiling, take a spoon and drop a little bit of the syrup into a bowl of really cold water. Take the syrup out of the cold water and test it: If it forms hard, brittle threads that break without bending at all, it has reached the hard-crack stage and is done. If the syrup is squishy or bends before breaking, it still needs to cook a little longer.

MELTING CHOCOLATE: We typically melt chocolate in a small pot over low heat. The key is to stir constantly with a rubber spatula until the chocolate is melted and smooth. You can also melt chocolate in the microwave: Place it in a glass bowl (or other microwave-safe bowl) and heat for 30 seconds on high power. Remove and stir. Continue to microwave in 15-second blasts, stirring between each one, until all the chocolate is melted.

Frosting Tips

⊘ For smooth frosting, always sift your powdered sugar. Sifting eliminates lumps and creates frosting as smooth as butter.

⊘ If you find that your frosting is too stiff, add a bit of milk or cream, a teaspoon at a time. If it's thin, add in powdered sugar ¼ cup at a time until you get the right consistency.

Tips for Brownies and Bars

⊘ Metal pans will cook brownie batter more quickly than ceramic or glass dishes will, so you may need to adjust the baking time slightly. You can check for doneness by inserting a toothpick into the center of the brownies. If it comes out clean, then they're done.

⊘ For a clean cut, skip the chef's knife: Allow brownies or bars to cool a little, then use a plastic knife to cut them. Works like a charm!

Cookie Tips

⊘ To make perfect-looking drop cookies, roll the dough into balls, place on the baking sheet and bake. Right after taking the cookies out of the oven, round out each cookie with the back of a metal spatula and top with extra chips or other toppings, depending on the recipe.

⊘ Our favorite chocolate chips are the Guittard brand. They are extremely high quality and, in our opinion, have the best flavor.

⊘ If you want your cookies to stay soft longer, try adding a piece of bread to your storage container or resealable plastic bag. The bread will help to absorb the air and will keep the cookies nice and moist.

CAKES AND CUPCAKES

"How do we like our eggs? Ummm, in a cake."

What makes a party more fun than a delicious cake or some beautiful cupcakes? What we love about these recipes is how versatile they can be to feed a small group, or a large crowd. We have used all these recipes time and time again at family gatherings or birthday parties. We guarantee each and every one will make whatever special event you are a part of more tasty and enjoyable!

JELL-O POKE CAKE

⏱ **PREP TIME:** 10 MINUTES
⏳ **COOK TIME:** 25 MINUTES
⏳ **COOL TIME:** 15 MINUTES
⏳ **CHILL TIME:** 3 HOURS
♡ **SERVES:** 15

✓ **FEED A CROWD**
✓ **MAKE AHEAD**

INGREDIENTS

1 (15.25-ounce) box white cake mix, plus any ingredients listed on box

1 (3-ounce) box strawberry Jell-O (or raspberry or cherry)

1 cup boiling water

1 cup cold water

1 (8-ounce) tub whipped topping (or 2 cups Homemade Whipped Cream, see below)

INSTRUCTIONS

1. Prepare cake as directed on the box and bake in a 9-x-13-inch baking dish. Let cool for 15 minutes.

2. Poke cake with a fork at ½–1-inch intervals.

3. Use hot and cold water to make Jell-O as directed on the package.

4. Spoon Jell-O liquid over the cake gradually until it is all absorbed.

5. Chill in the refrigerator for 3–4 hours. Top with whipped topping right before serving.

Scan me!

★ **BONUS RECIPE**

Homemade Whipped Cream

Place your mixing bowl and whisk attachment (or beaters if mixing with a hand mixer) in the freezer for about 10 minutes to chill. Once chilled, remove from the freezer and combine 2 cups heavy cream, ¼ cup powdered sugar and 2 teaspoons vanilla extract in your bowl. Start mixing on low speed, then increase to medium-high and mix until soft peaks form.

👍 **RECIPE TIPS**

☺ **Make Ahead:** *Because of the Jell-O, this cake needs to be refrigerated. It can be made and stored in the refrigerator up to 3 days. Just make sure to keep it tightly covered.*

☺ **Cupcake Version:** *Instead of making a 9-x-13-inch cake, make cupcakes according to the directions on the cake mix box. Once cupcakes have cooled, poke them with a fork or skewer, drizzle Jell-O into the holes and chill as directed above before adding whipped topping.*

ALSO TRY: Cream Puff Cake (page 209), Dirt Cake (page 210), Angel Food Ice Cream Cake (page 216), Lemon Lasagna (page 228)

CREAM PUFF CAKE

✓ **FEED A CROWD**

✓ **MAKE AHEAD**

INGREDIENTS

½ cup unsalted butter

1 cup water

1 cup all-purpose flour

4 eggs

1 (8-ounce) package cream cheese, softened

2 (3.4-ounce) boxes instant vanilla pudding

3 cups milk

1 (8-ounce) tub whipped topping (or 2 cups whipped cream)

TOPPINGS: chocolate syrup or white chocolate curls

Scan me!

INSTRUCTIONS

1. Preheat the oven to 400 degrees F.

2. Combine butter and water in a large pot and bring to a boil over high heat.

3. Reduce the heat to low, add flour and stir until mixture forms a ball. Remove from the heat.

4. Cool dough slightly, then beat in eggs *one at a time*, mixing between each addition. After adding the last egg, the dough will come together and will be smooth. Spread into a greased 9-x-13-inch baking dish.

5. Bake for 30 minutes, then cool completely. (NOTE: The dough should rise up the sides of the dish during baking.)

6. In a large bowl, beat the cream cheese until smooth.

7. In a separate bowl, whisk pudding mix and milk together until smooth. Add whipped cream cheese and beat until combined and smooth. Pour into the crust.

8. Spread whipped cream on top of pudding and refrigerate for at least 1 hour before serving.

9. Serve drizzled with chocolate syrup or topped with white chocolate curls.

ALSO TRY: Jell-O Poke Cake (page 208), Dirt Cake (page 210), Chocolate Fudge Sauce (page 270)

🖑 **RECIPE TIPS**

☺ **Make Ahead:** *This cake's components can be made 24 hours in advance and stored separately. Make the crust, and once cool, cover tightly with plastic wrap (while still in the pan) and store on the counter. Make filling and store in an airtight container in the refrigerator. When ready to assemble, add filling to the crust and top with whipped cream.*

DIRT CAKE

🕐 PREP TIME: 10 MINUTES
⏳ CHILL TIME: 3 HOURS
♡ SERVES: 12

✓ FEED A CROWD

✓ MAKE AHEAD

INGREDIENTS

1 (14.3-ounce) package Oreos

1 (8-ounce) package cream cheese, softened

½ cup unsalted butter, softened

1 cup powdered sugar

1 (16-ounce) tub whipped topping (or 4 cups Homemade Whipped Cream, page 208)

2 (3.4-ounce) boxes instant white chocolate or vanilla pudding

3 cups milk

1 teaspoon vanilla extract

Scan me!

INSTRUCTIONS

1. Crush all the Oreos in a large resealable plastic bag or in the food processor until they are crumbs. Press two-thirds of crushed cookies into the bottom of a 9-x-13-inch baking dish and set aside. Reserve the remaining crushed Oreos.

2. In a large bowl, beat cream cheese and butter together with a hand mixer until smooth. Mix in powdered sugar. Fold in whipped topping until well combined and set aside.

3. In a separate bowl, mix pudding, milk and vanilla. Let sit until thickened. Fold this mixture into the cream cheese mixture.

4. Carefully pour pudding/cream cheese mixture over the crumb crust in the pan.

5. Sprinkle with the reserved crushed Oreos. Refrigerate for 3–4 hours before serving.

👍 RECIPE TIPS

☺ **Make Ahead:** *Crush the Oreos as directed and keep them in a closed resealable plastic bag. Make the filling as directed and place in a large airtight container in the refrigerator for up to 24 hours. When ready to serve, assemble as directed above.*

☺ **Make It Look Like Dirt:** *Use chocolate pudding instead of white chocolate pudding. Once assembled, add some candy bugs and gummy worms to the top. You can also make this in individual cups: Add a scoop of crumbs to each cup, pipe in some filling, and top with more crumbs before adding the worms, dangling over the edges.*

★ BONUS RECIPE

Cheesecake Fruit Salad

We use the filling from this Dirt Cake for several other recipes, including our Cheesecake Fruit Salad. Make the cream mixture as described above, but halve the recipe: Beat 4 ounces softened cream cheese and 4 tablespoons softened unsalted butter together, mix in ½ cup powdered sugar and fold in 1 (8-ounce) tub whipped topping or 2 cups Homemade Whipped Cream (page 208). In a separate bowl mix 1 (3.4-ounce) box instant pudding, 1½ cups milk and ½ teaspoon vanilla extract, and fold into the cream cheese mixture. Then fold in 1 cup blueberries, 1 cup blackberries and 1 cup halved strawberries. Refrigerate for at least 1 hour before serving. This is great on its own or served in Swedish Pancakes (page 41) or crepes.

ALSO TRY: Jell-O Poke Cake (page 208), Cream Puff Cake (page 209), Lemon Lasagna (page 228), Fruit Pizza (page 229)

CHOCOLATE SHEET CAKE

PREP TIME: **15 MINUTES**

COOK TIME: **20 MINUTES**

SERVES: **24**

QUICK & EASY

FEED A CROWD

MAKE AHEAD

INGREDIENTS

CAKE:

2 cups all-purpose flour

2 cups sugar

½ cup unsweetened cocoa powder

1 tablespoon baking soda

1 teaspoon salt

2 eggs

1 cup buttermilk

1 cup hot water

⅔ cup vegetable oil

FROSTING:

½ cup unsalted butter

2 tablespoons unsweetened cocoa powder

5 tablespoons milk

1 teaspoon vanilla extract

3½ cups powdered sugar, sifted

TOPPING: sprinkles (optional)

Scan me!

INSTRUCTIONS

1. Preheat the oven to 350 degrees F.

2. To make the cake, mix flour, sugar, cocoa powder, baking soda and salt in a large bowl.

3. Add eggs, buttermilk, hot water and oil and beat together with a hand mixer until combined and smooth (it should be runny). Pour into a greased 11-x-15-inch baking dish.

4. Bake for 20 minutes, or until a toothpick inserted in the middle comes out clean.

5. To make the frosting, melt butter in a medium pot over low heat. Add cocoa powder, milk and vanilla and whisk until smooth. Add powdered sugar and whisk until smooth.

6. Remove from the heat and pour over the warm cake. Spread frosting quickly and add sprinkles right away, since frosting sets up fast.

ALSO TRY: White Sheet Cake (page 212), Brownies (page 220), Homemade Ice Cream (page 265)

🔥 RECIPE TIPS

☺ **Make Ahead:** *Make the cake as instructed, but do not add frosting. Once cool, cover with plastic wrap and store on the counter for up to 24 hours. When ready to serve, make frosting and add it to the cake.*

☺ **Feed a Crowd:** *This cake makes a lot, so it has become a staple for get-togethers and birthday parties in our house. We change out the sprinkles based on the occasion and usually serve it with different kinds of ice cream. If you like chopped pecans, you can add those too by mixing them into the frosting before spreading it onto the cake.*

WHITE SHEET CAKE

⏱ PREP TIME: 10 MINUTES

⧗ COOK TIME: 20 MINUTES

♡ SERVES: 24

✓ QUICK & EASY

✓ FEED A CROWD

✓ MAKE AHEAD

INGREDIENTS

CAKE:

1 cup unsalted butter

1 cup water

2 cups all-purpose flour

2 cups sugar

1 teaspoon baking soda

1 teaspoon salt

2 eggs, beaten

½ cup sour cream

½ teaspoon almond extract

FROSTING:

½ cup unsalted butter

⅓ cup milk

4½ cups powdered sugar, sifted

½ teaspoon almond extract

½ cup chopped walnuts (optional)

TOPPING: sprinkles (optional)

Scan me!

INSTRUCTIONS

1. Preheat the oven to 375 degrees F. Grease an 11-x-15-inch baking pan.

2. Combine butter and water in a large pot over medium-high heat and bring to a boil.

3. Remove from the heat and whisk in flour, sugar, baking soda, salt, eggs, sour cream and almond extract until smooth.

4. Pour into the prepared pan. Bake for 18–22 minutes, or until a toothpick inserted in the center comes out clean.

5. While cake is cooling, make frosting: Combine butter and milk in a medium pot over medium-high heat and bring to a boil. Remove from the heat and add powdered sugar and almond extract. Beat at medium speed with a hand mixer until it is a spreadable consistency.

6. Stir in walnuts. Spread frosting on top of cake and add sprinkles.

ALSO TRY: Chocolate Sheet Cake (page 211), Brownies (page 220), Blondies (page 221), M&M Chocolate Oat Bars (page 222), 7-Layer Bars (page 225)

👍 **RECIPE TIPS**

☺ **Make Ahead:** *Make the cake as instructed, but do not add frosting. Once cool, cover with plastic wrap and store on the counter for up to 24 hours. When ready to serve, make frosting and add it to the cake.*

☺ **Additional Toppings:** *This cake can also be topped with toasted coconut, sprinkles or any other variety of chopped nuts you like (we prefer chopped pecans).*

PINEAPPLE UPSIDE-DOWN CAKE

INGREDIENTS

1 cup unsalted butter, divided

1½ cups packed light brown sugar, divided

1 (20-ounce) can pineapple rings in juice

10 maraschino cherries

2 cups all-purpose flour

2 teaspoons baking powder

1 teaspoon salt

½ cup granulated sugar

2 eggs

½ cup milk

1 teaspoon almond extract

Scan me!

ALSO TRY: Lemon Bars (page 226), Banana Bars (page 227), Peach Cobbler (page 230), Homemade Ice Cream (page 265)

INSTRUCTIONS

1. Preheat the oven to 350 degrees F. Grease a 9-x-13-inch baking dish.

2. Melt ½ cup butter in a medium pot over medium heat. Set remaining ½ cup butter aside to soften.

3. Stir 1 cup brown sugar into butter in the pot and bring to a boil, stirring frequently. Continue boiling for 1 minute, then pour into the prepared pan.

4. Drain pineapple rings, reserving ½ cup of the juice, and place rings into the bottom of the pan. Place a cherry in the middle of each ring. Set aside.

5. In a medium bowl, whisk together flour, baking powder and salt. Set aside.

6. In another medium bowl, beat softened ½ cup butter, granulated sugar and remaining ½ cup brown sugar with a hand mixer until well combined. Add eggs and blend well.

7. Add flour mixture to wet mixture and beat until well combined.

8. While still mixing, add milk, ½ cup reserved pineapple juice and almond extract.

9. Carefully spread batter over pineapple slices.

10. Bake for 35–40 minutes, or until the middle is cooked through and a toothpick inserted in the center comes out clean. Let cool for at least 30 minutes.

11. Slide a sharp paring knife or a rubber spatula around the inner perimeter of the pan. Invert a serving platter larger than the cake over the top of the pan. Place one hand on the platter and one hand on the bottom of the pan, then flip. Allow the cake to sit for another few minutes with the pan still covering it, then carefully remove the pan and serve!

⏱ **RECIPE TIPS**

☺ **Make Ahead:** *This cake can be made ahead of time and stored, covered, at room temperature for 1–2 days or in the refrigerator for up to 3 days.*

EASY CHOCOLATE CAKE

⏱ PREP TIME: 10 MINUTES

⏳ COOK TIME: 30 MINUTES

⏳ COOL TIME: 30 MINUTES

♡ SERVES: 12

✓ FEED A CROWD

✓ MAKE AHEAD

INGREDIENTS

CAKE:

2 cups all-purpose flour

2 cups sugar

¾ cup unsweetened cocoa powder

2 teaspoons baking powder

1½ teaspoons baking soda

1 teaspoon salt

1 cup milk

2 eggs

½ cup vegetable oil

2 teaspoons vanilla extract

1 cup boiling water

CHOCOLATE BUTTERCREAM FROSTING:

4 cups powdered sugar, sifted

½ cup unsweetened cocoa powder

½ cup unsalted butter, softened

⅓–½ cup half-and-half

1 teaspoon vanilla extract

1 pinch salt

TOPPING: sprinkles (optional)

Scan me!

INSTRUCTIONS

1. Preheat the oven to 350 degrees F.

2. Line two 9-inch round pans with parchment paper and spray with nonstick spray.

3. In a large bowl, whisk flour, sugar, cocoa, baking powder, baking soda and salt together.

4. Whisk in milk, eggs, oil and vanilla until smooth. Stir in boiling water, mixing until smooth.

5. Divide batter evenly between the two pans. Bake for 30–35 minutes, or until a toothpick inserted in the center comes out clean.

6. Cool for 10 minutes in the pans, then invert cakes onto cooling racks. Let cool completely.

7. While cakes are cooling, make the frosting. In a medium bowl, combine powdered sugar, cocoa powder, butter, half-and-half, vanilla and salt, starting with a smaller amount of half-and-half. Beat together until smooth, adding enough additional half-and-half to get a spreadable consistency.

8. Place one cake layer on a cake stand or serving tray and spread about a cup of frosting on top. Place second cake layer on top, then frost sides and top of the cake. Add sprinkles. Serve immediately or cover and let sit overnight.

ALSO TRY: White Sheet Cake (page 212), Brownies (page 220), Homemade Ice Cream (page 265), Chocolate Fudge Sauce (page 270)

⚙ VARIATIONS

The best way to change this up is by changing the frosting: Vanilla Buttercream Frosting (page 215) or a fruity frosting like orange, raspberry or strawberry would be great!

★ BONUS RECIPE

Chocolate Cupcakes

Prepare cake batter as described above, but spoon batter into muffin tins, filling two-thirds full, and bake at 350 degrees F for 17–19 minutes, or until a toothpick inserted in the center comes out clean. Makes 24–30 cupcakes. Frost once cooled.

VANILLA CUPCAKES

⏱ **PREP TIME:** 15 MINUTES
⏳ **COOK TIME:** 20 MINUTES
♡ **SERVES:** 16

✓ FEED A CROWD
✓ MAKE AHEAD

INGREDIENTS

VANILLA CAKE:

1⅔ cups all-purpose flour

1 cup sugar

1½ teaspoons baking powder

¼ teaspoon baking soda

¼ teaspoon salt

¾ cup unsalted butter, melted

3 egg whites, room temperature

½ cup sour cream, room temperature

½ cup whole milk, room temperature

1 tablespoon vanilla extract

VANILLA BUTTERCREAM FROSTING:

1 cup unsalted butter, softened

3 cups powdered sugar

1 teaspoon vanilla extract

pinch salt

2–3 tablespoons milk or half-and-half

TOPPING: sprinkles (optional)

Scan me!

INSTRUCTIONS

1. Preheat the oven to 350 degrees F.

2. Line a 12-cup muffin tin with paper liners and set aside.

3. Whisk together flour, sugar, baking powder, baking soda and salt in a large bowl.

4. In a medium bowl, mix butter, egg whites, sour cream, milk and vanilla with a hand mixer. Pour wet ingredients into dry ingredients and mix until just combined, but do not overmix.

5. Scoop the batter into the prepared muffin tin, filling the cups two-thirds full.

6. Bake for 18–20 minutes, until the tops spring back when touched lightly. Remove from the oven and cool completely.

7. While cupcakes cool, make the frosting: Beat butter with a hand mixer on low speed until light and fluffy. Add powdered sugar, vanilla, salt and 1 tablespoon milk and mix. Add additional milk as needed to make a smooth frosting. Increase the speed to high and beat 3–5 minutes, until light and fluffy. Pipe onto the cooled cupcakes and decorate with sprinkles.

👍 **RECIPE TIPS**

☺ **Make Ahead:** *You can make both the cupcakes and frosting up to a day ahead of time, but wait to add the frosting to the cupcakes until just before serving. Store cupcakes in an airtight container on the counter. The frosting can be stored in a container in the refrigerator.*

☺ **Make It a Cake:** *Bake in a 9-x-13-inch baking dish for a thinner cake or in a 7-x-11-inch baking dish for a thicker cake. Bake at 350 degrees F for about 30 minutes for the thinner cake and about 40 minutes for the thicker cake, or until a toothpick inserted into the center comes out clean.*

⚙ **VARIATIONS**

This vanilla base is easy to change up with a variety of add-ins!

→ **FUNFETTI CUPCAKES:** Fold rainbow sprinkles into the batter before baking.

→ **CHOCOLATE CHIP CUPCAKES:** Fold mini chocolate chips into the batter before baking.

→ **HOLIDAY CUPCAKES:** Fold holiday sprinkles into the batter before baking.

ALSO TRY: Chocolate Sheet Cake (page 211), White Sheet Cake (page 212), Chocolate Buttercream Frosting (page 214)

ANGEL FOOD ICE CREAM CAKE

⏱ PREP TIME: **45 MINUTES**

⏳ COOK TIME: **30 MINUTES**

⏳ FREEZE TIME: **8 HOURS**

♡ SERVES: **16**

✓ FREEZER FRIENDLY

✓ FEED A CROWD

✓ MAKE AHEAD

INGREDIENTS

1 (16-ounce) box angel food cake mix, plus any ingredients listed on box

4 quarts ice cream (ideally 2–3 different flavors)

TOPPINGS: sprinkles, candies, crushed cookies or chocolates (optional)

Scan me!

INSTRUCTIONS

1. Make angel food cake as directed on the box and let cool completely.

2. While cake is cooling, remove ice cream tubs from the freezer to soften just enough to be able to spread.

3. Remove cake from the pan and tear it into small pieces.

4. To layer the cake: Spread about one-third of the softened ice cream in the bottom of an angel food cake pan, then add half the cake pieces from one of the bowls. Repeat layering, adding another layer of ice cream followed by the remaining half of the cake, and then finish with a final layer of ice cream. Freeze overnight.

5. To remove the cake from the pan, fill a large bowl with hot water and dip the bottom of the pan into the hot water for a few seconds. Place a plate on the top of the pan, then flip it over. The cake should slide right out onto the plate. The outer layer of the cake will be a little melted. Add any desired toppings at this point, then place cake back into the freezer to firm it up.

6. Freeze for at least 2 hours before cutting and serving.

👍 RECIPE TIPS

☺ **Keeping It Cold:** *If you are hoping to transport this cake to serve at an outdoor party, we suggest buying a block of dry ice. Store the cake with the dry ice in a cooler. Be sure to give the cake enough time to thaw a bit before serving.*

☺ **Ice Cream Flavors:** *We love to change the flavors up for this cake. Here are some of our favorite ice cream combos:*

Cookies and Cream + Cookie Dough

Lemon + Strawberry

Mint Chocolate Chip + Cookies and Cream

Birthday Cake + Cotton Candy (kids love this one!)

☺ **Make Ahead:** *After the ice cream cake has been assembled, put it in the freezer. Once frozen, wrap the entire frozen cake with plastic wrap, then again with aluminum foil. For best results use within 2 weeks.*

ALSO TRY: Cream Puff Cake (page 209), Dirt Cake (page 210), Homemade Ice Cream (page 265)

PUMPKIN DUMP CAKE

✓ PREPPED IN 5

✓ FEED A CROWD

INGREDIENTS

1 (29-ounce) can pumpkin puree

2 cups evaporated milk

4 large eggs

1 cup sugar

2 teaspoons ground cinnamon

1 teaspoon ground ginger

½ teaspoon ground cloves

1 (15.25-ounce) box yellow cake mix

1 cup chopped pecans

¾ cup cold unsalted butter

TOPPINGS: whipped cream or ice cream (optional)

Scan me!

INSTRUCTIONS

1. Preheat the oven to 350 degrees F. Grease and flour a 9-x-13-inch baking dish.

2. In a large bowl, mix pumpkin, milk, eggs, sugar, cinnamon, ginger and cloves. Pour into the prepared dish.

3. Sprinkle cake mix and chopped pecans on top.

4. Cut butter into thin slices and place all over the cake mix.

5. Bake for 1 hour and serve warm with whipped cream or ice cream.

ALSO TRY: Homemade Whipped Cream (page 208), Pumpkin Delight (page 234), Pecan Pie Bars (page 236), Homemade Ice Cream (page 265)

👍 RECIPE TIPS

☺ **Leftovers:** *We like to serve this warm, but if you have leftovers, cover and store in the refrigerator for 2–3 days. Reheat in the microwave at 30-second intervals until warm.*

☺ **No Yellow Cake Mix on Hand?** *You can use a pumpkin spice cake mix instead or make your own homemade mix. To make your own, whisk together 2¼ cups all-purpose flour, 1½ cups sugar, 3½ teaspoons baking powder, 1 teaspoon salt and 4 tablespoons unsalted butter. Use a pastry cutter to blend in the butter, and you've got a homemade yellow cake mix!*

PUMPKIN ROLL

⏱ **PREP TIME:** 20 MINUTES

⧖ **COOK TIME:** 15 MINUTES

⧗ **CHILL TIME:** 2 HOURS

♡ **SERVES:** 10

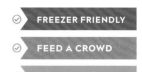

✓ FREEZER FRIENDLY

✓ FEED A CROWD

✓ MAKE AHEAD

INGREDIENTS

CAKE ROLL:

3 large eggs

1 cup granulated sugar

⅔ cup pumpkin puree

1 teaspoon lemon juice

¾ cup all-purpose flour

1 teaspoon baking powder

2 teaspoons ground cinnamon

1 teaspoon ground ginger

½ teaspoon ground nutmeg

½ teaspoon salt

powdered sugar, for sprinkling

FILLING:

1 cup powdered sugar

1 (8-ounce) package cream cheese, softened

4 tablespoons unsalted butter, softened

1 teaspoon vanilla extract

Scan me!

ALSO TRY: Pumpkin Dump Cake (page 217), Pumpkin Delight (page 234), Pumpkin Pie (page 235), Pecan Pie Bars (page 236)

INSTRUCTIONS

1. Preheat the oven to 375 degrees F. Line an 11-x-15-x-1-inch jelly roll pan with parchment paper and spray with nonstick spray.

2. In a large mixing bowl, beat eggs with a hand mixer for 5 minutes. Gradually beat in granulated sugar, then beat in pumpkin and lemon juice.

3. Whisk together flour, baking powder, cinnamon, ginger, nutmeg and salt in a small bowl, then add to the pumpkin mixture. Stir until well blended.

4. Pour batter into the prepared pan. Bake for 15 minutes, or until cake is completely set in the middle.

5. Sprinkle a flour sack–style dish towel generously with powdered sugar, and invert the hot cake onto the towel. Loosely roll up the cake and towel from the short side and let cool completely.

6. While cake is cooling, prepare the filling by beating all ingredients together with a hand mixer until smooth.

7. Unroll cake and spread filling to within ½ inch of the edges. Roll cake up again, without the towel this time, starting at the short side.

8. Wrap pumpkin roll in plastic wrap and place in the refrigerator. Chill for at least 2 hours to blend flavors.

9. To serve, unwrap the pumpkin roll and sprinkle with powdered sugar. Slice in 1-inch slices.

🔥 **RECIPE TIPS**

☺ **Make Ahead:** *The plastic-wrapped cake roll can be stored in the refrigerator for 1-2 days. You can also freeze the roll after wrapping in plastic; it will keep in the freezer for up to 2 months.*

☺ **Slicing:** *Cutting the roll from a frozen state makes for nice clean slices. Even if you aren't freezing it for longer-term storage, placing it in the freezer for 30-60 minutes will make it easier to slice. Place slices on a platter and allow to thaw before serving.*

BROWNIES, BARS AND PIES

"We must have pie. Stress cannot exist in the presence of pie." —David Mamet

If we ever find out that we have a large group to feed, and without much time to prep, our first instinct is to make one of these delicious bars or brownies. These recipes are all of the ones that we constantly get complimented on by family and friends (and it's a bonus that they are so easy). We also cannot forget about the pies in this book. Historically, pies have been very tricky for us, but after years of trying to find pies that are versatile and no-fail, we are happy to share these favorite pie recipes from our kitchen with you.

BROWNIES

⏲ PREP TIME: 10 MINUTES
⧗ COOK TIME: 25 MINUTES
⧗ COOL TIME: 10 MINUTES
♡ SERVES: 12

⊘ QUICK & EASY

⊘ FEED A CROWD

⊘ MAKE AHEAD

INGREDIENTS

1 cup unsalted butter, melted and cooled

2 tablespoons vegetable oil

1¼ cups granulated sugar

1 cup packed light brown sugar

4 eggs, room temperature

1 tablespoon vanilla extract

1 cup all-purpose flour

1 cup unsweetened cocoa powder

¾ teaspoon salt

½ teaspoon baking powder

1 cup chocolate chips (milk or semisweet), divided

TOPPINGS: sprinkles, toffee bits, crushed Oreos, crushed candies, chopped nuts (optional)

Scan me!

INSTRUCTIONS

1. Preheat the oven to 350 degrees F. Lightly grease a 9-x-11-inch baking dish and line with parchment paper and set aside.

2. In a medium bowl, combine melted butter, oil and both sugars and whisk well.

3. Add eggs and vanilla and mix for another 2 minutes.

4. In another bowl, sift together flour, cocoa, salt and baking powder.

5. Fold dry ingredients into wet ingredients and stir until just combined. Fold in ¾ cup chocolate chips.

6. Pour batter into the prepared baking dish and smooth out until even. Top with remaining ¼ cup chocolate chips and any other desired toppings and bake for 25–30 minutes, or until the middle no longer jiggles.

7. Let sit in the pan for 10–15 minutes, then remove from the pan and let cool completely before cutting.

👍 RECIPE TIPS

☺ **Make Ahead:** *Brownies will last 3–4 days in an airtight container at room temperature. They will last up to a week if stored in the refrigerator.*

☺ **Cutting Tip:** *Do you ever have trouble cutting your brownies into clean lines? Sometimes the brownies will tear or bunch up if you are trying to cut them with a regular knife. Try a plastic knife next time, and it will cut through the brownies like butter. So smooth, and way less mess!*

ALSO TRY: Blondies (page 221), Cookie Bars (page 223), Homemade Ice Cream (page 265), Chocolate Fudge Sauce (page 270)

BLONDIES

PREP TIME: 10 MINUTES
COOK TIME: 25 MINUTES
COOL TIME: 10 MINUTES
SERVES: 15

QUICK & EASY
FEED A CROWD
MAKE AHEAD

INGREDIENTS

1 cup unsalted butter, melted
1¼ cups packed light brown sugar
½ cup granulated sugar
2 large eggs plus 1 egg yolk, room temperature
2 teaspoons vanilla extract
2½ cups all-purpose flour
2 teaspoons cornstarch
1 teaspoon salt
½ teaspoon baking powder
⅔ cup white chocolate chips, plus more for topping
1 cup chopped walnuts (optional)

Scan me!

INSTRUCTIONS

1. Preheat the oven to 350 degrees F. Line a 9-x-13-inch baking dish with parchment paper and set aside.

2. In a large bowl, combine butter and both sugars. Use a wooden spoon to stir well.

3. Add eggs, egg yolk and vanilla. Mix well and set aside.

4. In a separate bowl, sift together flour, cornstarch, salt and baking powder. Slowly add to the butter mixture. Stir until just combined.

5. Fold in white chocolate chips and walnuts, then spread the batter evenly into the prepared pan.

6. Bake for 25–30 minutes, or until a toothpick comes out clean or with fudgy crumbs.

7. Remove from the oven and top with extra white chocolate chips, if desired. Let sit in the pan for 10–15 minutes, then remove from the pan and cool completely before cutting.

☝ RECIPE TIPS

☺ **Make Ahead:** *Blondies will last 3–4 days in an airtight container at room temperature. They will last up to a week if stored in the refrigerator.*

☺ **Cutting Tip:** *To make these easier to cut, line the pan with enough aluminum foil or parchment paper to overhang the pan on two sides so that it is easy to remove the whole blondie block. Once they have cooled, simply lift the entire block out of the pan and cut.*

ALSO TRY: Brownies (page 220), M&M Chocolate Oat Bars (page 222), 7-Layer Bars (page 225)

M&M CHOCOLATE OAT BARS

🕐 PREP TIME: 10 MINUTES

⏳ COOK TIME: 25 MINUTES

♡ SERVES: 15

✓ QUICK & EASY

✓ FEED A CROWD

✓ MAKE AHEAD

INGREDIENTS

1½ cups all-purpose flour

1½ cups quick-cooking rolled oats

1 cup packed light brown sugar

1 teaspoon salt

1 cup plus 2 tablespoons unsalted butter, softened, divided

1 (14-ounce) can sweetened condensed milk

1 (11.5-ounce) bag milk chocolate chips

1 cup plain M&M's

Scan me!

INSTRUCTIONS

1. Preheat the oven to 350 degrees F. Grease a 9-x-13-inch baking dish and set aside.

2. In a large bowl, mix flour, oats, brown sugar, salt and 1 cup butter with a spoon. Remove 1 cup of the mixture and set aside.

3. Press remaining mixture into the bottom of the prepared baking dish.

4. In a medium pot, combine condensed milk, chocolate chips and remaining 2 tablespoons butter over medium-low heat. Stir constantly until chips are melted and everything is mixed well.

5. Pour chocolate mixture over oat layer and spread evenly. Sprinkle reserved oat mixture over the chocolate.

6. Top with M&M's and bake for 25–30 minutes. Let cool completely in the pan before cutting.

ALSO TRY: Brownies (page 220), Blondies (page 221), 7-Layer Bars (page 225), Homemade Ice Cream (page 265)

👍 RECIPE TIPS

☺ **Make Ahead:** *These bars can be stored, covered tightly with plastic wrap, on the counter for up to 3 days. You can reheat in the microwave for about 15 seconds before serving, if desired.*

⚙ VARIATIONS

Easily change up these bars with different types of M&M's, such as white chocolate or peanut butter M&M's. This is not only a great way to change the flavor, but also to customize the bars for holidays by using the fun holiday-colored candies.

COOKIE BARS
(AKA PAN CHEWIES)

PREP TIME: 5 MINUTES
COOK TIME: 25 MINUTES
SERVES: 15

- PREPPED IN 5
- QUICK & EASY
- FEED A CROWD
- MAKE AHEAD

INGREDIENTS

2 cups packed light brown sugar

¾ cup unsalted butter, melted

2 eggs

2 teaspoons vanilla extract

2 cups all-purpose flour, sifted

1 teaspoon salt

1 teaspoon baking powder

¼ teaspoon baking soda

1½ cups chocolate chips (semisweet or milk)

Scan me!

INSTRUCTIONS

1. Preheat the oven to 350 degrees F. Grease a 9-x-13-inch glass baking dish and set aside.

2. In a medium bowl, combine brown sugar, butter, eggs and vanilla. Mix well with a wooden spoon.

3. Gradually add flour, salt, baking powder and baking soda. Stir until well combined and pour into the prepared baking dish.

4. Sprinkle with chocolate chips and bake for 24–28 minutes. Let cool completely in the pan before cutting.

ALSO TRY: Brownies (page 220), Blondies (page 221), M&M Chocolate Oat Bars (page 222)

🖒 RECIPE TIPS

☺ **Make Ahead:** *Covered tightly with aluminum foil or plastic wrap, these will keep on the counter for up to 3 days. To reheat, just place in the microwave for 15 seconds to make them gooey and warm.*

⚙ VARIATIONS

You can swap out the chocolate chips for a variety of other toppings to change up these bars. Here are some of our favorite combinations:

- White chocolate chips + butterscotch chips
- M&M's (we love to use the special M&M's for different holidays!)
- Chocolate chips + toffee bits or peanut butter chips

SUGAR COOKIE BARS

🕐 PREP TIME: 15 MINUTES

⏳ COOK TIME: 20 MINUTES

♡ SERVES: 15

✓ FEED A CROWD

✓ MAKE AHEAD

INGREDIENTS

BARS:

1¼ cups sugar

¾ cup unsalted butter, softened

1 (8-ounce) package cream cheese, softened

1 egg

1 tablespoon vanilla extract

1 teaspoon almond extract

1¾ cups all-purpose flour

1 teaspoon baking soda

1 teaspoon baking powder

FROSTING:

3½ cups powdered sugar

½ cup unsalted butter, softened

3–4 tablespoons milk

2 teaspoons vanilla extract

½ teaspoon almond extract

food coloring (optional)

TOPPING: sprinkles (optional)

Scan me!

INSTRUCTIONS

1. Preheat the oven to 350 degrees F. Grease a 9-x-13-inch baking dish and set aside.

2. Beat sugar, butter, cream cheese and egg together with a hand mixer in a medium bowl until well blended and a bit frothy, 2–3 minutes.

3. Add vanilla and almond extracts and mix well.

4. In a separate bowl, mix flour, baking soda and baking powder.

5. Add flour mixture to butter mixture and beat for a few minutes. Pour into a prepared pan and bake for 18–20 minutes. Let cool.

6. While the cake is cooling, make frosting by beating together powdered sugar, butter, milk, vanilla and almond extracts until well combined, starting with 3 tablespoons milk and adding more as needed to reach the desired texture. Add food coloring.

7. Spread over cooled cake and top with sprinkles.

ALSO TRY: Brownies (page 220), Blondies (page 221), Cookie Bars (page 223)

👍 **RECIPE TIPS**

☺ **Make Ahead:** *Make the bars as instructed, but do not frost. Store, covered tightly with plastic wrap, on the counter for 1 day or in the refrigerator for up to 3 days. Frost before serving. Frosting can also be made up to 24 hours ahead of time and stored, covered, in the refrigerator; it will need to be rewhipped before spreading on the bars.*

7-LAYER BARS

INGREDIENTS

1½ cups graham cracker crumbs

½ cup unsalted butter, melted

1 (14-ounce) can sweetened condensed milk

½ cup semisweet chocolate chips

½ cup milk chocolate chips

1 cup butterscotch chips

1 cup shredded coconut

1 cup chopped pecans

Scan me!

INSTRUCTIONS

1. Preheat the oven to 350 degrees F. Lightly grease a 9-x-13-inch baking dish with cooking spray and set aside.

2. In a medium bowl, combine graham cracker crumbs and butter. Pour into the prepared baking dish and press evenly over the bottom.

3. Pour sweetened condensed milk evenly over the graham cracker layer.

4. Sprinkle chocolate chips in an even layer, then do the same with butterscotch chips.

5. Next, sprinkle on coconut, and top it with a layer of chopped pecans.

6. Use a fork to firmly press down all the layers. Bake for 25 minutes.

7. Cool completely in the pan, then cut into squares, rectangles or diamonds for serving.

👍 **RECIPE TIPS**

☺ **Make Ahead:** *These can be made in advance and stored, covered tightly with plastic wrap, on the counter for up to 3 days. To reheat, just place in the microwave for about 15 seconds.*

⚙ **VARIATIONS**

You can swap out any of the topping ingredients or add additional layers to easily change up these bars! Try using chopped walnuts or sliced almonds instead of the pecans; substitute peanut butter chips for the butterscotch chips; or add a layer of crushed pretzels or mini marshmallows.

ALSO TRY: Brownies (page 220), Blondies (page 221), M&M Chocolate Oat Bars (page 222)

LEMON BARS

⊘ FEED A CROWD

⊘ MAKE AHEAD

INGREDIENTS

CRUST:

1 cup unsalted butter, room temperature

2 cups all-purpose flour

½ cup powdered sugar

½ teaspoon salt

LEMON LAYER:

4 eggs

5–6 tablespoons lemon juice

1¾ cups granulated sugar

⅓ cup all-purpose flour

TOPPING: powdered sugar

Scan me!

INSTRUCTIONS

1. Preheat the oven to 375 degrees F. Grease a 9-x-13-inch glass baking dish and set aside.

2. In a medium bowl, mix butter, flour, powdered sugar and salt with a pastry cutter or spatula. Pat mixture into the prepared dish.

3. Bake for 20 minutes. Make sure to not let it brown.

4. While crust is baking, blend eggs, lemon juice, granulated sugar and flour in a medium bowl with a hand mixer until frothy, about 30 seconds. Pour over warm crust.

5. Bake for an additional 22–24 minutes. Bars are done when the edges begin to turn golden brown and the middle is set and does not wobble.

6. Let cool completely in the pan. Sift powdered sugar over the top before cutting into squares.

👍 RECIPE TIPS

☺ **Make Ahead:** *These bars can be stored in an airtight container in the refrigerator for up to 7 days.*

☺ **Lemon Juice:** *Use freshly squeezed lemon juice. A medium-sized lemon will yield about 4 tablespoons of juice.*

ALSO TRY: Sugar Cookie Bars (page 224), Banana Bars (page 227), Lemon Lasagna (page 228), Fruit Pizza (page 229)

BANANA BARS

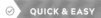

PREPPED IN 5

QUICK & EASY

FEED A CROWD

MAKE AHEAD

INGREDIENTS

BANANA CAKE:

1 cup unsalted butter, softened

1½ cups sugar

1 teaspoon baking soda

½ teaspoon salt

1½ cups mashed overripe bananas
(about 3 bananas)

2 eggs

1 cup sour cream

1 teaspoon vanilla extract

2 cups all-purpose flour

CREAM CHEESE FROSTING:

1 (8-ounce) package cream cheese, softened

½ cup unsalted butter, softened

2 cups powdered sugar

½ teaspoon vanilla extract

Scan me!

INSTRUCTIONS

1. Preheat the oven to 350 degrees F. Grease an 11-x-15-inch baking dish and set aside.

2. In a large mixing bowl, beat butter with a hand mixer for about 30 seconds. Add sugar, baking soda and salt and beat until combined. Add bananas, eggs, sour cream and vanilla and mix to combine. Add flour and mix to combine.

3. Pour into the prepared pan and spread evenly.

4. Bake for 25–30 minutes. Let cool in the pan.

5. While bars cool, make the frosting. In a medium bowl, beat cream cheese and butter with a hand mixer until smooth. Beat in powdered sugar and vanilla and mix until combined.

6. Spread frosting over cooled bars and cut into squares.

👍 RECIPE TIPS

☺ **Make Ahead:** *The bars and the frosting can be made in advance and stored separately. Cover both and place in the refrigerator for up to 24 hours. Wait to frost until ready to serve.*

☺ **Decorating:** *We like to decorate our bars with banana slices. Add them right before serving, since bananas will brown if put on too early. Other great toppings include chopped walnuts, caramel syrup, mini chocolate chips, chocolate shavings, sprinkles and berries.*

ALSO TRY: Blondies (page 221), Lemon Lasagna (page 228), Fruit Pizza (page 229)

LEMON LASAGNA

- PREP TIME: 10 MINUTES
- CHILL TIME: 1 HOUR
- SERVES: 16

⊘ **FEED A CROWD**

⊘ **MAKE AHEAD**

INGREDIENTS

CRUST:

1 (14.3-ounce) package Lemon Oreos (or Golden Oreos; about 36 cookies)

6 tablespoons unsalted butter, melted

FILLING:

1 cup powdered sugar

1 (8-ounce) package cream cheese, softened

½ cup unsalted butter, softened

1 (16-ounce) tub whipped topping (or Homemade Whipped Cream, page 208), divided

2 (3.4-ounce) boxes lemon instant pudding

3 cups milk

lemon slices, for garnish

Scan me!

INSTRUCTIONS

1. Crush Oreos in a food processor to a very fine texture. Place crushed Oreos in a large resealable plastic bag and add melted butter. Shake to mix until well combined.

2. Press buttered crumbs into the bottom of a 9-x-13-inch baking dish, making sure to cover the entire bottom.

3. In a medium bowl, blend powdered sugar, cream cheese, butter, and half of the whipped topping with a hand mixer. Blend well and pour over crust.

4. In another bowl, combine instant pudding and milk. Whisk together until pudding thickens, then pour over the cream cheese layer. Refrigerate for at least 5 minutes.

5. Top off with the remaining whipped topping and refrigerate at least 1 hour before serving. Add lemon slices for garnish.

⚙ **VARIATIONS**

You can easily change the flavor of this dessert using different pudding flavors and types of cookies. Some ideas include:

- Chocolate pudding with chocolate Oreos, topped with chocolate curls

- White chocolate pudding with Golden Oreos, topped with white chocolate curls

- Banana pudding with Golden Oreos, topped with banana slices

- Pumpkin pudding with Pumpkin Oreos or Golden Oreos, topped with white chocolate curls

- Pistachio pudding with shortbread cookies, topped with chopped pecans

---

👍 **RECIPE TIPS**

☺ **Make Ahead:** *This recipe can be made 24 hours ahead of time. Simply cover and refrigerate until ready to serve.*

ALSO TRY: Cream Puff Cake (page 209), Dirt Cake (page 210), Lemon Bars (page 226), Banana Bars (page 227)

FRUIT PIZZA

⏱ **PREP TIME:** 20 MINUTES
⧖ **COOK TIME:** 10 MINUTES
♡ **SERVES:** 12

✓ **FEED A CROWD**
✓ **MAKE AHEAD**

INGREDIENTS

PIZZA:

¾ cup sugar

½ cup unsalted butter

1 egg

1¼ cups plus 2 tablespoons all-purpose flour

1 teaspoon cream of tartar

½ teaspoon baking soda

⅛ teaspoon salt

fruit, for topping: bananas, strawberries, kiwis, blackberries, pineapples, blueberries

FROSTING:

1 (8-ounce) package cream cheese, softened

¾ cup powdered sugar

2 tablespoons pineapple juice (or vanilla extract)

Scan me!

INSTRUCTIONS

1. Preheat the oven to 350 degrees F.

2. In a medium bowl, cream together sugar, butter and egg with a hand mixer.

3. In another bowl, mix flour, cream of tartar, baking soda and salt.

4. Add dry ingredients to creamed mixture and mix until well combined and a soft dough forms.

5. Dip hands in flour and form a ball with the dough. Sprinkle dough ball with flour and roll out onto a lightly greased pizza pan (or large cookie sheet) until it is approximately ¼ inch thick and 11 inches in diameter. Leave 1–2 inches around the edges of the pan for dough to expand (it will be about 13 inches in diameter after baking).

6. Bake for 10 minutes, then let cool.

7. While crust cools, make the frosting. In a medium bowl, cream together cream cheese, sugar and pineapple juice with the hand mixer. Spread over cooled cookie crust.

8. Right before serving, add desired fruit in the pattern you prefer. (Tip: Dip bananas in pineapple juice to keep them from getting dark fast.)

9. Keep refrigerated for up to 3 hours until ready to serve.

👍 **RECIPE TIPS**

☺ **Make Ahead:** *You can prepare most of the ingredients a day beforehand, but do not assemble the pizza until 2–3 hours before serving. Cook, cool and cover the crust and store at room temperature for up to 24 hours. Store frosting in an airtight container in the refrigerator for up to 24 hours. Do not cut up fruits until ready to assemble pizza.*

☺ **Pressed for Time?** *If you do not have time to make a homemade crust, you can easily grab a package of sugar cookie dough from the market. Press the dough into the pan and bake at 375 degrees F for about 13 minutes.*

ALSO TRY: Banana Bars (page 227), Sugar Cookies (page 242), Cream Puffs (page 268)

PEACH COBBLER

⏱ PREP TIME: 5 MINUTES

⧗ COOK TIME: 40 MINUTES

♡ SERVES: 6

INGREDIENTS

½ cup unsalted butter

1 cup milk

1 cup all-purpose flour

1 cup sugar

2 teaspoons baking powder

pinch of salt

1 (15-ounce) can peaches

TOPPING: ground cinnamon (optional)

Scan me!

INSTRUCTIONS

1. Preheat the oven to 350 degrees F.

2. Set butter in a glass 9-x-9-inch baking dish and place in the oven to melt.

3. Meanwhile, in a medium bowl, mix milk, flour, sugar, baking powder and salt until well combined.

4. Take out the pan with the melted butter and pour batter mixture over it, making sure it spreads as evenly as possible.

5. Spoon peaches and their juice over batter. Do not mix. Sprinkle with cinnamon.

6. Bake for 38–44 minutes, or until the topping is cooked and golden brown. Serve warm.

👍 RECIPE TIPS

☺ **To Use Fresh Peaches:** *Combine 2 cups freshly sliced peaches (4-5 peaches, peeled, pitted and sliced) with ¾ cup sugar and a dash of salt in a saucepan and bring to a boil over high heat. Pour over batter in the 9-x-9-inch pan in place of the canned peaches. Do not mix! The rest of the recipe remains the same.*

☺ **Texture Tip:** *If you are worried about mushy and runny cobbler, mix some cornstarch into the peaches. In a small bowl, combine 1 teaspoon cold water and 1 teaspoon cornstarch, then stir mixture into the peaches. As the cobbler bakes, the hot liquid will activate the cornstarch.*

ALSO TRY: Lemon Bars (page 226), Lemon Lasagna (page 228), Fruit Pizza (page 229), Homemade Ice Cream (page 265)

GRAHAM CRACKER CRUST

PREP TIME: **5 MINUTES**

COOK TIME: **10 MINUTES**

COOL TIME: **1 HOUR**

MAKES: **1 CRUST**

PREPPED IN 5

QUICK & EASY

MAKE AHEAD

INGREDIENTS

1½ cups finely ground graham cracker crumbs

⅓ cup sugar

6 tablespoons unsalted butter, melted

Scan me!

INSTRUCTIONS

1. Preheat the oven to 375 degrees F.

2. In a medium bowl, mix graham cracker crumbs, sugar and melted butter until well blended.

3. Press mixture evenly into a 9-inch pie plate. Bake for 6–7 minutes and let cool completely (about 1 hour) before filling.

👍 RECIPE TIPS

☺ **Make Ahead:** *Cover the baked, cooled crust and store it in the refrigerator for 3 days or in the freezer for 3 months. When ready to assemble your pie, thaw crust to room temperature before filling.*

⚙ VARIATIONS

For a chocolatey pie crust, replace the graham crackers with original Oreos. You do not need to remove the Oreo filling—just crush them in a food processor and use the same way as graham cracker crumbs.

FILLINGS: The options are endless! Some of our favorite pies to make with a graham cracker crust include key lime pie, Cream Pie (page 233), Chocolate Cream Pie (page 233) and Pumpkin Pie (page 235)

PERFECT PIE CRUST

🕐 **PREP TIME:** 10 MINUTES

⏳ **CHILL TIME:** 2 HOURS 30 MINUTES

⏳ **COOK TIME:** 30 MINUTES

♡ **MAKES:** 2 CRUSTS

✓ **FREEZER FRIENDLY**

✓ **MAKE AHEAD**

INGREDIENTS

2¾ cups all-purpose flour

2 teaspoons sugar

1 teaspoon salt

1½ cups cold, unsalted butter

6–9 tablespoons ice-cold water

Scan me!

INSTRUCTIONS

1. In a medium mixing bowl, whisk together flour, sugar and salt.

2. Cut butter into tablespoons. Add to the dry ingredients. Using a pastry blender, cut butter into pea-sized pieces.

3. Add 6 tablespoons of water. Using a fork, mix until combined. If too dry, continue adding water until the crust comes together and is clumpy.

4. Turn the mixture out onto a lightly floured surface. Fold the dough into itself to knead lightly until it comes together. Form it into a ball and divide in half. Pat each half into a flat disc and wrap tightly in plastic wrap. Refrigerate for 2 hours.

5. Working with one disc at a time on a lightly floured surface, use a rolling pin to roll the dough into a 13-inch circle. Place into a 9-inch pie dish. Flute or crimp the edges (see Recipe Tips) and dock (poke all over) the bottom of the crust with a fork.

6. Refrigerate crust for 30 minutes.

7. To blind bake the crust, line it with parchment paper or aluminum foil and fill with pie weights, dry beans, or uncooked rice to prevent bubbling while baking.

8. Preheat the oven to 350 degrees F.

9. Bake for 13–15 minutes, then remove the weights and parchment or foil and continue baking for an additional 13–15 minutes, or until the bottom is fully baked through.

10. Let cool completely before filling.

ALSO TRY: Graham Cracker Crust (page 231), Cream Pie (page 233), Pumpkin Pie (page 235)

🖒 RECIPE TIPS

☺ **If Not Blind Baking:** *If you'll be using this crust for a recipe that doesn't require blind baking, such as a double-crust fruit pie, prepare the dough through Step 4, then follow your recipe's instructions for rolling out and baking the crust.*

☺ **To Flute a Pie Crust:** *Use two hands to pinch the crust (create a "flute") by pressing one thumb on the inside of the crust between your pinched thumb and index finger on the outside. Continue this wavy pattern all the way around the crust.*

☺ **To Freeze:** *We like to freeze the crust as discs. To do that, make the crust up to Step 4. After wrapping the discs in plastic wrap, place in a freezer-safe bag and freeze for up to 3 months.*

CREAM PIE

⟩ **FEED A CROWD**

⟩ **MAKE AHEAD**

INGREDIENTS

1 (9-inch) pie crust (store-bought or Perfect Pie Crust, page 232)

¾ cup sugar

3 tablespoons cornstarch

¼ teaspoon salt

2 cups milk

3 egg yolks, beaten

2 tablespoons unsalted butter

1 teaspoon vanilla extract

Scan me!

⚙ VARIATIONS

To change things up, this basic cream pie filling could be combined with other ingredients to make more pies.

⊕ **BANANA CREAM:** Slice 3–4 bananas and place into the bottom of the baked pie shell before adding the cream filling. Top with whipped cream and more banana slices.

⊕ **COCONUT CREAM:** Mix in 1 cup coconut flakes into the cream before pouring into the baked pie shell. Top with whipped cream and toasted coconut flakes.

ALSO TRY: Fruit Pizza (page 229), Cream Puff Cake (page 209), Perfect Pie Crust (page 232)

INSTRUCTIONS

1. Bake the pie crust in a 9-inch pie pan according to the package or recipe directions. Set aside to cool.

2. Whisk together the sugar, cornstarch, and salt in a medium saucepan. Add the milk slowly and whisk until combined.

3. Bring the mixture to a simmer over medium heat, stirring constantly to prevent the milk from scorching.

4. Once the mixture has reached a simmer, stir continuously for 1 minute, until thickened.

5. Remove from the heat and pour ½ cup of the mixture into the egg yolks, quickly stirring to prevent the eggs from curdling.

6. Pour the egg yolk mixture into the custard mixture and stir to combine.

7. Return the pot to medium heat and bring the custard back to a simmer. Simmer for 1 minute, stirring constantly.

8. Remove from the heat and stir in the butter and vanilla until smooth.

9. Pour the custard into a bowl, cover tightly with plastic wrap, and refrigerate until cooled to room temperature.

10. To assemble the pie, pour the custard into the cooled pie crust. Chill for at least 4 hours or overnight.

★ **BONUS RECIPE**

Chocolate Cream Pie

Combine 3 tablespoons unsalted butter and 1¼ cups semisweet chocolate chips in a large glass or metal bowl and set aside. Prepare custard as directed above, but add 2 tablespoons cocoa powder to the mixture in Step 2. Do not add butter in Step 8. After removing custard from the heat, stir in 2 teaspoons of vanilla extract. Place a strainer over the bowl of chocolate and butter and pour the hot chocolate custard mixture into the bowl, pressing it through the strainer to remove any lumps. Let sit for a couple of minutes, then stir until butter and chocolate are melted. Fill and chill the pie as directed in Steps 9 and 10.

👍 RECIPE TIPS

☺ **Make Ahead:** *Cream pies can be made 48 hours in advance. Gently cover with foil or plastic wrap and store in the refrigerator.*

PUMPKIN DELIGHT

⏱ **PREP TIME:** 20 MINUTES
⏳ **COOK TIME:** 15 MINUTES
⏳ **CHILL TIME:** 3 HOURS
♡ **SERVES:** 12

✓ **QUICK & EASY**
✓ **FEED A CROWD**
✓ **MAKE AHEAD**

INGREDIENTS

½ cup unsalted butter, softened
1 cup all-purpose flour
¾ cup chopped pecans, divided
1 (8-ounce) package cream cheese, softened
1 cup powdered sugar
3 cups whipped topping, divided
2½ cups milk
1 (15-ounce) can pumpkin puree
3 (3.4-ounce) packages white chocolate (or vanilla) instant pudding mix
1 teaspoon pumpkin spice

Scan me!

INSTRUCTIONS

1. Preheat the oven to 350 degrees F.

2. Mix butter, flour and ½ cup pecans together. Press into a greased 9-x-13-inch baking dish.

3. Bake for 15 minutes, then remove and let cool.

4. While crust cools, make the cream cheese layer. Blend cream cheese and powdered sugar in a medium bowl with a hand mixer, then fold in 1 cup of the whipped topping. Spread over the cooled crust.

5. Make the pudding layer by mixing milk, canned pumpkin, pudding mix, pumpkin spice and 1 cup whipped topping in a medium bowl until smooth. Spread over the cream cheese layer.

6. Spread remaining 1 cup whipped topping over the pudding and sprinkle with remaining ½ cup chopped pecans.

7. Chill in the refrigerator for 3 hours, or until set.

👍 **RECIPE TIPS**

☺ **Make Ahead:** *This can be made ahead and stored, covered, in the refrigerator for up to 2 days.*

☺ **Canned Pumpkin Puree:** *Some brands of pumpkin are more watery than others. If yours is watery, pour it into a strainer to remove the excess water before adding to the pudding. This will prevent the pumpkin layer from being runny.*

⚙ **VARIATIONS**

You can swap out the pecans and flour in the crust for graham cracker crumbs, crushed pretzels or crushed gingersnaps. For topping, try walnuts or toffee bits in place of the pecans.

ALSO TRY: Pumpkin Roll (page 218), Pumpkin Pie (page 235), Pecan Pie Bars (page 236)

PUMPKIN PIE

INGREDIENTS

4 large eggs

1 (29-ounce) can pumpkin puree

3 cups evaporated milk

1½ cups sugar

2 teaspoons ground cinnamon

1 teaspoon ground nutmeg

½ teaspoon ground cloves

1 teaspoon salt

2 (9-inch) pie crusts, unbaked (store-bought or homemade, page 232)

Scan me!

INSTRUCTIONS

1. Preheat the oven to 350 degrees F.

2. In a large bowl, lightly beat eggs with a hand mixer on low speed until well blended. Add pumpkin, evaporated milk, sugar, cinnamon, nutmeg, cloves and salt. Mix until well blended.

3. Place pie crusts in two 9-inch pie pans and poke holes in the crusts with a fork to prevent bubbles. Crimp edges of each crust.

4. Divide filling evenly between pie crusts and bake for 60–70 minutes, or until a knife inserted in the center comes out clean.

ALSO TRY: Homemade Whipped Cream (page 208), Pumpkin Dump Cake (page 217), Pecan Pie Bars (page 236), Homemade Ice Cream (page 265)

🔥 RECIPE TIPS

☺ **Make Ahead:** *Pumpkin pie can be kept loosely covered in the refrigerator for 3–5 days.*

☺ **Suggested Toppings:** *Dress your pie up with whipped cream, peanut brittle, sugared nuts (pecans are great!), a scoop of ice cream (vanilla, caramel or cinnamon) on each slice, mini chocolate chips or chocolate sauce.*

PECAN PIE BARS

⏱ **PREP TIME:** 10 MINUTES

⏳ **COOK TIME:** 50 MINUTES

♡ **SERVES:** 12

⊘ **FEED A CROWD**

⊘ **MAKE AHEAD**

INGREDIENTS

SHORTBREAD CRUST:

2 cups all-purpose flour

⅓ cup sugar

¼ teaspoon salt

¾ cup cold unsalted butter, cubed

FILLING:

1½ cups sugar

4 large eggs

1 cup light corn syrup

3 tablespoons unsalted butter, melted

1½ teaspoons vanilla extract

2½ cups chopped pecans

Scan me!

INSTRUCTIONS

1. Preheat the oven to 350 degrees F. Grease a 9-x-13-inch baking dish and set aside.

2. To make the shortbread crust: In a large bowl, mix flour, sugar and salt. Cut in cold butter to create coarse crumbs. Press into the bottom of the prepared dish and bake for 20 minutes.

3. Meanwhile, prepare the filling: Whisk sugar, eggs, corn syrup, melted butter and vanilla in a large bowl. Stir in pecans. Spread over hot crust as soon as it comes out of the oven.

4. Bake for 30–35 minutes more, until filling has set.

5. Cool completely in the pan before cutting into squares and serving.

ALSO TRY: Pumpkin Roll (page 218), Pumpkin Delight (page 234), Pumpkin Pie (page 235)

👍 **RECIPE TIPS**

☺ **Make Ahead:** *These bars can be made 24–48 hours in advance. Once cool, cover and store the entire slab in the refrigerator. Cut into squares just before serving.*

RICE KRISPIES TREATS

QUICK & EASY

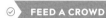
FEED A CROWD

MAKE AHEAD

GLUTEN-FREE

INGREDIENTS

3 tablespoons unsalted butter

1 (12-ounce) bag large marshmallows

8–8½ cups Rice Krispies cereal

1½ cups mini marshmallows

Scan me!

INSTRUCTIONS

1. In a large bowl, melt butter in the microwave for 30 seconds.

2. Add large marshmallows to the butter and microwave for 2–3 minutes.

3. Stir well and slowly add Rice Krispies. When all combined, toss in mini marshmallows, stir to mix and pour into a greased 9-x-13-inch pan.

4. Using wax paper or with greased hands, press mixture gently to spread evenly into all corners of the pan. Allow to set for at least 30 minutes before cutting and serving.

👍 RECIPE TIPS

☺ **Make Ahead:** *Store in an airtight container at room temperature for up to 3 days.*

☺ **Marshmallow Mods:** *It's easy to modify the recipe just a bit to make more while using a 16-ounce bag of marshmallows. Just use the larger bag and add 1 more tablespoon butter, 1½–2 cups more Rice Krispies and 2 more cups of mini marshmallows. Also note: 4 ounces of marshmallows = 16 large marshmallows.*

⚙ VARIATIONS

To change it up, try substituting Cocoa Krispies or Fruity Pebbles for Rice Krispies, or use different flavored marshmallows to create different flavors.

ALSO TRY: Scotcheroos (page 238), Puppy Chow (page 254), White Chocolate Trail Mix (page 264)

SCOTCHEROOS

○ **PREP TIME:** 5 MINUTES
⧖ **COOK TIME:** 15 MINUTES
⧖ **REST TIME:** 30 MINUTES
♡ **MAKES:** 20 SCOTCHEROOS

⊘ **PREPPED IN 5**
⊘ **QUICK & EASY**
⊘ **FEED A CROWD**
⊘ **MAKE AHEAD**
⊘ **GLUTEN-FREE**

INGREDIENTS

6 cups Rice Krispies cereal
1 cup sugar
1 cup creamy peanut butter
1 cup light corn syrup
1½ cups chocolate chips
1½ cups butterscotch chips

Scan me!

INSTRUCTIONS

1. Pour Rice Krispies into a large bowl and set aside.

2. In a medium pot over medium-high heat, bring sugar, peanut butter and corn syrup to a boil, making sure to stir constantly.

3. As soon as the mixture starts to boil, pour over cereal and mix well. Pour into a greased 9-x-13-inch pan and gently press down with a spatula to spread evenly into the pan.

4. In a small pot, melt chocolate and butterscotch chips together over low heat, stirring constantly. Pour over pressed Rice Krispies and let set for at least 30 minutes before cutting and serving.

👍 **RECIPE TIPS**

☺ **Make Ahead:** *Store in an airtight container at room temperature for up to 3 days.*

⚙ **VARIATIONS**

To add a pretty butterscotch swirl, after you have melted the chocolate and butterscotch chips together, melt a separate bowl of butterscotch chips. Spread the chocolate mixture evenly over the treat, then drizzle the plain butterscotch over the chocolate. Finally, use a toothpick to drag the butterscotch drizzle through the chocolate, creating a pretty pattern. You can also add sprinkles or crushed candies to the top of the chocolate layer before it sets.

ALSO TRY: Cookie Bars (page 223), Sugar Cookie Bars (page 224), Rice Krispies Treats (page 237)

COOKIES

"A balanced diet is a cookie in each hand."

Cookies just make everyone happier! Of all the desserts in this cookbook, the ones that we make the most often are the cookies. They are perfect for a quick, last-minute treat, or to brighten someone's day as a gift. Warm homemade cookies cannot be beat when trying to provide a little bit of love and service to others. These cookies have also been some of the first recipes our kids have used to begin learning to bake on their own, so they hold a special place in our hearts.

CHOCOLATE CHIP COOKIES

🕐 **PREP TIME:** 5 MINUTES

⏳ **COOK TIME:** 10 MINUTES

♡ **MAKES:** 36 COOKIES

✓ PREPPED IN 5

✓ QUICK & EASY

✓ ON THE TABLE IN 20

✓ FREEZER FRIENDLY

✓ FEED A CROWD

✓ MAKE AHEAD

INGREDIENTS

1 cup unsalted butter, softened (or ½ cup butter plus ½ cup vegetable oil)

1 cup packed light brown sugar

1 cup granulated sugar

2 eggs

3 cups all-purpose flour

1 teaspoon baking soda

1 teaspoon baking powder

1 teaspoon salt

1 teaspoon vanilla extract

2 cups chocolate chips (semisweet, milk, dark or a mix)

Scan me!

INSTRUCTIONS

1. Preheat the oven to 350 degrees F. Lightly grease a baking sheet and set aside.

2. In a stand mixer (or with a hand mixer in a large bowl), cream butter and both sugars. Add eggs and beat until fluffy.

3. Add flour, baking soda, baking powder, salt and vanilla, and mix until incorporated.

4. Fold in chocolate chips. Use a medium cookie scoop to scoop dough, roll into balls and place onto the prepared baking sheet.

5. Bake for 9–11 minutes.

6. Let cookies sit on the baking sheet for a few minutes, then remove to a rack to cool.

★ BONUS RECIPE

Pizookie

Use the same base chocolate chip cookie dough, but halve the recipe. Press dough into a greased 8–9-inch pan or cast iron skillet. Bake at 350 degrees F for 18–22 minutes. Serve gooey with Homemade Ice Cream (page 265).

⚙ VARIATIONS

These cookies are so easy to change up based on the add-ins and chips used. Other variations include:

➔ **M&M COOKIES:** Make cookies as directed above but use ½ cup butter and ½ cup oil. At Step 4, fold in ½ cup chopped M&M's, then continue dropping dough onto baking sheet. Top with whole M&M's and bake at 350 degrees F for 9–11 minutes.

➔ **COOKIES & CREAM COOKIES:** Add 1 cup white chocolate chips and 1 cup crushed Oreos to the dough before scooping, rolling and baking.

ALSO TRY: Snickerdoodles (page 241), Crinkles (page 244), Oatmeal Coconut Cookies (page 245), Gooey Butter Cookies (page 246)

SNICKER-DOODLES

- ⏱ **PREP TIME:** 10 MINUTES
- ⏳ **COOK TIME:** 10 MINUTES
- ♡ **MAKES:** 36 COOKIES

- ✓ **QUICK & EASY**
- ✓ **ON THE TABLE IN 20**
- ✓ **FREEZER FRIENDLY**
- ✓ **FEED A CROWD**
- ✓ **MAKE AHEAD**

INGREDIENTS

2¾ cups all-purpose flour
2 teaspoons cream of tartar
1 teaspoon baking soda
½ teaspoon salt
1 cup unsalted butter, softened
1½ cups plus ⅓ cup sugar, divided
2 eggs
1 teaspoon vanilla extract
2 tablespoons ground cinnamon

Scan me!

INSTRUCTIONS

1. Preheat the oven to 350 degrees F.

2. In a large bowl, mix together flour, cream of tartar, baking soda and salt. Set aside.

3. In another large bowl or in a stand mixer, cream together butter and 1½ cups sugar. Add eggs and vanilla and blend well.

4. Add dry ingredients to wet ingredients and mix well.

5. Combine remaining ⅓ cup sugar with the cinnamon in a small bowl.

6. Use a small cookie scoop to scoop out dough, roll into balls, and then roll in the cinnamon-sugar mixture twice.

7. Place 2 inches apart on an ungreased baking sheet.

8. Bake for 8–10 minutes.

9. Let cookies sit on the baking sheet for a few minutes, then remove to a rack to cool.

👍 RECIPE TIPS

☺ **Make Ahead:** *Prepare cookie dough and chill it in the refrigerator for up to 3 days. You can also bake cookies ahead and store in an airtight container for 4–5 days.*

☺ **To Chill or Not to Chill?** *If you like your cookies a little flatter, do not chill the dough. If you like your cookies more fluffy, chill dough for 1 hour before rolling and baking.*

ALSO TRY: Chocolate Chip Cookies (page 240), Gooey Butter Cookies (page 246), Soft Peanut Butter Cookies (page 247)

SUGAR COOKIES

⏱ PREP TIME: **10 MINUTES**

⏳ COOK TIME: **10 MINUTES**

♡ MAKES: **24 COOKIES**

- ⊘ QUICK & EASY
- ⊘ ON THE TABLE IN 20
- ⊘ FREEZER FRIENDLY
- ⊘ FEED A CROWD
- ⊘ MAKE AHEAD

INGREDIENTS

COOKIES:

¾ cup unsalted butter, softened

1 (8-ounce) package cream cheese, softened

1 cup granulated sugar

½ cup powdered sugar

1 teaspoon almond extract

1 egg

2¾ cups all-purpose flour

½ teaspoon baking powder

½ teaspoon salt

FROSTING:

4½ cups powdered sugar

⅓ cup unsalted butter, softened

¼ cup milk, plus more as needed

½ teaspoon vanilla extract

½ teaspoon almond extract

food coloring (optional)

Scan me!

INSTRUCTIONS

1. Preheat the oven to 375 degrees F. Lightly grease a baking sheet and set aside.

2. Cream butter, cream cheese, both sugars, almond extract and egg in a large bowl or stand mixer until fluffy.

3. In a medium bowl, combine flour, baking powder and salt.

4. Add dry ingredients to the creamed mixture and stir until a soft dough forms.

5. Roll out dough on a lightly floured surface to about ⅜ inch thick (roll thinner for more crunchy sugar cookies).

6. Cut with cookie cutters and bake for 9–12 minutes on the prepared baking sheet. Let cookies sit on the baking sheet for a few minutes, then remove to a rack to cool.

7. To make frosting: Mix all ingredients in a medium bowl with a hand mixer. If too thick, add a little more milk.

8. Frost cookies and let set before storing.

ALSO TRY: Cookie Bars (page 223), Sugar Cookie Bars (page 224), Snickerdoodles (page 241), Strawberry Cookies (page 248)

👍 **RECIPE TIPS**

☺ **Make Ahead:** *You can prepare the dough as directed, cover tightly, and store it in the refrigerator for 1–2 days before baking. Store baked cookies in an airtight container at room temperature for up to 5 days. Frost right before serving.*

NO-BAKE COOKIES

- ⏱ PREP TIME: 5 MINUTES
- ⧖ COOK TIME: 1 MINUTE
- ⧖ COOL TIME: 30 MINUTES
- ♡ MAKES: 24 COOKIES

PREPPED IN 5

QUICK & EASY

FEED A CROWD

GLUTEN-FREE

INGREDIENTS

2 cups sugar

¼ cup unsweetened cocoa powder

½ cup unsalted butter

½ cup milk

1 cup creamy peanut butter

1 tablespoon vanilla extract

3 cups quick-cooking rolled oats

Scan me!

INSTRUCTIONS

1. Combine sugar, cocoa powder, butter and milk in a medium saucepan over medium-high heat. Once it comes to a boil, start a timer and boil for 1 minute.

2. Remove from the heat and stir in peanut butter and vanilla until smooth, then stir in oats.

3. Drop heaping tablespoons onto a parchment paper–lined baking sheet and let cool for at least 30 minutes before serving.

♨ RECIPE TIPS

☺ **Make Ahead:** *Store in an airtight container at room temperature for up to a week. In an airtight container in the refrigerator, they can last up to 2 weeks.*

☺ **Can I Use Old-Fashioned Oats?** *You can—it just depends on what texture you prefer for your no-bake cookies. Quick-cooking oats are smaller and absorb liquid more easily, which makes the cookies more soft and chewy. If you use old-fashioned oats, the cookies will have a less chewy texture.*

ALSO TRY: M&M Chocolate Oat Bars (page 222), Crinkles (page 244), Soft Peanut Butter Cookies (page 247)

CRINKLES

- ⏱ **PREP TIME:** 5 MINUTES
- ⧗ **CHILL TIME:** 1 HOUR
- ⧗ **COOK TIME:** 10 MINUTES
- ♡ **MAKES:** 24 COOKIES

- ✓ **PREPPED IN 5**
- ✓ **FREEZER FRIENDLY**
- ✓ **FEED A CROWD**
- ✓ **MAKE AHEAD**
- ✓ **DAIRY-FREE**

INGREDIENTS

2 cups granulated sugar

1 cup unsweetened cocoa powder

½ cup vegetable oil

4 eggs

2 teaspoons vanilla extract

1⅔ cups all-purpose flour

2 teaspoons baking powder

½ teaspoon salt

½ cup powdered sugar

Scan me!

INSTRUCTIONS

1. In a medium bowl, combine granulated sugar, cocoa powder and oil and beat with a hand mixer on medium speed until mixed together.

2. Add eggs one at a time, beating until well combined after each addition. Stir in vanilla.

3. In a separate bowl, combine flour, baking powder and salt.

4. Add dry ingredients to the wet ingredients and stir until well combined. Chill for 1 hour.

5. Preheat the oven to 350 degrees F. Line a baking sheet with parchment paper and set aside.

6. Place powdered sugar in a bowl. Scoop out and roll dough into 1-inch balls and roll in powdered sugar until well coated. Place on the prepared baking sheet.

7. Bake for 9–11 minutes.

8. Let cookies sit on the baking sheet for a few minutes, then remove to a rack to cool completely.

ALSO TRY: Brownies (page 220), Cookie Bars (page 223), Chocolate Chip Cookies (page 240)

👍 RECIPE TIPS

☺ **Make Ahead:** *Baked cookies can be stored in an airtight container for 3–4 days at room temperature. Store dough in an airtight container in the refrigerator for up to 1 week before scooping, rolling and baking.*

OATMEAL COCONUT COOKIES

⏱ PREP TIME: 10 MINUTES

⏳ COOK TIME: 10 MINUTES

♡ MAKES: 24 COOKIES

- ✓ QUICK & EASY
- ✓ ON THE TABLE IN 20
- ✓ FREEZER FRIENDLY
- ✓ FEED A CROWD
- ✓ MAKE AHEAD

INGREDIENTS

1 cup granulated sugar

1 cup packed light brown sugar

1 cup unsalted butter

2 eggs

2 teaspoons vanilla extract

1 teaspoon almond extract (optional)

2½ cups all-purpose flour

2 cups quick-cooking rolled oats

1 cup sweetened coconut flakes

1 teaspoon baking soda

1 teaspoon baking powder

1 teaspoon salt

Scan me!

INSTRUCTIONS

1. Preheat the oven to 350 degrees F. Lightly grease a baking sheet and set aside.

2. In a large bowl or stand mixer, cream together both sugars, the butter, eggs, vanilla and almond extracts. Set aside.

3. In a separate bowl, mix flour, oats, coconut, baking soda, baking powder and salt together.

4. Add dry ingredients to the wet ingredients and mix well.

5. Use a small cookie scoop to scoop dough onto prepared baking sheet, and bake for 8–10 minutes.

6. Let cookies sit on the baking sheet for a few minutes, then remove to a rack to cool.

★ **BONUS RECIPE**

Oatmeal Chocolate Chip Cookies

To turn this recipe into Oatmeal Chocolate Chip Cookies, omit the coconut, add one 12-ounce bag of chocolate chips, and bake as directed above.

👍 **RECIPE TIPS**

☺ **To Freeze:** *Form the dough into balls, place them on a baking sheet and freeze for about 2 hours. Then transfer the dough balls to an airtight, freezer-safe container and freeze for 3–6 months. Bake as directed from frozen, adding a few extra minutes to the bake time.*

ALSO TRY: Chocolate Chip Cookies (page 240), Sugar Cookies (page 242), Gooey Butter Cookies (page 246)

GOOEY BUTTER COOKIES
(AKA CAKE MIX COOKIES)

INGREDIENTS

1 (8-ounce) package cream cheese, softened
½ cup unsalted butter, softened
1 egg
½ teaspoon vanilla extract
1 (15.25-ounce) box yellow cake mix
1 cup powdered sugar, plus more for dusting

Scan me!

★
BONUS
RECIPE

Gooey Monster Cookies

Make cookies as directed above, but use white cake mix. After mixing in the cake mix, divide batter into separate bowls for each color you want to make. Add one food coloring to each individual bowl and mix well. Chill for 30 minutes. Continue with Steps 3–5. Add candy eyeballs to cookies after baking, while they are still warm.

☝ **RECIPE TIPS**

☺ Make Ahead: *Store cookies in an airtight container in the refrigerator for 3–4 days.*

ALSO TRY: Sugar Cookies (page 242), Strawberry Cookies (page 248), Shortbread Cookies (page 249)

○ PREP TIME: **5 MINUTES**
⧖ CHILL TIME: **30 MINUTES**
⧖ COOK TIME: **10 MINUTES**
♡ MAKES: **24 COOKIES**

⊘ **PREPPED IN 5**
⊘ **FEED A CROWD**
⊘ **MAKE AHEAD**

INSTRUCTIONS

1. In a large bowl, beat cream cheese, butter, egg and vanilla with a hand mixer until fluffy.

2. Mix in cake mix until combined, and chill for 30 minutes.

3. Preheat the oven to 350 degrees F.

4. Place powdered sugar in a bowl. Scoop out and roll dough into 1½-inch balls and roll in powdered sugar until well coated. Place onto a lightly greased baking sheet.

5. Bake for 10–12 minutes.

6. Let cookies sit on the baking sheet for a few minutes, then remove to a rack to cool.

7. Sift more powdered sugar on top, if desired.

⚙ **VARIATIONS**

Change this up by using your favorite cake mix and adding your own embellishments. A few of our favorite combos include:

⊕ **CHOCOLATE ROLO CAKE MIX COOKIES:** Chocolate cake mix with a Rolo candy enclosed in each dough ball

⊕ **RED VELVET CAKE MIX COOKIES:** Red velvet cake mix with white chocolate chips

⊕ **FUNFETTI CAKE MIX COOKIES:** Funfetti cake mix with extra sprinkles

SOFT PEANUT BUTTER COOKIES

PREP TIME: **5 MINUTES**
COOK TIME: **10 MINUTES**
MAKES: **30 COOKIES**

- PREPPED IN 5
- QUICK & EASY
- ON THE TABLE IN 20
- FEED A CROWD
- MAKE AHEAD

INGREDIENTS

1½ cups creamy peanut butter (or crunchy)
1 cup unsalted butter, softened
1 cup packed light brown sugar
1 cup plus ½ cup granulated sugar, divided
2 eggs
2 tablespoons vanilla extract
2¼ cups all-purpose flour
1 teaspoon baking powder
1 teaspoon baking soda

Scan me!

INSTRUCTIONS

1. Preheat the oven to 350 degrees F.

2. In a large mixing bowl, beat together peanut butter, butter, brown sugar and 1 cup of granulated sugar. Add eggs and vanilla and mix until creamy.

3. In a separate bowl, combine flour, baking powder and baking soda. Whisk together, then pour into the butter mixture. Stir to combine.

4. Place remaining ½ cup of sugar in a bowl. Roll dough into 1–1½-inch balls and roll in sugar, making sure to coat all sides.

5. Place on a greased baking sheet and make a crisscross on top of each ball using a fork. Bake for 8–9 minutes.

6. Let cookies sit on the baking sheet for a few minutes, then remove to a rack to cool.

BONUS RECIPE

Peanut Butter Kiss Cookies

Make the recipe as directed above and bake for about 9 minutes. Remove from the oven and immediately add a Hershey's Kiss to each cookie.

👍 RECIPE TIPS

☺ **Make Ahead:** *Peanut butter cookies can be stored in dough form or after baking. To store cookie dough, wrap in plastic wrap and store in the refrigerator for 3 days. You can also form cookie dough balls, place them on a baking sheet and freeze for about 2 hours, then transfer them to a resealable plastic freezer bag and store them in the freezer for up to 3 months. Store baked cookies in an airtight container at room temperature for 7 days.*

☺ **Peanut Butter:** *Regular creamy peanut butter is definitely the best type of peanut butter to use. Natural peanut butter will not give you the same results.*

ALSO TRY: Chocolate Chip Cookies (page 240), Crinkles (page 244), Oatmeal Coconut Cookies (page 245)

STRAWBERRY COOKIES

⏱ PREP TIME: 10 MINUTES

⏳ COOK TIME: 10 MINUTES

♡ MAKES: 36 COOKIES

✓ QUICK & EASY

✓ ON THE TABLE IN 20

✓ FREEZER FRIENDLY

✓ FEED A CROWD

✓ MAKE AHEAD

INGREDIENTS

1 cup unsalted butter, softened

1 cup sugar

2 tablespoons strawberry Jell-O mix

2 eggs

1 teaspoon vanilla extract

2½ cups all-purpose flour

1 (3.4-ounce) package white chocolate instant pudding

1 teaspoon baking soda

½ teaspoon salt

1 (12-ounce) bag white chocolate chips

Scan me!

INSTRUCTIONS

1. Preheat the oven to 350 degrees F.

2. In a large bowl, cream butter, sugar and Jell-O mix together with a hand mixer. Add eggs and vanilla and mix well.

3. In a separate bowl, mix flour, pudding mix, baking soda and salt. Slowly add to the butter mixture, and mix well.

4. Fold in white chocolate chips.

5. Use a small cookie scoop to scoop and roll dough into 1½-inch balls, then place on a greased baking sheet.

6. Bake for 9–10 minutes.

7. Let cookies sit on the baking sheet for a few minutes, then remove to a rack to cool.

👍 RECIPE TIPS

☺ **Make Ahead:** *Store in an airtight container for 1 week at room temperature, or for 2 weeks in the refrigerator.*

⚙ VARIATIONS

Use vanilla instant pudding mix if you cannot find white chocolate pudding. Or change the flavor by substituting another flavor for the strawberry Jell-O mix, such as raspberry or cherry Jell-O.

ALSO TRY: Sugar Cookies (page 242), Oatmeal Coconut Cookies (page 245), Gooey Butter Cookies (page 246)

SHORTBREAD COOKIES

⏱ **PREP TIME:** 15 MINUTES
⏳ **COOK TIME:** 10 MINUTES
♡ **MAKES:** 48 COOKIES

✓ QUICK & EASY
✓ FREEZER FRIENDLY
✓ FEED A CROWD
✓ MAKE AHEAD

INGREDIENTS

2 cups unsalted butter, softened
1 cup sugar
2 teaspoons vanilla extract
4 cups all-purpose flour
1–2 tablespoons milk, as needed

Scan me!

INSTRUCTIONS

1. Preheat the oven to 350 degrees F.

2. In a large bowl, cream together butter and sugar with a hand mixer until light and fluffy. Add vanilla and mix well to combine.

3. Add flour and mix until the dough fully combines. Add milk as needed until the dough reaches the consistency of Play-Doh.

4. Scoop the dough into a cookie press. Hold the cookie press down on an ungreased, unlined baking sheet and press to form cookies.

5. Bake for 10–12 minutes, until very lightly golden on the bottom.

6. Let cookies sit on the baking sheet for a few minutes, then remove to a rack to cool.

👍 RECIPE TIPS

☺ **Make Ahead:** *Store in an airtight container at room temperature for 1 week or in an airtight container in the refrigerator for up to 2 weeks. You can also freeze them for 2–3 months.*

☺ **Decorating:** *The beauty of shortbread cookies is their simple elegance. The intricate design that a cookie press makes is all that is needed. If you do wish to decorate them, add a sprinkle of white sugar or colored sugar sprinkles before baking. If you have any smooth-top cookies, you can also add a drizzle of chocolate or dip a cookie halfway in melted chocolate.*

ALSO TRY: Snickerdoodles (page 241), Sugar Cookies (page 242), Gooey Butter Cookies (page 246)

GINGERSNAPS

⏱ **PREP TIME:** 5 MINUTES
⧗ **CHILL TIME:** 1 HOUR
⧗ **COOK TIME:** 10 MINUTES
♡ **MAKES:** 24 COOKIES

✓ PREPPED IN 5
✓ FREEZER FRIENDLY
✓ FEED A CROWD
✓ MAKE AHEAD

INGREDIENTS

1 cup sugar, plus more for rolling
¾ cup unsalted butter, softened
¼ cup molasses
1 egg
1 tablespoon applesauce
2¼ cups all-purpose flour
1½ teaspoons baking soda
1 teaspoon ground cinnamon
½ teaspoon ground cloves
½ teaspoon ground ginger
½ teaspoon ground nutmeg
¼ teaspoon salt

Scan me!

INSTRUCTIONS

1. In a large bowl, mix together sugar, butter, molasses, egg and applesauce with a hand mixer.

2. In a separate bowl, mix all remaining ingredients.

3. Combine dry ingredients with the wet ingredients and mix until combined.

4. Cover with plastic wrap and refrigerate for 1 hour.

5. Preheat the oven to 350 degrees F.

6. Shape dough into 1-inch balls and roll in white sugar. Place on an ungreased baking sheet and bake for 8–10 minutes. Cookies will puff up, then flatten.

7. Let cookies sit on the baking sheet for a few minutes, then remove to a rack to cool.

👍 RECIPE TIPS

☺ **Make Ahead:** *Place in an airtight container and store on the counter for up to 2 weeks.*

⚙ VARIATIONS

This classic cookie is easy to change up! We like to add white chocolate chips to the dough for a family favorite, or for the holidays, we add seasonal Hershey's Kisses to the top of each cookie once they are baked, just like the Peanut Butter Kiss Cookies (page 247). Because we love white chocolate, we also like to drizzle it on top after the cookies are baked, or dip half of each cookie in melted white chocolate, and let it set.

ALSO TRY: Snickerdoodles (page 241), Shortbread Cookies (page 249), Pumpkin Chocolate Chip Cookies (page 251)

PUMPKIN CHOCOLATE CHIP COOKIES

PREP TIME: **10 MINUTES**

COOK TIME: **10 MINUTES**

MAKES: **36 COOKIES**

INGREDIENTS

½ cup packed light brown sugar

½ cup granulated sugar

½ cup vegetable oil

1 egg

1 cup pumpkin puree

1 tablespoon vanilla extract

2 cups all-purpose flour

2 teaspoons baking powder

1 teaspoon baking soda

½ teaspoon salt

2 teaspoons ground cinnamon

⅓ teaspoon ground cloves (optional)

⅓ teaspoon ground nutmeg (optional)

1 cup semisweet chocolate chips

1 cup milk chocolate chips

 Scan me!

INSTRUCTIONS

1. Preheat the oven to 350 degrees F.

2. In a large bowl, whisk together both sugars and the oil. Add egg, pumpkin and vanilla and whisk until smooth.

3. In a medium bowl, combine flour, baking powder, baking soda, salt, cinnamon, cloves and nutmeg and whisk until blended.

4. Add dry ingredients to the wet ingredients and stir gently until just combined. Fold in both chocolate chips.

5. Use a small cookie scoop to scoop dough onto a lightly greased baking sheet. Bake for 10–12 minutes, or until set in the middle. Cool on the baking sheet for a couple of minutes, then remove to wire racks to cool.

👍 RECIPE TIPS

☺ **Make Ahead:** *Store the dough in an airtight container in the refrigerator for 1–2 days. Baked cookies can be stored in an airtight container or large resealable plastic bag for 2–3 days in a cool spot, or in the refrigerator for up to a week.*

☺ **Use a Spice Blend:** *Substitute 1 tablespoon pumpkin pie spice for the cinnamon, cloves and nutmeg, if needed.*

ALSO TRY: Chocolate Chip Cookies (page 240), Shortbread Cookies (page 249), Gingersnaps (page 250)

CANDY AND OTHER DESSERTS

"Stressed is desserts spelled backward."

One of the earliest and fondest cooking memories that we have is making homemade lollipops with my mom on Valentine's Day. It quickly has become a tradition for our family as well, along with other candy recipes for the holidays. All of these treats are perfect to build traditions around for gifting to others or just as a special treat to enjoy by yourself or as a family.

PUPPY CHOW
(AKA MUDDY BUDDIES)

⏱ PREP TIME: 10 MINUTES
⧗ COOK TIME: 5 MINUTES
♡ SERVES: 20

✓ QUICK & EASY

✓ ON THE TABLE IN 20

✓ FEED A CROWD

✓ MAKE AHEAD

✓ GLUTEN-FREE

INGREDIENTS

9 cups Chex cereal (rice or corn)

1 cup semisweet chocolate chips

½ cup creamy peanut butter

½ cup unsalted butter

1 teaspoon vanilla extract

1½ cups powdered sugar

Scan me!

INSTRUCTIONS

1. Place cereal in a large bowl and set aside.

2. In a medium saucepan over low heat, combine chocolate chips, peanut butter and butter and cook, stirring frequently, until melted. Remove from the heat and stir in vanilla.

3. Pour mixture over cereal, stirring until evenly coated.

4. Pour into a 2-gallon resealable plastic bag. Add powdered sugar. Seal bag and shake until well coated.

5. Spread out on a piece of waxed paper to cool, then serve immediately or transfer to an airtight container to store.

ALSO TRY: Candied Almonds (page 260), White Chocolate Popcorn (page 262), White Chocolate Trail Mix (page 264)

👍 RECIPE TIPS

☺ **Make Ahead:** *Place in an airtight container and store on the counter for 1–2 weeks.*

⚙ VARIATIONS

You can add a variety of ingredients to this classic treat to make it even better!

➔ **S'MORES:** Prepare Puppy Chow as directed, then mix in 4 cups Golden Grahams and 2 cups mini marshmallows.

➔ **COOKIES AND CREAM:** Add about 8 crushed Oreos to the bag along with the powdered sugar.

➔ **HOLIDAY:** Add 1 cup holiday M&M's or other holiday-colored candies to the mix.

CARAMEL APPLES

EQUIPMENT

6 skewers or popsicle sticks

INGREDIENTS

6 apples (Granny Smith, Fuji or Honeycrisp)

1 (11-ounce) bag Brach's Milk Maid caramels, unwrapped

3 tablespoons water

melted white chocolate candy coating (optional)

TOPPINGS: sprinkles, chopped nuts, crushed candy (optional)

Scan me!

ALSO TRY: Popcorn Balls (page 263), Churros (page 267), Funnel Cake (page 270)

INSTRUCTIONS

1. Wash apples and let them dry completely. This will help remove the wax that is on the apple skin, allowing the caramel to stick better.

2. Remove apple stems and insert skewers or popsicle sticks 1–2 inches in.

3. Place apples on a parchment paper–lined baking sheet and refrigerate for 1–2 hours.

4. In the top of a double boiler or in a medium pot over low heat, combine caramels and water and cook, stirring the entire time, until caramel is fully melted and reaches about 240 degrees F, 12–14 minutes.

5. Working one at a time, hold an apple by the stick, tilt the pot at an angle and swirl apple in caramel to coat. Gently tap to let excess caramel drip off, then place apple back on parchment paper. Once all apples have been dipped, refrigerate again for 30 minutes.

6. Once caramel has set, you can enjoy your apples as they are, or you can dip in melted candy coating, sprinkle on any desired toppings and let set at room temperature.

7. Store apples refrigerated, but remove from the refrigerator at least 30 minutes before serving.

👍 RECIPE TIPS

☺ **Make Ahead:** *Covered and refrigerated, caramel apples will keep for up to 2 weeks.*

☺ **Other Topping Ideas:** *The possibilities are endless—try topping these with mini M&M's, mini chocolate chips, mini marshmallows, shredded coconut, crushed Cinnamon Toast Crunch cereal, crushed graham crackers, crushed Butterfingers or crushed Oreos.*

COOKIES AND CREAM FUDGE

⏱ PREP TIME: 10 MINUTES

⧖ COOK TIME: 5 MINUTES

⧗ CHILL TIME: 4 HOURS

♡ SERVES: 16

✓ FEED A CROWD

✓ MAKE AHEAD

INGREDIENTS

1 (7-ounce) jar Marshmallow Fluff

2½ cups white chocolate chips

½ cup unsalted butter

1 cup sugar

½ cup heavy cream

½ teaspoon salt

20 Oreos, crushed

Scan me!

INSTRUCTIONS

1. Line a 9-x-9-inch baking dish with parchment paper. Set aside.

2. In a medium bowl, combine Marshmallow Fluff and white chocolate chips and set aside.

3. In a medium saucepan over medium heat, melt butter, then add sugar, cream and salt. Bring to a boil and cook, stirring, for 5 minutes.

4. Pour hot butter mixture into the bowl with white chocolate chips and Marshmallow Fluff and beat with a hand mixer until chips have melted and mixture is smooth.

5. Set aside about ¼ cup crushed Oreos. Fold remaining Oreos into marshmallow mixture and pour into the prepared pan. Sprinkle with reserved crushed Oreos.

6. Refrigerate for 4–6 hours. Cut into small squares before serving.

ALSO TRY: Caramel Apples (page 255), Homemade Lollipops (page 257), Candied Almonds (page 260)

☺ RECIPE TIPS

☺ **Make Ahead:** *This can be stored in an airtight container on the counter for up to 2 weeks.*

⚙ VARIATIONS

Switch up the flavor of this fudge by using different varieties of cookies in place of the Oreos. You can also fold in chopped candies, like white chocolate Reese's, Hershey's Kisses or candy canes, or chopped nuts such as pecans, walnuts or macadamia nuts.

HOMEMADE LOLLIPOPS

⏱ PREP TIME: **5 MINUTES**
⧗ COOK TIME: **15 MINUTES**
⧗ REST TIME: **10 MINUTES**
♡ SERVES: **16**

⊘ **FEED A CROWD**
⊘ **MAKE AHEAD**
⊘ **DAIRY-FREE**
⊘ **GLUTEN-FREE**

EQUIPMENT

16 lollipop sticks
16 metal or silicone lollipop molds
candy thermometer

INGREDIENTS

1 cup sugar
½ cup water
⅓ cup corn syrup
¼ teaspoon gel food coloring
3–5 drops LorAnn flavor oil, cherry or cinnamon

 *Scan me!*

INSTRUCTIONS

1. Insert sticks into molds. Place on a baking sheet and lightly spray with nonstick cooking spray. Put the baking sheet in the freezer while you make the candy.

2. In a medium saucepan, combine sugar, water and corn syrup over medium-high heat and bring to a boil. Do not stir the mixture once it starts to boil. Clamp a candy thermometer to the saucepan.

3. Cook to hard-crack stage—300 degrees F—then remove from the heat and add coloring and flavoring. Stir for 30–60 seconds and pour into molds.

4. Let sit for 10–15 minutes before removing the molds and taking the lollipops off the pan.

☝ RECIPE TIPS

☺ **Make Ahead:** *These can be wrapped in lollipop bags and stored at room temperature for up to 3 months.*

☺ **Molds:** *The easiest place to purchase molds is online.*

⚙ VARIATIONS

For Caramel Lollipops, add ½ cup melted butter to the candy mixture when it reaches 275 degrees F. Mix and bring temperature to 300 degrees F, then pour directly into lollipop molds. Let set for 15–20 minutes before removing molds and taking the lollipops off the pan.

ALSO TRY: Cookies and Cream Fudge (page 256), Homemade Toffee (page 259), Candied Almonds (page 260)

CHOCOLATE-COVERED STRAWBERRIES

- ⏱ **PREP TIME:** 10 MINUTES
- ⏳ **COOK TIME:** 5 MINUTES
- ⏳ **REST TIME:** 50 MINUTES
- ♡ **SERVES:** 12

- ✓ QUICK & EASY
- ✓ FEED A CROWD
- ✓ MAKE AHEAD
- ✓ GLUTEN-FREE

INGREDIENTS

1 pint strawberries (16–24 strawberries), rinsed and dried

1 (10-ounce) bag Ghirardelli milk chocolate melting wafers

2 ounces white melting chocolate, for drizzle

TOPPINGS: sprinkles, chopped nuts, shredded coconut, mini chocolate chips (optional)

Scan me!

INSTRUCTIONS

1. Line a baking sheet with parchment paper. Place strawberries and a hot pad right next to your saucepan.

2. Place milk chocolate in a medium saucepan over low heat and cook, stirring constantly with a rubber spatula, until melted, about 5 minutes. When chocolate is completely smooth, remove from the heat and set pot on the hot pad.

3. Hold the pot of chocolate at an angle. Grab a strawberry by the stem and dip both sides in the chocolate. Allow excess chocolate to drip off and wipe bottom of strawberry on the edge of the pan before placing on the parchment (this will help prevent chocolate from pooling). Repeat to dip all the strawberries. Let sit 5 minutes.

4. Once first layer of chocolate has set, repeat the process to double dip each strawberry, again being sure to wipe off the excess chocolate before returning the berries to the parchment. This will make them extra chocolatey and smooth on the outside. Let strawberries sit on your counter until hard, about 30 minutes.

5. Melt white chocolate as described in Step 2 and transfer to a piping bag or a resealable plastic bag with a small hole cut in the corner. Drizzle back and forth over dipped strawberries, then immediately add any desired toppings. Let sit for about 15 minutes to set.

👍 RECIPE TIPS

☺ **Make Ahead:** *These can be made up to 48 hours in advance. Place a sheet of wax paper at the bottom of an airtight container. Add a layer of strawberries, then top with another piece of wax paper. Repeat to store layers separated by pieces of wax paper. Store in the refrigerator.*

☺ **Chocolate Pairing:** *You can choose any two contrasting chocolate types for dipping and drizzling your strawberries. Some of our favorites include Ghirardelli Melting Wafers (milk, white or dark), candy coating, Baker's Baking Bar (semisweet or white) and Guittard chocolate chips.*

ALSO TRY: Fruit Pizza (page 229), Cream Cheese Fruit Dip (page 273), Caramel Dip (page 274)

HOMEMADE TOFFEE

- PREP TIME: 10 MINUTES
- COOK TIME: 15 MINUTES
- REST TIME: 2 HOURS
- SERVES: 12

FEED A CROWD

MAKE AHEAD

GLUTEN-FREE

EQUIPMENT

candy thermometer

INGREDIENTS

2 cups salted butter

2 cups sugar

2 teaspoons vanilla extract

¼ teaspoon salt

2 cups milk chocolate chips

½ cup chopped pecans

Scan me!

INSTRUCTIONS

1. Line a 7-x-12-inch jelly roll pan with parchment paper.

2. Combine butter, sugar, vanilla and salt in a large, heavy-bottomed saucepan over medium heat. Clamp a candy thermometer to the saucepan.

3. Cook, stirring occasionally, until melted and smooth, then bring to a boil while whisking constantly.

4. Continue whisking the mixture as it boils until it reaches 290 degrees F or the hard-crack stage. This will take 10–15 minutes, and the mixture will be amber-caramel in color.

5. When it reaches hard-crack stage, immediately pour toffee into the prepared pan.

6. Let sit for 1–2 minutes, then sprinkle chocolate chips on top. After 1 more minute, spread chocolate smooth with an offset or rubber spatula and sprinkle chopped pecans on top.

7. Let sit at room temperature for 2 hours to harden, then cut into pieces with a thick, sharp knife.

👍 RECIPE TIPS

☺ **Make Ahead:** *Toffee can be stored in an airtight container at room temperature for 1–2 weeks. You can also refrigerate it to extend the shelf life to about 3 months.*

⚙ VARIATIONS

To change up your toffee, switch out the milk chocolate chips for semisweet, dark, or white chocolate, or use chopped almonds, toffee bits, candy cane bits or holiday sprinkles in place of the pecans.

ALSO TRY: Cookies and Cream Fudge (page 256), Homemade Lollipops (page 257), Candied Almonds (page 260)

CANDIED ALMONDS

⏱ **PREP TIME:** 5 MINUTES
⧖ **COOK TIME:** 1 HOUR
♡ **SERVES:** 12

⊘ PREPPED IN 5
⊘ FEED A CROWD
⊘ MAKE AHEAD
⊘ DAIRY-FREE
⊘ GLUTEN-FREE

INGREDIENTS

1 egg white
1 teaspoon cold water
4 cups whole raw almonds
½ cup sugar
½ teaspoon ground cinnamon
¼ teaspoon salt

Scan me!

INSTRUCTIONS

1. Preheat the oven to 250 degrees F. Lightly grease a 10-x-15-inch jelly roll pan and set aside.

2. In a small bowl, lightly beat egg white. Add water and beat until frothy. Add almonds and stir until well coated.

3. In a separate bowl (or in a resealable plastic bag), mix sugar, cinnamon and salt. Sprinkle over nuts and toss to coat, then spread nuts evenly on the greased pan.

4. Bake for 1 hour, stirring occasionally, until golden. Let cool before enjoying.

👍 **RECIPE TIPS**

☺ **Make Ahead:** *You can make these in advance and store in an airtight container for 1 week at room temperature, 2 weeks in the refrigerator or 2 months in the freezer.*

⚙ **VARIATIONS**

Change up the flavor of your candied almonds by adding 2 teaspoons vanilla extract or vanilla bean paste, adding 2 teaspoons pumpkin pie spice or replacing the cinnamon with a pinch of cayenne pepper.

ALSO TRY: Puppy Chow (page 254), Chocolate-Covered Strawberries (page 258), Homemade Toffee (page 259)

CARAMEL MARSHMALLOW POPCORN

⏱ PREP TIME: **5 MINUTES**

⧗ COOK TIME: **10 MINUTES**

⧗ REST TIME: **10 MINUTES**

♡ SERVES: **8**

✓ PREPPED IN 5

✓ QUICK & EASY

✓ FEED A CROWD

✓ GLUTEN-FREE

INGREDIENTS

1 (3.2-ounce) bag plain microwave popcorn

½ cup unsalted butter

1 cup packed light brown sugar

1 tablespoon light corn syrup

20 large marshmallows (or 3 cups mini marshmallows)

Scan me!

INSTRUCTIONS

1. Pop popcorn and place in a large bowl, removing any unpopped kernels.

2. Melt butter in a medium saucepan over medium-low heat. Add brown sugar and corn syrup and cook, stirring, until well blended. Add marshmallows and stir continuously until all melted, about 5 minutes.

3. Pour mixture over popcorn and mix well. Spread popcorn out on parchment paper or a greased baking sheet and let sit for about 10 minutes to set up.

ALSO TRY: Puppy Chow (page 254), Candied Almonds (page 260), White Chocolate Popcorn (page 262)

👍 RECIPE TIPS

☺ **Choose Your Favorite Popcorn:** *One 3.2-ounce bag of microwave popcorn contains 5 tablespoons of unpopped kernels, which makes 10–11 cups of popped popcorn. So for this recipe, you can buy 11 cups of plain prepopped popcorn, pop 5 tablespoons of your own kernels, or pop 1 bag of plain microwave popcorn.*

WHITE CHOCOLATE POPCORN

⏱ **PREP TIME:** 5 MINUTES

⧗ **COOK TIME:** 10 MINUTES

⧗ **REST TIME:** 15 MINUTES

♡ **SERVES:** 12

- ✓ PREPPED IN 5
- ✓ QUICK & EASY
- ✓ FEED A CROWD
- ✓ MAKE AHEAD
- ✓ GLUTEN-FREE

INGREDIENTS

2 (3.2-ounce) bags plain microwave popcorn

1 (24-ounce) package vanilla bark (or candy coating)

1 cup M&M's

Scan me!

INSTRUCTIONS

1. Pop popcorn and pour into a large bowl, removing any unpopped kernels.

2. Break vanilla bark into squares and place in a medium pot over low heat. Cook, stirring constantly with a rubber spatula, until melted. Remove from the heat.

3. Pour melted melted vanilla bark (or candy coating) over popcorn and mix until coated.

4. Add M&M's and mix, then spread popcorn out onto a parchment paper–lined baking sheet. Let sit for 15 minutes, until hardened.

Churro Popcorn

★ **BONUS RECIPE**

Follow the recipe above but omit the M&M's. Combine 2 tablespoons sugar and 1 teaspoon ground cinnamon, and sprinkle over popcorn as soon as you spread it onto the parchment paper–lined baking sheet. Let sit until hardened.

👍 **RECIPE TIPS**

☺ **Make Ahead:** *In an airtight container at room temperature, this popcorn will keep for up to 1 week.*

ALSO TRY: Puppy Chow (page 254), Chocolate-Covered Strawberries (page 258), Caramel Marshmallow Popcorn (page 261)

POPCORN BALLS

QUICK & EASY

ON THE TABLE IN 20

FEED A CROWD

MAKE AHEAD

GLUTEN-FREE

INGREDIENTS

2 (3.2-ounce) bags plain microwave popcorn

2½ cups powdered sugar

1 cup mini marshmallows

¾ cup light corn syrup

4 tablespoons margarine (or unsalted butter), plus more for your hands

2 teaspoons cold water

a few drops food coloring of choice

Scan me!

INSTRUCTIONS

1. Pop popcorn and pour into a large bowl, removing any unpopped kernels.

2. In a medium pot over medium-high heat, combine powdered sugar, marshmallows, corn syrup, margarine, water and food coloring. Heat and stir until the mixture comes to a boil.

3. Carefully pour over the popcorn, stirring to coat each kernel.

4. Let cool a bit, then butter your fingers so you can easily handle and shape popcorn into 3–4-inch balls before they cool.

5. Wrap with plastic wrap and store at room temperature.

ALSO TRY: Rice Krispies Treats (page 237), Scotcheroos (page 238), Puppy Chow (page 254)

👍 **RECIPE TIPS**

☺ **Make Ahead:** *Wrap balls with plastic wrap and store at room temperature for up to 5 days.*

☺ **Serving Suggestion:** *Make the balls a little bit smaller and insert a popsicle stick into the middle of each one before wrapping to eliminate some of the mess and stickiness that comes with these.*

WHITE CHOCOLATE TRAIL MIX

- ⏱ **PREP TIME:** 5 MINUTES
- ⏳ **COOK TIME:** 5 MINUTES
- ⏳ **REST TIME:** 1 HOUR
- ♡ **SERVES:** 12

- ⊘ **PREPPED IN 5**
- ⊘ **QUICK & EASY**
- ⊘ **FEED A CROWD**

INGREDIENTS

2 cups Rice Chex cereal

2 cups plain Cheerios

2 cups mini pretzels

2 cups M&M's

1–2 cups peanuts (salted or unsalted)

1 (24-ounce) package white almond bark

Scan me!

INSTRUCTIONS

1. In a large bowl, combine Chex, Cheerios, pretzels, M&M's and peanuts and mix well.

2. Break almond bark into pieces and melt in a medium pot over low heat, stirring constantly until smooth.

3. Pour melted bark over cereal mixture and mix well.

4. Spread out onto wax paper or onto a parchment paper–lined baking sheet. Let set for 1 hour, then break into pieces to serve.

ALSO TRY: Puppy Chow (page 254), White Chocolate Popcorn (page 262), Popcorn Balls (page 263)

👍 **RECIPE TIPS**

☺ **Dress It Up:** *Make a holiday version (like Christmas or Valentine's Day!) by using holiday M&M's that are specific colors. If you are feeling extra fancy, throw in some colorful sprinkles, too.*

HOMEMADE ICE CREAM

⏱ **PREP TIME:** 45 MINUTES

⏳ **FREEZE TIME:** 4 HOURS

♡ **SERVES:** 10

FREEZER FRIENDLY

FEED A CROWD

MAKE AHEAD

GLUTEN-FREE

INGREDIENTS

2 cups heavy cream

2 cups half-and-half

1 cup sugar

1 tablespoon vanilla extract

Scan me!

INSTRUCTIONS

1. In a medium bowl combine all ingredients, stirring to dissolve the sugar completely.

2. Pour into an ice cream maker, filling no more than two-thirds full. (If you have extra mixture, just store it in a container in the refrigerator until you can churn it.)

3. Freeze cream mixture according to the manufacturer's directions. For those whose ice cream makers use ice, adding rock salt to the ice in your ice cream maker can lower the temperature and speed up the freezing process. Serve immediately or store in covered containers in the freezer.

⚙ VARIATIONS

There are so many ways to change up this ice cream—just make sure any add-ins are cold, and mix them in during the last 2 minutes of churning in the ice cream maker. Here are some of our favorites:

- ⊕ **COOKIES AND CREAM:** Add 1½ cups coarsely chopped Oreos.
- ⊕ **VANILLA MALT:** Add ¾ cup malted milk powder.
- ⊕ **SALTED CARAMEL:** Add ¼ teaspoon salt, and a drizzle of caramel sauce.
- ⊕ **PEACHES AND CREAM:** Add 1 (15-ounce) can sliced peaches (drained and diced) or 3 medium peaches, peeled and sliced.

☝ RECIPE TIPS

☺ **No Ice Cream Maker?** *No problem! To make this without an ice cream maker, place a shallow container (glass or metal work best) in the freezer to chill. Prepare cream mixture as described above and pour into the chilled container. Store in the coldest part of your freezer until almost firm but still soft enough to be stirred, about 1 hour. Stir mixture with a spoon or hand mixer, then return to the freezer. Over the next 3 hours, mix the ice cream with a spoon or hand mixer every 30 minutes to help it stay aerated and creamy. After 3 hours, serve or store in covered containers in the freezer.*

ALSO TRY: Chocolate Sheet Cake (page 211), White Sheet Cake (page 212), Brownies (page 220), M&M Chocolate Oat Bars (page 222), Peach Cobbler (page 230)

ARROZ CON LECHE

PREP TIME: 5 MINUTES
COOK TIME: 40 MINUTES
SERVES: 10

PREPPED IN 5

FEED A CROWD

MAKE AHEAD

GLUTEN-FREE

INGREDIENTS

7 cups water

1 cup long-grain white rice

2 cinnamon sticks

1 (14-ounce) can sweetened condensed milk

1 (12-ounce) can evaporated milk

1 cup whole milk

TOPPING: ground cinnamon

Scan me!

INSTRUCTIONS

1. Combine water, rice and cinnamon sticks in a large saucepan over medium-high heat. Bring to a boil, uncovered, and cook for 16–18 minutes.

2. Drain any remaining liquid, remove cinnamon sticks and return rice to the pan over medium-high heat. Add sweetened condensed milk, evaporated milk and whole milk and bring to a boil.

3. Reduce the heat to low and cook for about 20 minutes, stirring constantly. The milk can easily burn, so it is important to stir constantly as it thickens.

4. Divide rice among serving cups and sprinkle with cinnamon. Serve warm.

☺ RECIPE TIPS

☺ **Make Ahead:** *Just store in the refrigerator in an airtight container for a few days. We reheat it in a pot and add a bit more cinnamon to the top before serving.*

⚙ VARIATIONS

For a more intense cinnamon-flavored rice pudding, add 1 teaspoon of cinnamon in Step 2 when adding the milks. You can also add raisins at this point, if you wish.

TOPPINGS: Try topping each serving with a sprinkle of brown sugar, nutmeg or coconut or with a drizzle of honey.

ALSO TRY: Easy Cinnamon Rolls (page 48), Dirt Cake (page 210), Churros (page 267)

CHURROS

⏱ PREP TIME: 10 MINUTES

⌛ COOK TIME: 25 MINUTES

♡ MAKES: 16 CHURROS

FEED A CROWD

INGREDIENTS

CHURROS:

1½–2 cups vegetable oil, for frying

1 cup water

½ cup unsalted butter, cut into pieces

¼ teaspoon ground cinnamon

¼ teaspoon salt

1¼ cups all-purpose flour

3 large eggs

½ teaspoon vanilla extract

TOPPING:

½ cup sugar

1 teaspoon ground cinnamon, divided

Scan me!

INSTRUCTIONS

1. Fill a heavy-bottomed pot with 1½–2 inches of oil and heat over medium-high heat to about 360 degrees F.

2. To make the topping: Whisk together sugar and cinnamon in a shallow dish and set aside.

3. To begin the churros: Combine water, butter, cinnamon and salt in a small saucepan. Bring the mixture to a rolling boil over medium heat, then reduce the heat to low.

4. Add flour and stir to form a ball. Remove from the heat and let cool for 5 minutes.

5. Add eggs one at a time, stirring until combined after each addition. Add vanilla.

6. Add a large star tip to a piping bag and spoon dough into the piping bag. Pipe dough over the hot oil and cut at 1–3 inches long. Repeat until churros fill the pan, making sure to leave room between churros. Fry until golden brown, 2–3 minutes on each side.

7. Remove churros from oil with a slotted spoon and place on a paper towel–lined plate.

8. While still warm, roll in cinnamon/sugar mixture. Repeat with remaining dough. Serve warm.

👍 RECIPE TIPS

☺ **Dip Pairings:** *Churros are great with their cinnamon-sugar coating, but are even better with an assortment of dips. A few of our favorites include Chocolate Fudge Sauce (page 270), Caramel Dip (page 274), strawberry sauce and white chocolate fudge sauce.*

ALSO TRY: Snickerdoodles (page 241), Popcorn Balls (page 263), Funnel Cake (page 270)

CREAM PUFFS

FEED A CROWD

MAKE AHEAD

INGREDIENTS

1 cup water

5 tablespoons plus 1 teaspoon unsalted butter

1 tablespoon granulated sugar

⅛ teaspoon salt

1 cup all-purpose flour

4 eggs

1 cup heavy cream

¼ cup powdered sugar, or more or less to taste

Scan me!

ALSO TRY: Cream Puff Cake (page 209), Popcorn Balls (page 263), Churros (page 267)

INSTRUCTIONS

1. Preheat the oven to 450 degrees F. Line two baking sheets with parchment paper or silicone liners and set aside.

2. In a medium saucepan over medium heat, combine water, butter, granulated sugar and salt and bring to a simmer. Once a simmer is reached, remove from the heat and stir in flour all at once until the mixture forms a ball. Let stand for 5 minutes.

3. Add the eggs one at a time, mixing well by hand or with a hand mixer between each addition. Mix until the dough is smooth and shiny.

4. Transfer dough to a pastry bag fitted with a large tip (or a resealable plastic bag with a hole cut in the corner). Pipe small (1–1½-inch) rounds of dough onto the prepared baking sheets, spacing about 1 inch apart. Use your finger to press down the little peaks at the top of the dough, so the puffs are smooth. (Tip: Make sure all the cream puffs are the same size, so they all cook at the same rate.)

5. Bake for 10 minutes, then lower the temperature to 350 degrees F and bake for 15 minutes more. The puffs are done when they are lightly browned and the insides are hollow. Let the puffs cool completely.

6. While the puffs cool, beat cream with a hand mixer or by hand, using a wire whisk, until firm peaks form. Beat in the powdered sugar a little at a time until the whipped cream is as sweet as you prefer.

7. When puffs are cool, split each cream puff in half using a serrated knife.

8. Place a scoop of whipped cream onto the bottom half of each puff. Top with the other half and dust with powdered sugar before serving.

☝ RECIPE TIPS

☺ **Make Ahead:** *You can store the unbaked pastry dough in an airtight container or pastry bag in the refrigerator for up to 2 days. Baked shells can also be stored, unfilled, in an airtight container at room temperature for 1–2 days. Filled puffs are best served right away, but can be made a couple hours ahead of time and refrigerated.*

STRAWBERRY PRETZEL SALAD

⏲ **PREP TIME:** 10 MINUTES
⧗ **COOK TIME:** 10 MINUTES
⧖ **CHILL TIME:** 4 HOURS
♡ **SERVES:** 12–15

✓ **FEED A CROWD**

✓ **MAKE AHEAD**

INGREDIENTS

2½ cups crushed pretzels
½ cup sugar, divided
⅔ cup unsalted butter, melted
12 ounces cream cheese, softened
2 tablespoons milk
1 cup whipped topping
2 cups boiling water
1 (6-ounce) box strawberry Jell-O mix
1½ cups cold water
4 cups sliced strawberries

Scan me!

INSTRUCTIONS

1. Preheat the oven to 350 degrees F.

2. In a medium bowl, mix crushed pretzels, ¼ cup sugar and the butter. Press into the bottom of a 9-x-13-inch baking dish. Bake for 10 minutes and let cool.

3. In another bowl, beat cream cheese, remaining ¼ cup sugar and milk together with a hand mixer. Fold in whipped topping and spread over the crust to the edges. Refrigerate until ready to use.

4. In a large, heatproof bowl, combine boiling water and Jell-O mix and stir for 2 minutes until dissolved. Stir in cold water and refrigerate for 1–2 hours, or until thickened.

5. Stir strawberries into thickened Jell-O and spoon into crust over the cream cheese layer.

6. Refrigerate for at least another 3 hours before serving.

ALSO TRY: Lemon Lasagna (page 228), Chocolate-Covered Strawberries (page 258), Cream Cheese Fruit Dip (page 273)

🖐 RECIPE TIPS

☺ **Make Ahead:** *Because this needs several hours to set in the refrigerator, it is best made the morning of or the day before serving. It will keep, refrigerated, for 3–4 days.*

⚙ VARIATIONS

Pair up any flavor Jell-O with its fruit counterpart, such as cherry Jell-O with cherries or raspberry Jell-O with raspberries, or try mixing flavors, such as lime Jell-O paired with strawberries.

FUNNEL CAKE

PREP TIME: 5 MINUTES

COOK TIME: 25 MINUTES

SERVES: 6

PREPPED IN 5

QUICK & EASY

MAKE AHEAD

INGREDIENTS

vegetable oil, for frying

2 cups all-purpose flour

1 teaspoon baking powder

½ teaspoon salt

1½ cups milk

2 eggs

TOPPINGS: whipped cream, fruit, Chocolate Fudge Sauce (see below), caramel sauce, powdered sugar

Scan me!

INSTRUCTIONS

1. Pour about 1 inch vegetable oil into a frying pan and heat over medium-high heat to 375 degrees F.

2. In a medium bowl, whisk together flour, baking powder, salt, milk and eggs.

3. Pour batter into a funnel, blocking the tip of the funnel with your finger, or use a squeeze bottle. Position funnel over the hot oil and slowly move your finger so batter comes out in a steady stream. Make circular and crisscross motions to form a funnel cake. Fry for 1–2 minutes, or until golden brown.

4. Using tongs, flip funnel cake and fry the other side for 1–2 minutes.

5. Remove to a paper towel–lined plate to drain.

6. Repeat with the remaining batter. Serve funnel cakes warm with desired toppings.

Chocolate Fudge Sauce

★ BONUS RECIPE

Combine 2 cups powdered sugar, ¾ cup semisweet chocolate chips, ½ cup unsalted butter and 1 (12-ounce) can evaporated milk in a medium pot over medium-high heat. Bring to a boil and cook for 8 minutes, stirring constantly. Use on top of funnel cakes, ice cream and more.

👍 **RECIPE TIPS**

☺ **Choose Your Tool:** *Although they're called "funnel cakes," squeeze bottles actually work even better than funnels for making these. Clean an old ketchup bottle or something similar and pour the batter into it to make frying easier.*

☺ **Make Ahead:** *You can make the batter ahead of time and store it in an airtight container in the refrigerator for 2–3 days before making funnel cakes.*

⚙ **VARIATIONS**

➔ **FOR FUNNEL CAKE FRIES:** Follow the instructions as written, but pipe batter in long straight lines into oil. Fry until golden and remove.

➔ **FOR FUNNEL CAKE BITES:** Use a cookie scoop to drop the batter into the oil. Fry until golden brown and remove.

ALSO TRY: Strawberry Jam (page 63), Homemade Whipped Cream (page 208), Homemade Ice Cream (page 265), Churros (page 267)

BEIGNETS

⏱ PREP TIME: 10 MINUTES
⏳ RISE TIME: 1 HOUR
⏳ COOK TIME: 20 MINUTES
♡ MAKES: 18 BEIGNETS

✓ FEED A CROWD

✓ MAKE AHEAD

INGREDIENTS

¾ cup warm water (110–115 degrees F)

1 teaspoon rapid rise yeast

1 egg, lightly beaten

½ cup heavy cream

2 tablespoons shortening

¼ cup granulated sugar

1 teaspoon salt

1 dash nutmeg

3¼ cups all-purpose flour

1 quart vegetable oil, for frying

½ cup powdered sugar

Scan me!

INSTRUCTIONS

1. Place warm water in a small bowl. Sprinkle yeast on top and stir to dissolve. Allow yeast to activate (about 5 minutes).

2. In a large mixing bowl or stand mixer, combine egg, cream, shortening, granulated sugar, salt and nutmeg. Mix to combine.

3. Pour in activated yeast and mix.

4. Add flour to the mix. Use the dough hook attachment on a stand mixer and mix on medium speed until all ingredients are combined and the dough is smooth but still slightly sticky.

5. Form a ball with the dough and place in a greased bowl. Cover and let rise for about 1 hour.

6. Heat 3 inches of oil in a deep-sided, heavy pot over medium-high heat until oil reaches between 360 and 370 degrees F.

7. On a lightly floured surface, roll out the dough until it is ½ inch thick, making sure not to overwork the dough. Cut into 2½-inch squares.

8. Working in batches, fry beignets in the hot oil until golden brown (1–2 minutes on each side).

9. Use tongs to remove the beignets from the hot oil. Place on a paper towel–lined plate to drain. While beignets are still warm, dust them completely with powdered sugar. Serve immediately.

🔖 RECIPE TIPS

☺ **Make Ahead:** *You can make the dough and store it, covered, in the refrigerator for up to 3 days. Even though it is in the refrigerator, it will slowly rise. Let the dough come to room temperature before rolling and cutting.*

☺ **Keep Warm:** *After frying, place beignets on a baking sheet in a 200 degree F oven for up to 30 minutes before serving.*

☺ **Toppings:** *Serve with Chocolate Fudge Sauce (page 270) or Caramel Dip (page 274).*

ALSO TRY: Cream Puff Cake (page 209), Cream Puffs (page 268), Funnel Cake (page 270)

CREAM CHEESE FRUIT DIP

⏱ **PREP TIME: 10 MINUTES**

♡ **SERVES: 14**

- ✓ QUICK & EASY
- ✓ ON THE TABLE IN 20
- ✓ FEED A CROWD
- ✓ MAKE AHEAD
- ✓ GLUTEN-FREE

INGREDIENTS

1½ cups powdered sugar
1 (8-ounce) package cream cheese, softened
1 teaspoon vanilla extract
1 (8-ounce) tub whipped topping
1 (7-ounce) jar Marshmallow Fluff
strawberries, pineapple, grapes or pound cake
    pieces, for serving

Scan me!

INSTRUCTIONS

1. In a medium bowl, beat powdered sugar, cream cheese and vanilla together, with a hand mixer on low speed, until well mixed.

2. Fold in whipped topping and Marshmallow Fluff.

3. Chill until ready to serve. Serve with fruit or pound cake for dipping.

ALSO TRY: Caramel Dip (page 274), Apple Brickle Dip (page 275)

👍 RECIPE TIPS

☺ **Make Ahead:** *This dip can be made 5–7 days in advance. Store in an airtight container in the refrigerator and mix thoroughly before serving.*

☺ **Serving Tip:** *To serve cut fruit alongside this dip without it turning brown, squeeze a lemon over the fruit and gently toss. This will ensure the fruit lasts longer for serving.*

CARAMEL DIP

⏱ **PREP TIME:** **5 MINUTES**
⧗ **COOK TIME:** **10 MINUTES**
♡ **SERVES:** **10**

✓ PREPPED IN 5
✓ QUICK & EASY
✓ ON THE TABLE IN 20
✓ FEED A CROWD
✓ MAKE AHEAD
✓ GLUTEN-FREE

INGREDIENTS

½ cup unsalted butter
2 cups packed dark brown sugar
1 (14-ounce) can sweetened condensed milk
1 cup light corn syrup
2 tablespoons water
1 teaspoon vanilla extract
sliced apples, for serving

Scan me!

INSTRUCTIONS

1. Melt butter in a small saucepan over medium heat.

2. Add all remaining ingredients and cook, stirring constantly, until sugar is dissolved, 6–7 minutes.

3. Remove from the heat and let cool before serving. Serve with apples or any other desired dippers.

ALSO TRY: Cream Cheese Fruit Dip (page 273), Apple Brickle Dip (page 275)

👍 RECIPE TIPS

☺ **Make Ahead:** *This dip can be made up to 1 week in advance. Store in an airtight container in the refrigerator.*

☺ **What to Dip?** *Apples are our favorite, but pretzels, strawberries, bananas, pound cake or marshmallows are also great dippers.*

APPLE BRICKLE DIP

🕐 PREP TIME: **5 MINUTES**
♡ SERVES: **8**

✓ PREPPED IN 5
✓ QUICK & EASY
✓ ON THE TABLE IN 20
✓ MAKE AHEAD
✓ GLUTEN-FREE

INGREDIENTS

1 (8-ounce) package cream cheese, softened
½ cup packed light brown sugar
½ cup granulated sugar
1 teaspoon vanilla extract
1 (8-ounce) package Heath Toffee Bits
sliced apples (Gala, Fuji or Honeycrisp),
   for serving

Scan me!

INSTRUCTIONS

1. In a medium bowl, beat cream cheese, both sugars and vanilla with a hand mixer.

2. Fold in toffee bits and refrigerate until ready to serve.

3. Serve with sliced apples for dipping.

👍 RECIPE TIPS

☺ **Make Ahead:** *You can make this dip 3–5 days ahead of time. Store in an airtight container in the refrigerator.*

☺ **More Dipping Ideas:** *Though this dip was created for apples, you can certainly use other delicious dippers such as pineapple spears, berries, graham crackers, pretzels, vanilla wafers, Oreos or gingersnaps.*

ALSO TRY: Cream Cheese Fruit Dip (page 273), Caramel Dip (page 274)

DRINKS

"When life hands you lemons, make lemonade. But if it doesn't hand you water and sugar, too, your lemonade will be lousy."

Homemade drinks are so underrated! They are among the easiest recipes, can easily be made for small or large groups, work for multiple meals during the day, and can even be a great stand-alone treat! Nothing gets our kids more excited at dinnertime or at a picnic than whipping out one of our favorite drink recipes. Try any of these, and you will not be disappointed!

HELPFUL TIPS + INFORMATION

How Much to Serve

HOW MUCH TO SERVE GUESTS: A glass of punch, soda or juice is usually 6–8 ounces. Guests will typically drink 1–2 glasses during the first hour of a party and 1 glass for every hour after.

Serving Tips

- ⊘ **CARBONATED DRINKS:** Carbonation in punch will only last for a few hours, so add sodas and other carbonated ingredients just before serving.

- ⊘ **KEEP HOT DRINKS HOT:** The ideal temperature for hot beverages like cocoa is 140°F. Serve in a slow cooker on the warm setting with the lid off to keep them at just the right temperature.

- ⊘ **KEEP COLD DRINKS COLD:** To avoid diluting a cold drink, mix the ingredients ahead of time, but hold the ice until just before serving, or keep extra punch in the refrigerator or in a cooler, and refill the beverage dispenser as needed. You can also get creative with your ice to keep drinks cold without diluting them:

  - ○ Instead of using plain ice, make a small batch of punch in advance and freeze it in ice cube trays. As the punch cubes melt, they will add more flavor and not water down the drink.

  - ○ Instead of adding ice cubes, use frozen fruit in a complementary flavor to keep drinks cold.

Fun Ways to Spruce Up a Drink

- ⊘ One of our favorite ways to garnish drinks is to add sugar to the rim of each glass. You'll need a bowl of fruit juice and a bowl of sugar. Dip the rim of the glass in the juice, then dip into the sugar and let dry before pouring in the drink.

- ⊘ Add a scoop of ice cream to any cold drink or punch and serve as-is, or mix together to turn it into a float.

- ⊘ Garnish individual glasses with a wedge of lemon or lime on the rim so your guests can add a spritz of fresh citrus juice.

- ⊘ When serving punches in a large batch, add fresh-cut fruit or berries to the beverage dispenser for a pop of color and extra flavor.

Use Up Leftovers

Pour leftover drinks into popsicle molds to freeze and turn into a cold treat.

PINK PUNCH

⏱ **PREP TIME:** 5 MINUTES
♡ **SERVES:** 12

✓ PREPPED IN 5
✓ QUICK & EASY
✓ ON THE TABLE IN 20
✓ FREEZER FRIENDLY
✓ FEED A CROWD
✓ MAKE AHEAD
✓ DAIRY-FREE
✓ GLUTEN-FREE

INGREDIENTS

1 (46-ounce) can Dole pineapple juice, cold
1 cup pink lemonade mix
1 (2-liter) bottle Sprite, cold

Scan me!

INSTRUCTIONS

1. Combine pineapple juice and lemonade mix in a large pitcher or punch bowl.

2. Right before serving, add Sprite and mix well. Add ice.

👍 **RECIPE TIPS**

☺ **Make Ahead:** *You can make the pineapple-lemonade mixture ahead and keep it refrigerated for up to 24 hours. Wait to add the soda until right before serving.*

☺ **Presentation:** *This punch looks so delicious and pretty in a glass pitcher, bowl or beverage dispenser. To really make it shine, add sliced lemon rounds and pineapple rings. You can even include strawberries, raspberries or cranberries.*

⚙ **VARIATIONS**

Change it up by using classic lemonade mix, blue raspberry lemonade mix or cherry limeade lemonade mix in place of the pink lemonade.

ALSO TRY: Cherry Limeade (page 281), Lemonade (page 282)

OCEAN WATER

✓ PREPPED IN 5

✓ QUICK & EASY

✓ ON THE TABLE IN 20

✓ DAIRY-FREE

✓ GLUTEN-FREE

INGREDIENTS

⅔ cup water

⅔ cup sugar

1 liter Sprite or 7UP

1 tablespoon coconut extract

blue food coloring

 *Scan me!*

INSTRUCTIONS

1. Combine water and sugar in a microwave-safe bowl and microwave for 45 seconds, then stir until sugar is dissolved.

2. Pour into a pitcher and add Sprite, coconut extract and 3–4 drops food coloring. Mix well.

3. Add ice right before serving.

ALSO TRY: Pink Punch (page 279), Cherry Limeade (page 281), Frozen Hot Chocolate (page 285)

👍 **RECIPE TIPS**

☺ **Serving Suggestions:** *There are so many fun ways to serve this up. Try adding Swedish Fish for the kids, adding a mini umbrella to each glass, serving out of a coconut-shaped cup or using seashell- or sea creature–shaped molds to create ocean-themed ice cubes.*

CHERRY LIMEADE

○ **PREP TIME:** 5 MINUTES

♡ **SERVES:** 1

⊘ **PREPPED IN 5**

⊘ **QUICK & EASY**

⊘ **ON THE TABLE IN 20**

⊘ **DAIRY-FREE**

⊘ **GLUTEN-FREE**

INGREDIENTS

2 maraschino cherries

2 lime wedges

1 (12-ounce) can 7UP or Sprite

2 tablespoons maraschino syrup

Scan me!

INSTRUCTIONS

1. Place cherries and 1 lime wedge in the bottom of a serving glass.

2. Add ice, then pour in 7UP.

3. Add maraschino syrup and juice from remaining lime wedge.

👍 RECIPE TIPS

☺ **The Ice Makes the Drink:** *We use Sonic's ice because it's airy and chewy. It also takes longer to melt than other ice, which helps the drink last longer without getting watered down.*

☺ **Maraschino Syrup:** *There's no need to purchase a separate bottle of maraschino syrup; just use the syrup from the maraschino cherry jar.*

ALSO TRY: Pink Punch (page 279), Lemonade (page 282)

LEMONADE

⏱ **PREP TIME:** 20 MINUTES

⏳ **CHILL TIME:** 30 MINUTES

♡ **SERVES:** 10

✓ FREEZER FRIENDLY

✓ FEED A CROWD

✓ MAKE AHEAD

✓ DAIRY-FREE

✓ GLUTEN-FREE

INGREDIENTS

1½ cups sugar

8 cups water, divided

1½ cups freshly squeezed lemon juice (from about 8 lemons)

Scan me!

INSTRUCTIONS

1. To get the most juice from the lemons, you will want to soak them in hot water for about 10 minutes.

2. While the lemons are soaking, make the syrup: Combine sugar and 1 cup water in a saucepan and bring to a boil. Stir until sugar has dissolved. Remove from the heat and allow to cool. Once syrup has reached room temperature, cover and place in the refrigerator to chill for 30 minutes.

3. Remove lemons from the hot water and allow them to cool enough to handle. Firmly roll each lemon on the countertop a few times. Cut lemons in half and juice them. Remove all the seeds but leave the pulp. Set juice aside until syrup has chilled.

4. To mix the lemonade, combine chilled syrup, lemon juice and remaining 7 cups water in a pitcher. Stir and serve over ice.

👍 **RECIPE TIPS**

☺ **Make Ahead:** *Lemonade can be made ahead and stored in a pitcher in the refrigerator for 5–7 days.*

⚙ **VARIATIONS**

↻ **LIMEADE:** Simply substitute the lemons for limes.

↻ **STRAWBERRY LEMONADE:** Place about 1 cup sliced strawberries in a bowl with 2 tablespoons sugar. Let sit for 5 minutes, then mash with a fork or use a food processor to puree. Mix strawberry puree into the lemonade, using more or less to taste.

ALSO TRY: Pink Punch (page 279), Cherry Limeade (page 281)

HALLOWEEN PUNCH

PREP TIME: **10 MINUTES**
COOK TIME: **5 MINUTES**
CHILL TIME: **1 HOUR**
SERVES: **16**

INGREDIENTS

1 (46-ounce) can pineapple juice, divided
1 (3-ounce) package orange gelatin
1 (64-ounce) bottle orange juice
1 (2-liter) bottle Sprite or 7UP, cold
1 quart orange sherbet

Scan me!

INSTRUCTIONS

1. In a small pot over medium-high heat, bring 1 cup pineapple juice to a boil. Stir in gelatin until dissolved. Remove from the heat and let cool. Transfer to a large container.

2. Add orange juice and remaining pineapple juice. Chill in the refrigerator for at least 1 hour.

3. Just before serving, pour into a large punch bowl, add Sprite and mix well. Top with scoops of sherbet.

👍 RECIPE TIPS

☺ **Make It Festive:**

Fill a rubber glove with water and freeze it. When ready to serve, add the rubber glove to the punch bowl and you'll have a floating hand keeping things cool.

Serve the punch from a black cauldron. This is especially fun when you use dry ice!

To make it extra-festive, serve in clear cups and draw pumpkin faces on the outside.

⚙ VARIATIONS

For a green Halloween version, use lime gelatin in place of the orange gelatin, limeade in place of the orange juice and lime sherbet in place of the orange sherbet to make it a festive Witch's Brew.

ALSO TRY: Holiday Punch (page 284), Apple Cider (page 286)

HOLIDAY PUNCH

- 🕐 **PREP TIME:** 5 MINUTES
- ⏳ **CHILL TIME:** 1 HOUR
- ♡ **SERVES:** 12

- ✓ PREPPED IN 5
- ✓ FEED A CROWD
- ✓ MAKE AHEAD
- ✓ DAIRY-FREE
- ✓ GLUTEN-FREE

INGREDIENTS

8 cups lemonade

4 cups cranberry juice

4 cups orange juice

1 (2-liter) bottle Sprite, chilled

1 cup fresh cranberries

1 orange, sliced

Scan me!

INSTRUCTIONS

1. Combine the lemonade, cranberry juice and orange juice in a large glass punch bowl. Refrigerate for 1–2 hours.

2. Right before serving, add Sprite and mix. Top with cranberries, orange slices and ice.

ALSO TRY: Pink Punch (page 279), Apple Cider (page 286), Eggnog (page 287)

👍 RECIPE TIPS

☺ **Keep It Cold:** *Consider freezing some of the punch into ice cubes—before you place the lemonade-juice mixture in the refrigerator to chill, pour a bit of it into an ice cube mold and freeze. This will help the punch stay cold longer, and when the cubes do melt, the punch will not get watered down. Another idea is to freeze the cranberries before adding to the punch bowl. They will also keep the punch cool without watering it down.*

☺ **To Serve in Rimmed Glasses:** *Pour sugar into a bowl or plate that is larger than the rim of your glasses. Moisten each glass's rim with lemon or orange juice, then dip it in the sugar.*

☺ **Make Ahead:** *Mix together the fresh fruit juices (cranberry juice, lemonade and orange juice) and refrigerate for at least 1 hour. When ready to serve, stir in Sprite (or any lemon-lime soda) and mix.*

FROZEN HOT CHOCOLATE

⏱ PREP TIME: 5 MINUTES

♡ SERVES: 2

✓ PREPPED IN 5

✓ QUICK & EASY

✓ ON THE TABLE IN 20

✓ GLUTEN-FREE

INGREDIENTS

2 cups milk

3 (1.38-ounce) packets hot cocoa mix

3 cups ice

whipped cream (optional)

chocolate curls (optional)

Scan me!

BONUS RECIPE

INSTRUCTIONS

1. Combine milk, hot cocoa mix and ice in a blender. Blend until mostly smooth.

2. Pour into two glasses and top with whipped cream and chocolate curls.

ALSO TRY: Pink Punch (page 279), Lemonade (page 282)

Homemade Hot Cocoa

Sift 2½ cups powdered sugar, 2 cups powdered milk (or instant nonfat dry milk), 1 cup unsweetened cocoa powder and ¼ teaspoon salt into a large bowl. Mix to combine well. Pour into storage containers and add mini marshmallows, if desired. Store in a sealed container at room temperature for up to 6 months. To make cocoa, mix ¼ cup hot cocoa mix with ¾ cup warm milk.

👍 **RECIPE TIPS**

☺ **How Much Cocoa Should I Use?** *If your favorite hot cocoa comes in a canister rather than in packets, not to worry. One packet contains about 2½ tablespoons cocoa mix, so for this recipe you'll need about 7½ tablespoons hot cocoa mix.*

APPLE CIDER

PREP TIME: 15 MINUTES
COOK TIME: 2 HOURS
SERVES: 12

- ⊘ FEED A CROWD
- ⊘ MAKE AHEAD
- ● SLOW COOKER
- ⊘ DAIRY-FREE
- ⊘ GLUTEN-FREE

INGREDIENTS

10 large apples (we use 5 Gala and 5 Honeycrisp)
16 cups water
¾ cup sugar
1 tablespoon ground cinnamon
1 tablespoon ground allspice
6 cinnamon sticks

Scan me!

INSTRUCTIONS

1. Quarter each apple and remove the core. Place apple slices in a large stockpot and add water.

2. Stir in sugar, cinnamon, allspice and cinnamon sticks. Bring to a simmer over medium heat, then cover the pot with a lid and continue simmering for 2 hours.

3. Stir well, then carefully strain the apple mixture through a fine-mesh sieve. Discard solids from the sieve. Line the sieve with cheesecloth and strain the cider again.

4. Serve warm, or refrigerate for 1–2 hours until cold.

👍 RECIPE TIPS

☺ **Slow Cooker Directions:** *Add all ingredients to the slow cooker and cook on high for 3–4 hours or low for 6–8 hours, stirring occasionally. Continue with Steps 3 and 4.*

☺ **Waste Not:** *Instead of discarding the apples after straining the cider, transfer the cooked, soft apples to a food processor and blend to make applesauce. Add cinnamon or other spices to taste.*

☺ **Make Ahead:** *This cider can be made ahead and stored in the refrigerator for about a week. For longer storage, freezing is recommended. When freezing, be sure to allow at least a 2-inch head space because the cider will expand during freezing and can rupture the container.*

⚙ VARIATIONS

For caramel apple cider, stir in 2 tablespoons caramel sauce before serving.

ALSO TRY: Halloween Punch (page 283), Holiday Punch (page 284), Eggnog (page 287)

EGGNOG

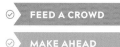
FEED A CROWD

MAKE AHEAD

GLUTEN-FREE

INGREDIENTS

6 large eggs, separated

1 cup sugar, divided

6 cups milk

2 tablespoons vanilla extract

½ teaspoon ground nutmeg

dash of salt

1 cup heavy cream, chilled

Scan me!

INSTRUCTIONS

1. Place a medium metal or glass mixing bowl in the refrigerator to be used later.

2. In another medium bowl, beat egg whites with a hand mixer until stiff. Fold in ¾ cup sugar, a few tablespoons at a time. Set aside.

3. In a large mixing bowl, beat egg yolks until they turn a lemon-yellow color. Mix in remaining ¼ cup sugar a few tablespoons at a time. Then mix in milk, vanilla, nutmeg and salt. Set aside.

4. Remove the chilled bowl from the refrigerator. Pour in heavy cream and whip until soft peaks form.

5. Add the egg-white mixture and the whipped cream to the egg-yolk mixture and use a wooden spoon to stir together. Chill until cold, about 2 hours.

ALSO TRY: Holiday Punch (page 284), Apple Cider (page 286)

👍 **RECIPE TIPS**

☺ **Make Ahead:** *Eggnog is best when chilled for a couple of hours before serving. Keep it covered in an airtight container in the refrigerator for up to 1 week.*

INDEXES

"Organized people are just too lazy to look for things."

So Easy doesn't just apply to the recipes! This book was created to be "So Easy" to use as well. To make finding the right recipe quicker and easier, we have included tags to help you navigate quickly to the recipe that will work best for the occasion that you are planning for. These indexes give you several ways of perusing the book and finding that recipe that is perfect for the moment at hand.

Recipe Tag Index

This tag index will help you decide which recipe fits best with the occasion, craving, holiday, or feast that you are planning for. The corresponding color-coded tags can be found on each individual recipe.

RECIPE LIST WITH PAGE NUMBERS	PREPPED IN 5	QUICK & EASY	ON THE TABLE IN 20	FREEZER FRIENDLY	FEED A CROWD	MAKE AHEAD	SLOW COOKER	DAIRY-FREE	GLUTEN-FREE
7-Layer Bars, 225		X			X	X			
7-Layer Dip, 87		X			X	X			X
Almond Poppy Seed Bread, 76	X			X		X			
Angel Food Ice Cream Cake, 216				X	X	X			
Apple Brickle Dip, 275	X	X	X			X			X
Apple Cider, 286					X	X	X	X	X
Arroz con Leche, 266	X				X	X			X
Asian Ramen Salad, 110		X	X		X	X			
Baby Back Ribs, 168					X			X	
Bacon-Wrapped Smokies, 92				X	X	X		X	X
Baked Potatoes, 139						X			X
Baked Salmon, 173	X							X	X
Baked Ziti, 201		X			X	X			
Banana Bars, 227	X	X			X	X			
Banana Bread, 81				X		X			
Beef Goulash, 194					X	X	X		
Beef Stroganoff, 200		X			X		X		
Beignets, 272					X	X			
Belgian Waffles, 42				X		X			
Best Chili Soup, 126							X	X	X
Biscuit Egg Casserole, 51	X	X			X	X			
Biscuits and Gravy, 50	X	X							
Black Bean and Corn Salsa (aka Cowboy Caviar), 155		X	X		X	X		X	X

RECIPE LIST WITH PAGE NUMBERS

	PREPPED IN 5	QUICK & EASY	ON THE TABLE IN 20	FREEZER FRIENDLY	FEED A CROWD	MAKE AHEAD	SLOW COOKER	DAIRY-FREE	GLUTEN-FREE
Chicken Tacos, 188		X			X				X
Chicken Tetrazzini, 193					X	X			
Chimichangas, 185						X			
Chocolate Chip Cookies, 240	X	X	X	X	X	X			
Chocolate Muffins, 80				X		X			
Chocolate Sheet Cake, 211		X			X	X			
Chocolate-Covered Strawberries, 258		X			X	X			X
Churros, 267					X				
Cilantro-Lime Rice, 149	X	X							X
Cinnamon Bread, 72				X		X			
Cinnamon Roll Cake, 46					X	X			
Classic Burgers, 160		X	X					X	
Coffee Cake, 47					X	X			
Cookie Bars (aka Pan Chewies), 223	X	X			X	X			
Cookies and Cream Fudge, 256					X	X			
Cornbread, 71	X	X		X	X	X			
Cream Cheese and Chicken Taquitos, 186	X	X			X	X			X
Cream Cheese Bean Dip, 89	X	X			X	X	X		X
Cream Cheese Fruit Dip, 273		X	X		X	X			X
Cream Pie, 233					X	X			
Cream Puff Cake, 209					X	X			
Cream Puffs, 268					X	X			
Creamed Corn, 138	X	X	X						
Creamy Swiss Chicken, 177	X								X
Crinkles, 244	X			X	X	X		X	
Deviled Eggs, 93						X			X
Dirt Cake, 210					X	X			
Donuts, 45					X	X			

RECIPE LIST WITH PAGE NUMBERS

	PREPPED IN 5	QUICK & EASY	ON THE TABLE IN 20	FREEZER FRIENDLY	FEED A CROWD	MAKE AHEAD	SLOW COOKER	DAIRY-FREE	GLUTEN-FREE
Easy Chocolate Cake, 214					X	X			
Easy Cinnamon Rolls, 48				X	X	X			
Easy Garlic Knots, 66		X	X		X	X			
Easy Homemade Biscuits, 65				X	X	X			
Easy Homemade White Bread, 61				X		X		X	
Easy Lasagna, 195				X	X				
Egg Drop Soup, 131		X	X					X	
Eggnog, 287					X	X			X
Empanadas, 189					X	X		X	
Energy Balls, 55				X		X		X	X
Fettuccine Alfredo, 198	X								
Flautas, 187					X	X			X
Flour Tortillas, 70					X	X			
French Bread, 63				X	X	X		X	
French Toast, 43	X	X	X			X			
French Toast Bake, 44				X	X	X			
Fried Egg Rolls, 99			X	X	X	X		X	
Fried Pickles, 97								X	
Fried Rice, 147	X	X	X						
Fried Zucchini, 98		X							
Frozen Hot Chocolate, 285	X	X	X						X
Fruit Pizza, 229					X	X			
Fruit Salad, 105					X	X		X	X
Fruit Smoothie, 56	X	X		X		X			X
Fry Bread, 69					X	X		X	
Funeral Potatoes, 146					X	X			X
Funnel Cake, 270	X	X				X			
Garlic Prime Rib, 162	X				X			X	X

RECIPE LIST WITH PAGE NUMBERS	PREPPED IN 5	QUICK & EASY	ON THE TABLE IN 20	FREEZER FRIENDLY	FEED A CROWD	MAKE AHEAD	SLOW COOKER	DAIRY-FREE	GLUTEN-FREE
General Tso's Chicken, 180	X	X	X	X				X	
German Pancakes, 40	X	X			X				
Gingersnaps, 250	X			X	X	X			
Glazed Lemon Zucchini Bread, 75				X		X			
Gooey Butter Cookies (aka Cake Mix Cookies), 246	X				X	X			
Graham Cracker Crust, 231	X	X				X			
Green Bean Bundles, 135		X				X			X
Green Bean Casserole, 137	X				X	X	X		
Green Chile Chicken Enchiladas, 183						X			X
Guacamole, 88		X	X		X	X		X	X
Halloween Punch, 283						X			X
Ham and Cheese Quiche, 54				X	X	X			
Hawaiian Haystacks, 176	X						X		
Heavenly Rolls, 68				X	X	X			
Holiday Punch, 284	X				X	X		X	X
Homemade Ice Cream, 265				X	X	X			X
Homemade Lollipops, 257					X	X		X	X
Homemade Mac and Cheese, 142					X	X	X		
Homemade Salsa, 153		X	X		X	X		X	X
Homemade Toffee, 259					X	X			X
Homemade Tortilla Chips, 151		X				X			X
Italian Sausage Pasta, 196	X	X	X						
Jell-O Poke Cake, 208					X	X			
Kid-Friendly Spaghetti, 199	X				X				
Lemon Bars, 226					X	X			
Lemon Lasagna, 228					X	X			
Lemonade, 282				X	X	X		X	X
M&M Chocolate Oat Bars, 222		X			X	X			

RECIPE LIST WITH PAGE NUMBERS

	PREPPED IN 5	QUICK & EASY	ON THE TABLE IN 20	FREEZER FRIENDLY	FEED A CROWD	MAKE AHEAD	SLOW COOKER	DAIRY-FREE	GLUTEN-FREE
Macaroni Salad, 113		X	X		X	X			
Marinated Steak, 161	X							X	
Mashed Potatoes, 145						X			X
Meatloaf, 164	X			X	X	X		X	
Monte Cristo Sandwiches, 169	X	X	X						
Mozzarella Sticks, 95		X			X	X			
No-Bake Cookies, 243	X	X			X				X
Oatmeal Coconut Cookies, 245		X	X	X	X	X			
Ocean Water, 280	X	X	X					X	X
Orange Julius, 57	X	X		X					X
Pancakes, 39	X	X		X	X				
Parmesan Sweet Potato Cubes, 141		X							X
Parmesan-Crusted Pork Chops, 167		X							
Pasta Salad, 114					X	X			
Peach Cobbler, 230	X	X							
Pecan Pie Bars, 236					X	X			
Perfect Pie Crust, 232				X		X			
Pico de Gallo, 152		X	X		X	X		X	X
Pigs in a Blanket, 166	X	X	X		X	X		X	
Pineapple Upside-Down Cake, 213					X	X			
Pink Punch, 279	X	X	X	X	X	X		X	X
Pizza Dip, 91	X	X			X	X			X
Pizza, 202		X		X	X	X			
Popcorn Balls, 263		X	X		X	X			X
Pot Roast, 165	X			X			X		
Potato Breakfast Casserole, 52	X	X			X	X			
Potato Salad, 112					X	X			X
Pulled Pork, 171	X			X	X	X	X	X	X

RECIPE LIST WITH PAGE NUMBERS

Recipes by Category

They say a picture is worth a thousand words, well . . . Here are 214,000 delicious words' worth of pictures to help you quickly see what recipe might fit best with whatever you are planning.

BREAKFAST

Belgian Waffles, 42

Biscuit Egg Casserole, 51

Biscuits and Gravy, 50

Breakfast Potatoes, 38

Breakfast Strata, 53

Cinnamon Roll Cake, 46

Coffee Cake, 47

Donuts, 45

Easy Cinnamon Rolls, 48

Energy Balls, 55

French Toast, 43

French Toast Bake, 44

Fruit Smoothie, 56

German Pancakes, 40

Ham and Cheese Quiche, 54

Orange Julius, 57

Pancakes, 39

Potato Breakfast Casserole, 52

Scrambled Eggs, 37

Swedish Pancakes, 41

BREADS & MUFFINS

Almond Poppy Seed Bread, 76

Banana Bread, 81

Blueberry Muffins, 77

Bread Bowls, 64

Cheesy Garlic Bread, 67

Chocolate Muffins, 80

Cinnamon Bread, 72

Cornbread, 71

Easy Garlic Knots, 66

Easy Homemade Biscuits, 65

Easy Homemade White Bread, 61

Flour Tortillas, 70

SOUPS

Best Chili Soup, 126

Broccoli Cheese Soup, 122

Chicken Dumpling Soup, 124

Chicken Noodle Soup, 120

Egg Drop Soup, 131

Slow Cooker Beef Stew, 123

Slow Cooker Cheesy Potato Soup, 121

Slow Cooker Chicken Tortilla Soup, 128

Slow Cooker Green Chile Chicken Enchilada Soup, 129

Slow Cooker Spinach Tortellini Soup, 125

Taco Soup, 130

Tomato Basil Soup, 119

White Chicken Chili, 127

SIDES

Baked Potatoes, 139

Black Bean and Corn Salsa (aka Cowboy Caviar), 155

Brown Sugar–Glazed Carrots, 136

Cilantro-Lime Rice, 149

Creamed Corn, 138

Fried Rice, 147

Funeral Potatoes, 146

Green Bean Bundles, 135

Green Bean Casserole, 137

Homemade Mac and Cheese, 142

Homemade Salsa, 153

Homemade Tortilla Chips, 151

Mashed Potatoes, 145

Parmesan Sweet Potato Cubes, 141

Pico de Gallo, 152

Roasted Vegetables, 140

Spanish Rice, 148

Street Corn (Esquites), 150

Sweet Salsa Verde, 154

Twice-Baked Potatoes, 144

MEAT

Baby Back Ribs, 168

Baked Salmon, 173

Brown Sugar Ham, 172

Cheese Enchiladas, 184

Chicken Nuggets, 178

Chicken Pot Pie, 179

Chicken Tacos, 188

Chimichangas, 185

Classic Burgers, 160

Cream Cheese and Chicken Taquitos, 186

Creamy Swiss Chicken, 177

Empanadas, 189

Flautas, 187

Garlic Prime Rib, 162

General Tso's Chicken, 180

Green Chile Chicken Enchiladas, 183

Hawaiian Haystacks, 176

Marinated Steak, 161

Meatloaf, 164

Monte Cristo Sandwiches, 169

Parmesan-Crusted Pork Chops, 167

Pigs in a Blanket, 166

Pot Roast, 165

Pulled Pork, 171

Roast Chicken, 174

Roast Turkey, 175

Slow Cooker Brisket, 163

Sweet and Sour Chicken, 181

Sweet Pork, 170

Teriyaki Chicken, 182

Tostadas, 190

PASTA AND PIZZA

Baked Ziti, 201

Beef Goulash, 194

Beef Stroganoff, 200

Cheesy Pasta Bake, 197

Chicken Tetrazzini, 193

Easy Lasagna, 195

Fettuccine Alfredo, 198

Italian Sausage Pasta, 196

Kid-Friendly Spaghetti, 199

Recipe Index